IT'S ALL ABOUT TREO

IT'S ALL ABOUT TREO

Life and War with the World's Bravest Dog

Dave Heyhoe

with

Damien Lewis

Quercus

First published in Great Britain in 2012 by
Quercus
55 Baker Street
Seventh Floor, South Block
London
W1U 8EW

All images supplied courtesy of the author except

Page 2, top Marco Di Lauro/Getty Images
Page 3, top and bottom Matt Cooke
Page 9, top and bottom Marco Di Lauro/Getty Images
Page 15, top Murray Sanders/Daily Mail/Rex Features
Page 16, Matt Cooke

A CIP catalogue record for this book is available
from the British Library

HB ISBN 978 1 78087 396 1
TPB ISBN 978 1 78087 397 8
Ebook ISBN 978 1 78087 398 5

10 9 8 7 6 5 4 3 2 1

Text and plates designed and typeset by Ellipsis Digital Ltd

Printed and bound in Great Britain by Clays Ltd, St Ives plc

For

The lads and lasses of Ranger Company, the Royal Irish Regiment, and for all the Military Working Dog teams that put themselves in harm's way to deliver us from evil.

And Lance Corporal Ken Rowe and Ranger Justin Cupples, who never made it back.

D. H.

For Steve Clarke, for the love of dogs.

D. L.

AUTHOR'S NOTE

Where necessary a number of names, dates and place names have been changed to protect people's identities and obscure sensitive information.

ACKNOWLEDGEMENTS

Special thanks to the following, without whom this book would never have been written. The team at Quercus: Richard Milner, Joshua Ireland, Caroline Proud, Mike McGrath, Digby Halsby at Flint, Annabel Merullo, Laura Williams, Jonathan Sissons and team at PFD. The Abbott family, who gave Treo a second chance. Author Damien Lewis, who helped give me the strength to put mine and Treo's story into words. Thank you also to James Ede and staff at Congleton Veterinary Centre for your continued support of Treo and military working dogs.

CHAPTER ONE

I glance at Treo. I'm worried about how he's coping with the suffocating heat and the thudding beat of the whocka-whocka. Its giant twin rotor blades are screaming above our heads as we swoop earthwards, the helo coming in low and fast and weaving this way and that in an effort to avoid enemy fire.

I'm sitting on a fold-down canvas seat to one side of the giant helicopter's hold, Treo facing forwards and sandwiched between my knees. The rear ramp's already been lowered, so my dog and I can dive off it as soon as the aircraft hits the dirt. The wind is rushing in like a howling gale, mixed with the heady scent of burning avgas from the aircraft's twin turbines.

Treo's a handsome-as-hell black Labrador–spaniel cross, and he's my most trusted friend. In the world of war-dogs he's known as a toughie and a troublemaker, not a licky, soppy kind of mutt. But right now I can tell that he's in need of some real comfort from his 'dad'.

He feels my gaze upon him, and cranes his head around in an effort to make eye contact. The whites of his eyes flash this way and that as he searches for me, his shiny black muzzle pointing vertically at the roof above.

I reach down and get my arm around his neck, pulling him in until his head's leant to one side and cradled on my thigh.

I hold him close and whisper into his velvety-soft ear: 'It's OK, lad, Dad's here and he's not going to let anything happen to you, not ever . . .'

But as I say those words I pray that I've got the power to deliver on them – that I truly can bring my dog out of this one uninjured and alive. When dog and handler are as close as Treo and me, emotions run up-leash and down again. He knows I'm excited to be here, but that I'm hugely apprehensive and nervous for him.

He throws me this glance, his coal-bright amber eyes like pools of trusting fire. Over the years we've spent together I've learned to read his every look. This one says: *Wherever the hell it is you're taking me, Dad, I'm sticking by your side. And as long as I'm with you I know it's going to be all right.*

I tell him that it is. I tell him that he's right. I tell him that I'll protect him with my very life if I have to; no one's going to shoot or blow up my best buddy, my dog.

On one level, it doesn't matter what words exactly you say to your dog, it's how you say them that matters. I'm using my high-pitched 'praise' voice as I talk, letting Treo know I'm happy with him and that all's good between us. But he and I have lived and worked together for so long now that we've formed a special, much deeper connection. I truly believe that my dog can understand every word that I say, and that's the magic of the bond between us.

The Chinook lurches earthwards and flares out, preparing to land. We descend into a howling 'brown-out' – a thick, choking dust storm kicked up by the rotor blades. Luckily, I've remembered to pack Treo's 'doggles', Perspex goggles that strap onto your dog's head. As we go belting down the Chinook's open ramp, we're both sporting our protective eyewear so as to prevent the sand from getting blasted into our eyes and blinding us.

We hit the ground running, and as we exit the chopper the handler and dog team we're replacing are ready to go pounding up the open ramp to take our place. It's too noisy to exchange more than the briefest of words. The handler stuffs a scribbled note into my hand: *Dave, welcome to Sangin. Only 186 days to go – you know the rest!*

Seconds later they're swallowed up by the aircraft's gaping hold, the whine of the rotors screaming to fever pitch as the Chinook claws into the air. I crouch amongst a heap of our 'K9' – military working dog – equipment, trying to shield Treo from the crushing downwash of the rotor blades. The belly of the helicopter vanishes into the dark and howling sandstorm, whisking handler and dog back towards Camp Bastion . . . and safety.

Treo and I have just taken over as the Arms Explosives Search dog team here in Sangin, Helmand Province, Afghanistan – more commonly known as 'IED Central'. This is arguably the most dangerous place in the world's most dangerous war zone right now. Yet that's it: our handover's done. The man-and-dog team that preceded us has got the hell out, and with them has gone all the knowledge that they accumulated during their six-month tour. Still, I do my best to see the funny side of it: *welcome to Sangin. Only 186 days to go . . .*

With the helicopter gone the dust storm gradually abates. Treo and I are able to take stock of our surroundings. We've been dropped on the helipad – a stretch of parched, arid sandy terrain – which sits in the midst of the Sangin DC (District Centre), a vast compound that serves as the British Army's headquarters here.

The entire place is dominated by the squat shape of the District Centre itself, which resembles something from out of the Alamo. It's like a dun-coloured layer cake; one made from pockmarked concrete and shrapnel-riddled sandbags, and decorated with glistening spools of razor wire. The whip-like silhouettes of radio antennae sprout from four corners of the war-blasted building, and every bullet-torn window and doorway vomits rolls of camouflage netting.

Clustered around the foot of the building are scores of squat, ugly, makeshift shelters. The walls are made of thick HESCO barriers – a wire-mesh system filled with earth to form blast-proof structures – with sandbags overhead. There are thick tufts of grass sprouting out of the roofs, testimony to the length of time the British Army has spent under siege here.

It's towards one of those shelters that Treo and I make our wary way, in search of somewhere to house one man and his dog. Although a dog and handler have been here before us, there's very little on site for an animal's welfare. All the base can offer to house Treo is a small metal cage, with some sheets of cardboard flung over for shade.

As soon as I put him in there his ears flop down and his head droops to the floor unhappily. He glances up at me with a dejected, hangdog look: *What have I done to deserve this?*

I reach into one of the side pockets of my rucksack and pull out a vacuum-wrapped bone. It's one of dozens I've carried out from the UK. I pass it through the bars, in an effort to try to cheer him up a little.

'Here you go then, big lad, have a chew on that . . .'

He sniffs at the proffered bone but doesn't take it, which is so unlike my dog. He leaves me to drop it onto the floor of his cage. This isn't Treo at all. Normally, he loves nothing more than a good gnaw on a big, juicy bone. This is his way of showing me how unhappy he is in these dingy and cramped quarters.

It's a first rule in the working-dog world that only a well rested and well looked after animal will give 100 per cent. A dog that feels uncared for will be unhappy and will work way below par. Treo and I have come here on a life-or-death mission sniffing out the bombs, and in my book anything less than 100 per cent is just not good enough.

In addition to being dark and horribly claustrophobic, the cage also provides zero cover from enemy fire. From our pre-deployment briefings I know that Sangin's getting shot-up, mortared and rocketed on a daily basis. So, first priority is going to be to build my dog and me some proper, decent bomb- and bulletproof quarters.

By the time I've got Treo half settled it's last light, and we've got no time for any of that now. I fetch him out of his cage, for there's no way he'll get any rest in there. We bed down side by side on my cot, with him cuddling up to me for security. I give him a good long scratch behind the ears where I know he likes it best, and I talk him to sleep as gunfire crackles in the darkness all around us.

I lie awake, a bundle of worry. The commander of the resident unit – Bravo Company, 40 Commando, Royal Marines –

has already let me know that he wants Treo and me out on their patrols right away. Sangin's been nicknamed IED Central for a very good reason: British soldiers keep getting hit by murderous improvised explosive devices (IEDs) here. Yet from the moment Treo and I set out for Afghanistan our journey's been dogged by trouble, and we could hardly be less prepared for the war-torn streets of Sangin town.

A few days back we'd deployed from the 104 Military Working Dog Unit, based at North Luffenham, Rutland. We were two dozen human-and-dog teams, including Arms Explosive Search (AES) dogs, Infantry Patrol (IP) dogs, and Patrol Dogs. IP dogs are trained to go out on the front line and detect the enemy from afar, whereas patrol dogs are trained to provide security at military bases and other installations.

We deliberately deployed two weeks early to Afghanistan, planning to use the extra time to get the AES dogs acclimatised to the withering heat, and their noses adjusted to the smells here. Treo's an AES dog, which means he's trained to find weapons and to detect a range of explosive odours – including C4, detonation cord, water gel, TNT and dynamite. But scents tend to differ wherever it is you're searching – especially when you've got a nose as sensitive as Treo's – and we'd planned to spend those two weeks training with local arms and explosives, to get the dogs tuned in.

But it sure didn't happen that way. The first we knew that we were being sent directly into the field was when our giant Galaxy transport aircraft touched down at Camp Bastion. I was just getting Treo out of his transportation crate when word was passed around the aircraft's echoing hold – *Get your kit ready, you're going out tomorrow!* And that's how we learned that we were heading directly into the jaws of war.

The commander of the 104, Captain Martin Thompson, called us together to explain what was what. After our sergeant major, Frank Holmes, I am the third most senior rank, and the only one of the more senior guys getting sent into the field. That didn't worry me much. I'm infantry trained, and in my thirty-eight years I've gained more combat experience than most of the young soldiers being sent into Afghanistan. What did worry me was heading into the heart of war with 'green' dogs; ones who'd had no chance to acclimatise, or to get their noses in.

The 104 is seen as being the elite of the British military working dog world, and we're often deployed to support Special Forces operations. Our CO explained to us that being from the 104 we could handle it, and that we'd 'acclimatise on the job'. We'd have to ease our dogs into their first missions, carefully controlling how often they went out and for how long, so they didn't burn themselves out, or worse still miss any IEDs.

We're all of us total pros and we hail from a fine unit, so none of us whinged too much. But if we'd had those two weeks to properly acclimatise and prepare, who knows how differently things might have turned out.

In a way I guess it was understandable, but our OC gave the three female AES handlers the real cushy postings. Ali Sutherland got Kabul, which is nicknamed 'Kabutlins' by the British soldiers. Foot patrols in the Afghan capital were done with the floppy-jungle-hat, softly-softly approach, reflecting the perceived threat level. Marianne Hay had got given the military base at Kandahar, complete with swimming pool, Pizza Hut and

Dunkin' Donuts. And Debbie Cafful got Lashkar Gar, the capital of Helmand Province, which is also slipper city.

I know those lasses well, having trained them and their dogs over the months and the years. There's not one amongst them would have baulked at being sent to the most dangerous of bases in Afghanistan. They're as brave and capable as the lads, and I know they'd have gone anywhere asked of them, but the RAVC's hierarchy is determined to protect them. God knows it'd be one hell of a public relations disaster to get a woman-and-dog team killed here.

That left the boys to take the murder postings. Dan Barron had been sent up to Kajaki, with his liver-and-white spaniel, Harvey. Dan's one of the nicest blokes you could ever meet, with his funny, high-pitched Preston accent, and a habit of dropping his aitches. Dan's only problem is his drinking: like most of us, he thinks he's ten men when he's got the beer inside him. He loves his 'Arvey, and I know it'll destroy him if his dog steps on one of the thousands of deadly land mines planted up around the Kajaki area.

Then there's Sean Cheetham, all seven-foot beanpole of him, with his black Labrador, Max. Sean's got a wonderful good nature, and he'd do anything for you, although he sure loves doing his cheeky impersonations of my thick Mancunian accent. Sean and I are great friends, which makes me all the more worried that he'd got posted to the die-hard Taliban stronghold of Musa Qala. I've got a feeling Sean's going to go up there a boy and come back very much a man.

The seventh member of the 104's AES team is young Ken Rowe. You can't help liking Ken. He's a good-looking, gobby

Geordie who winds me up something proper, but I love him all the same. His confidence and brash ways remind me of myself at his age – twenty-something and ready to take on the world.

Ken's got a fantastic dog, a snowy-white Lab called Sasha. If there's one dog in the 104 that can rival Treo's abilities, it's her. She's the only one that Treo truly respects. He recognises her superlative search capabilities, and she's also Treo's bit of skirt. Whenever he's around Sasha he goes all bashful, like an adolescent with a crush. It's hardly surprising: she is one hell of a classy-looking girl.

With some K9 teams the love between handler and hound becomes so strong that the dog actually stops working properly. That was the case with Sasha and her first handler, Marianne. Reluctantly, Marianne had to give Sasha up and hand her over to Ken. She feared that she and her dog had grown too close, and that their ability to seek out the bombs had become impaired by their love for each other.

I've never had that problem with Treo. No matter how much love I give him, he always wants to work. I don't believe there's anything will ever stop him doing what we do so well together. Whenever I take him down the local hardware store at home, he's straight over to the bottles of weedkiller, sitting on his haunches and staring up at them: *Look what I've found, Dad.* (Weedkillers can be used to make explosives.) He can't stop being a working dog. It's what he loves.

Ken and Sasha got together only recently, but they've formed a fantastic team, one of the 104's very best. Here in Afghanistan they've been given Inkerman – a base that's arguably as volatile as Sangin, but somewhat smaller. There are more firefights at Inkerman, but there are far fewer IEDs. It's a more traditional, less sneaky kind of war the Taliban are waging there. But after Sangin I figure it's the next worst posting in terms of your chances of getting blown up or killed.

I'm worried for Ken, Sean and Dan, plus their dogs. Dead worried. They're new to combat and they've been posted to places that are pretty close to hell. They're lone teams parachuted into a variety of regiments, and I know the horrendous work rate that'll be expected of them and their dogs. But I'm confident that each has the personality to shine through and to win friends, which will help them cope with the loneliness, the exhaustion and the sheer relentless knife-edge terror of it all.

I've trained and worked and lived with those lads since 2003, when we first deployed to Northern Ireland together. I've coached them tirelessly for Afghan ops, trying to give them the kind of infantry know-how that I learned in my original unit, the Cheshire Regiment. But I'm not kidding myself that it's going to be easy for them, or risk- and trauma-free.

In a tiny unit like ours involved in such life-or-death work, everyone becomes close. Ken, Dan and Sean were up at my house for Christmas, just a few weeks prior to deploying to Afghanistan. I'd made sure we had a proper good time of it, and that was really my family Christmas.

I'd bought this giant turkey from a local Lincolnshire farmer to feed all of my boys. I was getting it ready for the oven when Ken tapped me on the shoulder. He had one of those smug grins on his face, which always serve to wind me up a treat.

'What you doing for Christmas dinner then, Dave? Turkey stuffed with giblets?'

'What's that supposed to mean, you ungrateful little so-and-so?' I shot back at him.

'You ain't removed the giblets, have you?'

I peered inside the greasy white flesh and I could see that Ken was right – I hadn't. I could half remember my mum removing the turkey's innards at Christmas so she could pack it full of stuffing. I started to reach inside the big, cold slab of turkey to do likewise.

Ken was laughing outright now. 'That's its bloody neck! You've got to go in the other way, and ram your hand up its arse . . .'

I stepped back and gestured at the big, pimply white carcass. 'There you go then, mate, you have a go.'

Ken point-blank refused. As far as he was concerned I'd invited him over for Christmas dinner, so all the hard work was going to be done by me. Somehow, I muddled through, and a few hours late we sat down to the mother of all feasts. And every time one of us finished off a hunk of juicy turkey, we made sure to toss the bone to Treo. He was in heaven, was my boy, and the rest of my team seemed pretty happy with the feasting.

Ken, Dan and Sean are like the honorary members of the Dave Heyhoe family, especially since I've got next to no hope of ever having kids of my own. I'm no oil painting, yet somehow I've managed to snare some lovely girlfriends in my time. But with none has there ever been the barest hint of a pregnancy. A few years back I'd gone to see an Army doctor, to have a quiet chat about it all. He in turn referred me to a local hospital.

There I had to go through the embarrassing ritual of

producing a sperm sample so the doctors could take a good look. The result that came back was that I had a less than 5 per cent chance of ever fathering a child, my sperm count was so low. And so it was that I'd learned that I was more or less infertile.

I'd always seen myself as being a very 'manly' kind of bloke, and this just didn't feel right somehow. Dave Heyhoe was half the man that he'd thought he was. And that in turn made the lads from the 104 – Ken, Dan and Sean – even more like my family. And as for Treo, he's like the son that I'll never have.

It's typical of the cheek of those lads that even on the Chinook ride out to Sangin, they were still winding me up.

'Sangin's nothing more than Blackpool with a bloody river running through it.'

'Enjoy your holiday by the water whilst we get the murder postings!'

'Hope you packed your suntan lotion and your lilo.'

I volunteered Treo and me for Sangin. I did so because I've got sixteen years' infantry experience, and if anyone can handle IED Central then I can. I've done years of hands-on soldiering, so it's only right that Treo and I get the most dangerous posting of all.

There are four platoons from Bravo Company stationed here, and they're an elite unit who'll want a K9 team on every one of their patrols. We're expected to get straight on with sniffing out the bombs, having had zero time to settle in. I've put one condition on our doing so: the boss of the 104 has to get a second K9 team sent out to serve alongside us. Without another man-and-dog team, Treo and I are going to be burned out in a matter of days.

I've done two decades of soldiering and I'm a veteran of Northern Ireland, Bosnia and Iraq. It's been my role in the 104 to prepare our dog teams for Afghanistan. Most of the handlers are combat virgins, and they're walking into the fire. If I lose a single man, woman or dog I know that I'll never get over it: I'll always blame myself for not bringing them all home. I'll spend the rest of my life wondering if I could have done something more in the training, something that would have made the difference between their living and dying.

We seven AES teams are tasked with covering the entire British war effort here in Afghanistan. Treo and I were the first to be dropped on the ground, with the other teams flying onwards to their bases. As my dog and I exited the Chinook, I said my goodbyes to the young lads and lasses and their dogs. Just as Treo sees me as his dad, so do they, and it was tough letting them go. But I've got every faith in them.

I'm 100 per cent certain none will turn away from their task, even though they're heading out to do the most dangerous job in the world.

CHAPTER TWO

On our first morning in Sangin Treo and I are introduced to the two surprise members of our team – Jihad and Sandbag. Bravo Company has adopted two Afghan strays as their mascots. Jihad looks like a collie–German shepherd cross, and she's a sleek and beautiful dog. Sandbag is an impossible-looking Labrador–poodle cross, with the body and legs of a pot-bellied pig.

Jihad and Sandbag are the old dogs here in Sangin, and they're understandably keen to meet the new arrival, Treo. I'm keen for him to get to know Jihad in particular, because I'm told she goes on every patrol with the lads. As for Sandbag, she looks too fat to go anywhere, but I'm told she's a cheeky little mutt who everyone loves to hate, and that she's great for morale. But before they can meet and greet Treo, I've got to check the both of them over.

Jihad and Sandbag may be great for boosting morale, but they're crawling with ticks. I get an alcohol wipe and put it on the tick's back, which forces its head and jaws to withdraw, allowing me to safely remove and to kill it. I can tell that Jihad's recently had a litter of puppies, for her teats and belly are saggy.

Her vulva's badly infected and I'll need to get it treated, or she'll get septicaemia and die.

I order a batch of drugs off the 104's veterinarian, based at Camp Bastion. She promises to get them sent out to me, but only when she can manage to get them onto a flight, and only if none of the working dogs is in need of the medicines. It's the best we can manage, and I just have to hope I get the drugs into Jihad in time to cure her.

My inspection done, I allow Treo some face-time with Jihad, and I can tell he thinks she's a girl with some class. At first he tries acting all cool – body rigid, mouth clamped shut, stubby tail rock-still. But as soon as they start sniffing each other's undersides he loses it, getting this big, dopey smile on his face. Jihad doesn't have any such qualms: she's flirting with him outrageously. Treo gives me a *So what next, Dad?* look.

Jihad's not quite had the Sasha effect on Treo, but he's yet to see her in action out on patrol. Treo's a typical dog, and he's not going to hold back hitting on Jihad just because of Sasha. But I can't let them get too close quite yet. Jihad's a stray and she's very likely riddled with disease, and I can't take the risk of Treo catching anything. I'll allow him a good bit of innocent fun, but not to take it any further.

If Jihad and Sandbag are going to be honorary members of my K9 team, I figure they'll need some credentials. I manage to get a call through to home via the base's satellite phone. I speak to my folks, tell them about the two new members of my team, and get a couple of bone-shaped aluminium dog tags ordered – one inscribed 'Jihad', the other 'Sandbag'. Welcome to the family.

*

Next priority is to get Treo's nose in. I've been warned that Bravo Company need us for a major operation, and time's running. I ask the Afghan National Army soldiers co-located with the British forces if they have any local weaponry and explosives that I can use to train my dog. They hand me a pineapple-shaped warhead for a Rocket Propelled Grenade (RPG), plus an AK47 assault rifle.

I find a deserted corner of the base. I take the RPG and start jumping on it pointy-nose-downwards, to drive it into the earth. I've got Treo locked in his dingy cage, and I need to bury the warhead good and proper, to really test him. I'm almost done when this Royal Marine comes running over screaming his head off. He's going nuts.

'NOOOOOOO!'

Apparently, the RPG round is live, and I've come that close to blowing myself to bits. I stop what I'm doing, check the safety cap is screwed on *very* firmly, and proceed to bury it a little more carefully. The ruckus over the RPG incident has attracted a lot of attention and by the time I've gone and fetched Treo we've got something of an audience.

I release my dog and give him the magical words: 'Seek on, lad, seek on.'

He makes a beeline for the location of the RPG and stops right over it, his eyes staring at the ground where it's buried. He turns to me, and I'm about to tell him what a good boy he is and give him a big well done, when he notices all the onlookers. Not wanting to miss the chance of putting in a top perform-ance, he proceeds to cock his leg and to pee all over the buried round.

It's some way to make a first impression with those Royal Marine lads. It's also typical Treo. He's got a real mischievous, rebel streak. The rufty-tufty Marines break into a spontaneous round of applause at Treo's pissing-on-the-explosives trick, and I figure they have us pegged now as the joker man-and-dog team. First I tried to blow myself up with the RPG; now Treo's peed on it. What a performance.

It reminds me of the time when Treo and I were working as the then Prime Minister Tony Blair's personal security detail. I'd sent my dog for a good sniff around his hotel room, and Treo couldn't resist jumping onto the Prime Minister's bed. Before I could stop him he'd done a big luxurious doggy roll, giving his back a good scratch as he went – one that left black Treo hairs all over the pristine white sheets.

The next morning we ran into the Prime Minister having breakfast. He fixed Treo with a look – *I know what you did. You think it's funny. Well I don't* – and gave me a wry kind of a smile before telling me how lucky it was that he loved dogs.

I try explaining to the Royal Marines that peeing on something is not Treo's normal way of indicating that he's found explosives. But my words are lost in a gale of laughter: *Yeah, course not, mate, we believe you.*

We train our dogs to track a scent to the point of greatest danger – the strongest concentration of the odour in the air – but never to touch the explosives, and certainly not to pee on it! But Treo's been parachuted into a strange environment, he's been locked up in the cage from hell all morning, and he's a black dog in the boiling heat of the Afghan day. I reckon we've got to cut him some slack.

We're facing a five a.m. start the following day, and I've got a shedload of stuff to prepare. I'll carry enough dried food to last Treo four days, just in case we get marooned out there, plus a couple of ration packs for me. I'll carry three Camelbaks of water, a medical kit specially made for Treo, and one for me. I'll also have my own personal weapon, a stubby SA80 carbine, and several magazines of spare ammunition. We handlers carry the Stubby – a shortened assault rifle – because it's easier to use when trying to control our dogs.

I'll also be decked out in body armour, grenades, a bayonet and radio kit. Basically, I'll have everything the Royal Marine lads are carrying, plus all the gear for my dog. It's one hell of a lot of weight to lug around on your back. Treo will be on-leash when we're not searching, but off-leash when we are. I need him to be able to range freely and to follow his nose wherever it takes him.

Equally importantly, I'll need to ease myself into a new mindset. I've got to start thinking like a Taliban, and double guessing where they'll have planted their killer devices. Treo and I will be out front, leading patrols, studying the ground for any tell-tale signs that a bomb's been planted. We'll have to rely on the Royal Marines to be our eyes and ears and our protection out there.

The Taliban know what the dogs can do by now. They know we're the single biggest threat to their murderous IEDs. So I'll have the added pressure of always being watchful for Treo, to make sure they don't capture or kill him. I've made Treo a solemn promise that I'm going to bring him out of this alive, and I'm determined to deliver. I'll be asking him to risk his life for me and for the patrol. In return I'll sacrifice myself if I have to, but they're not getting my dog.

We'll be hitting the search area at the hottest time of the day, putting Treo under immense pressure and risking heat exhaustion. My worry is for my dog first and foremost, but also for the safety of the entire patrol. A cool and rested dog is far more efficient at detecting the threat than a hot, exhausted and frustrated one. I've raised my concerns with the Commanding Officer of Bravo Company, but he's told me that the plan is the plan. We've got to run with it.

At first light the following morning Treo and I mount up a Viking armoured vehicle, one of three forming our patrol. With a crunch of grinding gears the metal-skinned beast gets under way, and we nose through the darkened gates of the base and out into bandit country. We turn right, heading north up route 611 towards Inkerman, Ken and Sasha's posting.

There are some forty young guns of Bravo Company distributed across the Vikings, plus a handful of the Afghan National Army (ANA) soldiers co-located with us here at Sangin. And there's Jihad, of course, the new honorary member of my K9 team.

I can sense that the Bravo Company lads are more than a little curious as to just what Treo and I can do. The story of the RPG round and Treo's leg-cocking incident has done the rounds, and there's been a good deal of sniggering. I guess this is make-or-break time: we're really going to have to prove ourselves out there.

It's seven o'clock by the time we've pushed the fifteen kilometres north to the start point for the patrol. We dismount in a patch of deserted bush. We're to move south from here on foot, clearing terrain as we go. Before we get under way, the patrol commander, a young and thrusting corporal, asks me what call sign the patrol is to use to address the dog team. We've all got personal radios clipped to our helmets, for comms between patrol members.

I've noticed that this Royal Marines lot don't appear to go in for nicknames or light-hearted call signs very much. They seem far too serious for that. Instead, they address each other by their surnames or by rank mostly, and it's all a bit too formal – not to mention grim-sounding – for my liking.

'Sir, it's probably best just to call me "Dave Dog",' I tell him. 'Or just plain "Dog", 'cause I've noticed there's another Dave on the patrol.'

He gives me this look, like I'm taking the piss or something. Ever since I joined the 104, my nickname has been Dave Dog. It's become such a part of me that it's the name everyone uses for me down my local boozer, and it's the name I use on the pub's pool league. I figure it's as fine a call sign as any, now that Treo and I are at war.

'Everyone else calls me Dog,' I tell him.

'Right, Dog it is,' the patrol commander confirms, a little reluctantly. 'Right, erm . . . *Dog*, I want you out front of the patrol, and every compound cleared from here back to Sangin. Let's go.'

'Hold it just a minute, sir,' I say. 'What's the set-up, protection-wise, for me and my dog?'

For a moment he stares at me, like he can't believe I'm questioning an order and holding up his patrol. I don't give a shit.

I'm thirty-eight years old to his mid-twenties. I'd reached the rank of sergeant in the Cheshires before taking a demotion back to lance corporal, which is the only way to get entry into dog handler training. They'll only take you if you're willing to sacrifice your rank, simply to get your K9.

More importantly, no one can order me what to do with my dog. I may be embedded with his patrol as the 'search element', but my dog remains 100 per cent my responsibility at all times.

'It's like I said, dog handler,' he replies impatiently, 'you and your dog will be out front—'

'Sir, there's something you need to know here,' I cut in. 'When we start the search I will be totally focused on my dog. I'll be looking to the ground at his front, scanning for potential IEDs. I need to be eyes-on my dog, to make sure he doesn't shoot off around a corner out of sight. If I'm looking down at my dog, I can't be looking out for the Taliban. I need to be able to concentrate on Treo one hundred per cent, and without worrying about us getting shot or blown up.'

'Everyone faces the same threat—'

'No, sir, they don't. My dog and me – we're at the tip of the spear. If the enemy's waiting in ambush, we'll be the first to get it. If there's a device planted out there, my dog and me will be first onto it. What I need is two of your lads, one to either side of the track a fair distance behind us, providing security. If either of us triggers a device, we'll take the blast. The lads on security should be far enough back to survive. But I need to know that I can rely on them for every second that we're searching—'

'Understood,' the patrol commander cuts in.

He barks an order at a couple of burly Commandos that they're to be on my shoulder, providing the dedicated dog team security.

That done, I turn to face the narrow path that snakes through the bush. I stand there in the blinding early morning sunlight surveying the route ahead. Treo is at my feet, to my left as always, but he can sense my fear and indecision, and it's unsettled him.

Before heading out to Afghanistan, we'd studied the kinds of devices the Taliban are using here. The most common is the cellphone-triggered IED. The bomb is dug into a road or a path like this one, just below where a patrol will be passing. When the bomb maker sees a column of British soldiers approaching, he dials the phone. His call sends the circuit live, which detonates the bomb. If it's a vehicle convoy moving at speed it's hard to time the detonation right. It's much easier with a patrol on foot moving along a path, and led by one man and his dog.

I pull out Treo's reward – a bog-standard fluorescent green tennis ball – and instantly my dog knows we're here to search. The ball is the key. It's how handler and dog train together from the very start. You begin by rolling a ball into a room, and letting the dog run in to play with it. You then put a target scent (such as an explosive) inside a box, and roll the ball up to the box. The dog smells the scent at the same time as grabbing the ball, and you call him back and tell him he's a good boy. Now he's linked the scent to the ball and to play: *If I find the scent I find the ball, and so I get to play.*

On that basic premise you build layer upon layer of further training. The dog never knows that he's in any danger; that he's searching for this deadly killer device. Once I send Treo into the Afghan bush, to him this will be just a game. If he could talk he'd probably be saying to me, *Jesus, Dad, where've you brought me – don't you think it's a bit too hot to play out here?*

The sun's not fully up yet but I can feel the cold sweat dripping down my back, and the thrumming, juddering, pounding heartbeat of fear – fear for myself, but fear mainly for my dog. My stomach's knotted tight as a fist, and my legs feel like they're going to jelly.

I unleash my dog to let him have his head. I take the first step, Treo stepping out beside me.

I whisper: 'Seek on, boy, seek on.'

And so we start the walk.

Treo's off, his stumpy tail flicking from side to side, his nose suspended a few centimetres above the earth swinging this way and that as he scans for the killer scent. I guide him with hand signals and sweeping arm movements, plus the occasional whispered 'get over', to bring him back to where I want him.

'Heel', 'sit down', 'stay', 'come', 'leave' and 'no' – those are the basic verbal commands we teach the dogs. We add in the search-specific stuff later. But over the years Treo and I have developed our own special language known only to the two of us. Much of our communication is instinctive and unspoken, but I guess that I'm also a bit of a dog whisperer.

As we step out leading the patrol I'm nattering away to my dog: 'Come on lad, this way; good lad, up and over that ditch, mind your pawsies as you go . . .'

I'm talking to him as if he were my best mate, because that's exactly what he is to me. To me, such behaviour is all perfectly normal. It's just the heat and the crushing fear that I'm not used to, knowing that we'll be first onto the Taliban guns or their bombs. But I can sense the stares from the Commando lads behind me as I mutter and chatter to my dog.

'Good boy, keep going, get on then – good lad!' I tell him, as I guide him to the left and right of the path.

My constant, good-natured mutterings give Treo the confidence he needs to keep pushing on in either direction. If I detected the slightest hint of danger up ahead, he knows that I'd reel him in.

'Good laaaaad,' I tell him, as he swings his muzzle this way and that above the hard-packed earth, hoovering up the scent in great, greedy gasps. I elongate the 'lad', so it lasts three or four times the normal length, which is all part of the special language we've built between us.

I'm hyper-alert to Treo's slightest change in behaviour: a pause, and his stubby tail going rigid for an instant, or anything that might indicate he's onto the scent of a bomb. I keep telling myself that this is what my dog and I came here for – to save lives. Yet at the same time I know that if we mess up it could cost the lives of the Marines on this patrol, not to mention my own.

One wrong move, one tiny lapse of concentration, and that could lead to myself and those Bravo Company lads getting blown to bits. I do not want that on my conscience, not even posthumously.

But worst of all I know that if I let Treo put one paw wrong, it could so easily be his last.

CHAPTER THREE

We've pushed ahead for a good hour along a confusing maze of narrow pathways and alleys that thread between mud-walled compounds. Each patch of terrain we cross is a completely new and nerve-racking experience, especially since the Bravo Company lads keep issuing warnings that the Taliban are shadowing us, waiting for their moment to attack.

I've seen no visible signs of the enemy, and in any case I'm the search dog handler so I've got to concentrate 100 per cent on my task. But it's a horrible, eerie feeling that the enemy are out there, watching our every move, and knowing that I can't afford to look out for them, or ready my weapon for an attack.

In spite of my nervousness, nothing seems to faze my dog. Just about every compound that we pass seems to have an Afghan fighting hound tethered in it. As soon as they can smell Treo they start barking. He glances up, gives a shake of his coat, then glances back at me: *So, it's some dumb dog. Big deal.*

Then he's got his nose to the ground again, moist nostrils soaking up the scent all around him. He doesn't seem bothered in the slightest, and especially since he knows he's got Jihad out there riding shotgun for him.

Jihad's running a constant security cordon around the patrol. A fighting dog starts barking and she's there, fronting up to it and barking right back in its face. She's providing a fine early warning system, one that enables Treo and me to box around any dog-based threat. We won't see her for twenty minutes or so, and then she pops her head out of the bush, all bright-eyed and bushy-tailed: *All right, guys?*

Treo took to Jihad from the very start. In part it's because she's a good-looking girl but there's something more to it now. It's like Jihad's saying: *Hey, pal, you're in my patch now and I've got your back*. It's as if they're working as a team, and coordinating between them how best to search and clear this area of any threat.

Jihad returns from having faced down a particularly noisy fighting dog, and Treo gives her a *thanks for that – you're a doll* look. His little black stump of a tail is wagging furiously. She flashes him a cool, laid-back smile, revealing a perfect set of canines: *Any time, handsome, any time.*

Treo's only got a stump for a tail because I had to get it docked. On operations in Northern Ireland he used to wag it so hard that he'd bash it against walls, and on several occasions he actually broke it. Each time I had to bandage and splint it, keeping him off work for several days until it was healed.

Two months before deploying to Afghanistan I decided we had to get it done. In the Afghan heat a broken tail could easily get infected and put Treo out of action. Worst-case scenario it could give him septicaemia, in which case his entire bloodstream would become infected and he could die.

After he'd been docked, Treo came around from the anaesthetic, took one look at the bandaged stump where his tail used to be and rolled his eyes at me: *I thought that's what you'd brought me here for. Oh well, tail gone – time to crack on.*

Doing a big operation like this can impact upon a dog's ability to search, but I felt I had to take the risk. I was dreading going out on our next search exercise in case losing his tail had ruined Treo as an AES dog. But it didn't seem to have had any effect at all. Treo was still Treo – a world-beating bomb-detection machine. Which is a good thing really, now that we're out here facing the enemy and with half a dozen kilometres of paths and alleyways still to search.

We're approaching maybe our fiftieth compound of the day, the sun's high and we're roasting. Every time Treo raises a paw and places it onto the baking earth I freeze up and tense myself for a blast. I have to force myself to keep moving forwards, and the sweat's pouring off me in bucket-loads.

The temperature out here must be pushing well past forty degrees, and if it's this hot for me, how must it be for Treo, all wrapped up in his glossy black coat of fur? But nothing seems to slow my dog, not even the burning Afghan sun that's beating down upon him.

There's a savage burst of ferocious barking off to one side of a building up ahead, and I figure there must be the biggest Afghan fighting dog ever tethered in there. Treo pauses for an instant, glances in the direction of the snarls, his ears pricked forwards to siphon up the sound.

He glances back at me: *And? Are we scared, Dad? Who's he kidding?*

His head goes down and he's snuffling again, sifting every

wind-blown molecule on the baking-hot, bone-dry air. I can hear his lungs pumping as he sniffs his way forward, siphoning individual scents through his muzzle, his brain searching for the handful that we're looking for – the ones that will give him his reward, a play with his beloved ball.

I hear a second, more familiar round of barking now – Jihad fronting up to that fighting dog and telling it to back the hell off. *That's our girl.*

We're almost at the compound when Treo shows the first classic symptoms of a change in behaviour – indicating to me that he's onto something. His nose starts to suck up the air in great, heaving gasps, nostrils flaring as he savours the scent. His head sways this way and that as he tries to pinpoint the direction from which the smell is coming, and then he's making a beeline for the doorway of that mud-walled compound.

This is our first ever patrol in Afghanistan, and this the first sign of my dog showing a real interest in something. The thought keeps flashing through my mind: *what the hell is he onto here?* It could be completely mundane, like a pile of goat poo. Treo is a dog, after all, and sometimes he does get distracted by all the usual doggy smells. But the way he's behaving it's far more likely to be an arms cache, hidden explosives, or maybe an IED that's primed and ready to blow.

'Careful, lad, careful,' I whisper. 'What is it you think you're onto here?'

He glances back at me. I can read his eyes: *You know, Dad, I need to get a closer sniff – but there's something in there, that's for sure.*

Treo knows he's in an alien environment and he knows that

this is serious. He knows it's the real deal. He can sense the fear and the potential for violence rippling through the hot Afghan air, not to mention the tension that I'm feeling. He knows we've upped the ante big time, and that he's got to get in there and find something for me, for his dad.

At my signal one of the Bravo Company lads on my shoulder boots open the galvanised iron door leading into the compound. It flies inwards with an almighty crash. The moment it's open Treo darts inside, his nose pulling him forwards like a magnet towards a giant lump of steel.

For a second I stand on the threshold, watching him track the scent that's right on the end of his nose. Momentarily the fear that's inside me holds me back. That fear is fuelled by the host of Afghan faces that have turned towards my dog and me in shock, surprise and real enmity. Whoever it is that lives in this compound, they definitely do not want us in here.

And then I get a grip: *Dave, bloody get inside and step up to your dog. You can't let him do this alone.*

I stride across the dirt floor until I'm right by Treo's side. A row of eyes to the left of us – all male, all openly hostile – are glued to my dog as he noses his way ahead, steadily, stealthily, each paw-step taking him further in the direction that he's heading. Ahead of my dog there's a shed-like building. Suddenly I know for sure that's where he's heading. Question is: *what the hell is there inside it?*

As Treo creeps steadily onwards every second seems to last a lifetime. I place one boot in front of the other, feeling like I'm moving through a slow-mo scene of pure, icy fear. I've never experienced anything like this before. It's evil, and it's only my link to my dog that keeps me moving forward. *If Treo can do this, so can I.*

He reaches that shed, his nose glued unerringly to the door. I can sense that he's about to plonk his butt down – to sit at source. He's telling me: *Dad, it's in there.*

The last thing I want for him to do is to sit at source. If it's a pressure-plate IED, all it will take is for Treo to plant a paw – or worse still his stubby black stump of a tail – onto the ground, and that'll be enough to compress the device, so making the electrical contact and sending it live. At which point my dog and my closest friend in life will be blown all to hell.

Before he can actually plonk his butt down, I signal Treo back to me. I use a soft, short whistle, which is all it ever takes. An instant later he's at my side, but still he's got his eyes glued firmly to that dark and shadowed doorway.

I turn to speak to the patrol commander. I indicate the shed. 'I think my dog's onto something. It's in there.'

The guy looks doubtful. Very. 'Are you sure, *Dog*?' He shakes his head, kind of irritably. 'I don't much like all this calling you "Dog" business . . .'

I feel like saying: *Do I give a shit, sir? My dog's onto a scent so you can call me bloody Angel Toes if you like – just go and open the door . . .*

Instead, I indicate the shed again: 'Sir, whatever my dog's onto, it's in there.' I turn to look at the line of locals watching us intently. 'And whatever it is, it doesn't look as if Johnny-local there wants us finding it either.'

The patrol commander strides across to the door. I can tell that he thinks my dog's found jack, but I know differently. I yank

Treo back by his harness and tense myself for the blast. He rips open the door, then stops dead in his tracks. His figure is silhouetted in that dark doorway as if he's turned to stone.

He lets out a long, low whistle: '*Bloody hell.*'

He turns around and he's got this look on his face – *we just hit the jackpot.* He yells for some of his lads to get over, and together they start doing a search of the shed's insides. It turns out there are some three-dozen empty illume rounds in there, plus raw explosives. British and allied forces use a lot of illume – a blinding flare round that renders darkness into bright, fluorescent daylight – during night operations when they need light to find the enemy.

But the Taliban have discovered a different use entirely for spent illume rounds. When packed with any home-made or cheap commercial explosive like TNT, they make perfect IEDs. Blast alone doesn't kill someone: it requires lethal metal projectiles that shred skin and flesh and shatter bone. When the explosive is detonated it blasts the illume shell into a thousand jagged shards of steel shrapnel.

The shed is packed full of prime IED-making material. With over thirty illume rounds in there, it's more than enough to kill thirty British soldiers, and to maim many more. There are also spools of electrical wire, sheets of waterproof plastic, metal plates and rolls of insulation tape, plus rakes of pliers, tinsnips, soldering irons and batteries.

It's day one, mission one, and what Treo has discovered here is a bomb-making factory.

I'm chuffed to bits at Treo's find. I slip the tennis ball out of my pocket, and Treo's instantly shifted his attention from the explosives find to his beloved prize. He's got his eyes glued to the ball: *Oooh! Oooh! Can I, Dad? Can I? Can I get a play with my ball?* I make as if to throw it one way, and throw it the other, but Treo's too smart to buy the dummy. Instead, he scampers off and grabs it triumphantly in his delighted jaws.

When working with an arms explosives search dog, you never know what it is that he's onto. So to discover that it's a bomb factory, and not an IED that's primed to blow you all sky high, is a real bonus. We've been on the ground for less than two hours, and Treo's shown that he's the dog's bollocks of search work – not that I ever doubted him.

We've done loads of search work in Northern Ireland before now. We've found bits and pieces of lethal kit, but nothing remotely like a bomb-making factory. This is a totally different level. My dog and I came out here this morning as the joke team that tries to blow up live explosives, or pee on them. Treo's find is the first big step in turning all of that around.

Unsurprisingly, the Bravo Company lads loathe the Taliban bomb makers. There isn't a man amongst them who hasn't lost a good friend to an IED. Planting IEDs is a cowardly, sneaky way to fight a war. They are banned under all the rules of war, because they are indiscriminate killers. Here in Afghanistan 80 per cent of them end up hitting innocent Afghan civilians; mostly women and children. So in a sense, Treo and I are here as much to save the Afghan people as our fellow soldiers.

The Bravo Company lads bring forward their interpreter – their 'terp' – to question the guy we figure is the chief IED-maker. He's a young, skinny Afghan male who looks to be only just out of puberty. He's got a short, wispy beard, and he keeps tugging at it nervously and glancing over at the elders. The look on their faces says it all: it's as if they can't believe that this black dog has come in here and his nose has led him right to their bomb-making factory. Unfortunately for him, our suspect bomb maker seems loath to answer any questions.

The Bravo lads are on the last few weeks of their tour by now, with five long months behind them. They've developed an absolute pathological hatred of the bomb makers. Tempers are running high and so the patrol commander orders me to get the suspect out of the way and to use Treo to stand guard over him. Of course, Treo isn't a guard dog. He's an arms and explosives search dog. But the distinction seems a little academic in the heat of things. I'm part of this patrol, and wherever possible I'll do as much as my dog and I can to get the job done.

I march the suspect around the back of the compound. We come to a halt with Treo giving him the evil eye. The young Afghan starts pleading for his life in a mixture of broken English and the local lingo. I can't understand all that he's saying, but I can read the terror in his eyes. The interpreter explains that we've taken him to the toilet area, which is where the Taliban would take you to deliver a punishment beating, and in preparation for an execution.

The young Afghan fears I'm about to kill him, or to get Treo to bite him half to death. As I try to reassure him – suspect bomb maker or not, he's still human and I'm no murderer – I realise that this is my first up-close encounter with a local. He's shaking like a leaf and the fear in his eyes unnerves me. He seems convinced that I'm about to slot him, and that I'll enjoy every minute of it.

I'm not a small bloke. I'm six foot two and fifteen stone, though I'm sure the weight's going to start dropping off with six months of patrols like this one ahead of us. But I didn't think that I looked like your typical cold-blooded murderer. I guess the Taliban have got to the locals to such a degree that this is what they think of us – that we're ruthless executioners.

In truth, I'm horrified. As for Treo, he's looking at the skinny Afghan as if to say: *What's he done so wrong, Dad?* If Treo knew that this was the guy trying to blow up his dad, he'd grab him by the trouser leg and not let go. But he doesn't know, and all he can sense is the smell of fear and desperation about him.

I'm trying to get the interpreter to talk the guy down from his terror, when a couple of the Afghan National Army (ANA) lads sidle up to us. They've found some photos of the guy posing with weapons and bomb-making kit. They're convinced that he's a major player – a bomb-making mastermind out here. They start firing questions – and I figure threats – at the prisoner.

Before I can stop them, they start dragging him back towards the compound. I fear they're going to kick the living daylights out of him in front of the elders. Right now he's got his own fellow Afghans about to beat him to within an inch of his life. He probably is a bomb maker. He probably is trying to kill us. But unless we can show human compassion and decency, we're no better than the enemy we're trying to fight.

I step into the line of fire, Treo one pace ahead of me baring his fangs and issuing a low and throaty growl.

It's my dog that makes the ANA guys back off. As with most Afghans, they seem to have a deep, ingrained fear of dogs. In this they're the complete opposite of us. There's not a bloke on the patrol that hasn't had a smile or a good word for Treo, and that was before he found the bomb-making factory. As one of my fellow handlers was fond of telling me back home, for us Brits, 'God is dog spelled backwards.'

The ANA guys take one more look at Treo and decide discretion is the better part of valour. They turn on their heels and they're gone.

Twenty minutes later the bomb-making factory has been dismantled and its contents bagged up. We move out with the prisoner in tow. Treo and I push ahead, and after what we've found here our spirits are sky high. We're walking on clouds. Thirty shells amount to thirty IEDs, so that's thirty blokes saved from horrible injury or worse. And there's no better feeling than going to war to save the lives of your fellow soldiers.

When we're a good distance from the compound we go firm, so we can take a much-needed breather. We've stopped beside a river and I decide to let Treo go for it. He's in there like a flash, sploshing and splashing about, and he's loving it.

After a good twenty minutes' rest the patrol commander gives the order to move out, which means Treo and me taking up pole position again.

I call my dog: 'Come on, lad, get here. Time to get going again on those tired pawsies.'

Unfortunately, Treo's having none of it. He glances up at me: *Aw, come on, Dad, it's paradise in here . . .*

The patrol commander tells me that we've got to move because the Taliban are closing in. There's an edge to his voice now that I haven't detected before. Stay static too long and we're a sitting target, he explains. I tell him that Treo's a dog, and that he's got to cool down. But at the same time I can sense the threat all around us, and my instinct is screaming danger.

I call my dog again, more forcibly this time: 'Treo, get here, now!'

He lifts his head from the river: *Ears full of water, Dad, I can't hear you!*

The patrol commander's becoming more and more impatient. 'Dog, we've got to move – like now.'

'Sir, I know.' I nod in Treo's direction. He's doing somersaults and rollicking in the water. 'But my dog's still a dog . . .'

I know exactly how Treo's feeling. He's a big, solid black dog, so he's got the worst of all possible coat colours for being in the furnace of the Afghan heat. He's in the river thinking *this is lovely – and you want me to come out there and follow that hard, sun-baked track . . .* But the longer I stand here with everyone watching me, the more wound-up I get, especially as we're about to get ambushed at any moment.

'Come on!' I yell at him. 'GET HERE – NOW!'

He glances over his shoulder, his muzzle showing a wet, toothy grin: *Dad, you want me, come and get me . . .*

I know I've got no choice but to go in.

I scramble down the muddy bank and slide into the water. I wade across to Treo and grab him by his harness. I try to kill my anger, and I do my best to haul him onto dry land with humour and a smile. I've got no choice, really: the entire patrol seems to have formed up to watch and the lads are rolling about with laughter. We're about to get smashed by the Taliban and there's this comedy scene playing out before them. They're loving it.

I dump Treo on the path, squat down and get my face right up close to his, noses touching and eye-to-eye. 'Now, you listen to me, lad . . .'

His ears droop almost imperceptibly, and I can see the look in his eyes: *Hey, Dad, I was only joking – I'm sorry.*

'You ignore me, big lad, you go out of my sight, lose me and I don't know what's happening to you, then we're going to have big fisticuffs. Last thing I need is a cloth-eared dog when there's a great big shitfight about to kick off all around us.'

This is the most that I'll ever discipline my dog. It's enough. I see his ears go down further, and that apologetic look in his big, brown soppy eyes.

I glance up and I can see that the Bravo lads have witnessed this moment between us – man and dog. I'm being incredibly intimate with Treo, and I can tell that they understand, *they get it*. Treo and I have been together for five years. I can count the days that we've spent apart on one hand. A lot of people can't understand it, but we've formed a relationship that's closer than I've had with just about any human.

A lot of the Bravo Company blokes have served together for that kind of time too. They understand the bond that forms between soldiers – and in my case, between man and dog – in combat. They know how close you get to your mates, especially when you're daily walking the knife-edge between life and death.

No sooner have I finished admonishing Treo than I hear a distinctive, muffled crump. It's followed an instant later by the banshee howl of an incoming mortar round. It slams into the patch of river where Treo was having his bath, hurling water and mud and debris high into the air.

If I'd hauled him out seconds later they'd have got him: that mortar round would have made mincemeat out of my dog.

An instant later all hell breaks loose. Mortar rounds start screaming through the air, and there's the sharp staccato beat of gunfire as rounds smash into the terrain all around us. The bush has erupted with fire, shredded undergrowth and chunks of blasted dirt raining down to every side.

The Bravo lads start running hell for leather, charging through the undergrowth and making for the nearest solid cover.

The platoon commander turns and screams at Treo and me: 'You coming with us or what!'

CHAPTER FOUR

My dog and I join the mad scramble as the Taliban hammer rounds into our position. For several seconds we charge about like headless chickens, before the adrenalin kicks in and we're taking proper cover. Treo and I are down in the dirt, and still there are rounds cracking and snarling past our heads.

We're being hosed down by an enemy in a compound some two hundred metres to the east of us. I get my body – and my body armour – between Treo and the enemy bullets, to shield him. *No way is anyone shooting my dog.*

Most K9 blokes aren't infantry-ready. They're dog handlers first and foremost, and they're the best in the world at what they do, but they've got little combat training or experience under fire. It just so happens that I was infantry before going for K9.

In an instant my training kicks in and I'm returning fire with my stubby SA80, pumping rounds into the enemy target. Treo's down beside me on his belly and he's got a pained look on his face: *All this noise – let me know when you're done.*

I see spent shell cases from my Stumpy go flying through the air, glistening and glinting in the sunlight. A couple of them land on Treo's back, where his hair's still gleaming wet from the river. He shakes them off irritably. They come out of the weapon burning hot and I can tell that he's not best pleased. *What you trying to do, Dad, singe my fur off?*

Treo's jumpy and I can tell that he's well spooked. But still he's holding it together, which is how I was hoping he'd react to being in combat. We've had the dogs out on the ranges in the UK to try to get them used to loud explosions and gunfire. Plus we've had them out on exercises under simulated war-fighting conditions, trying to rehearse what it would be like to sniff out the bombs on the front line. But there's nothing like being in your first fight for real.

Treo and I are positioned right next to Bravo Company's machine-gunner. All morning he's been hauling a big, heavy general purpose machine gun plus ammo through the bush, and he's keen to unload some of it on the bad guys. He opens up, the pounding percussions letting rip next to our heads. Treo's ears flap like mad, and he jumps right across me, landing on the opposite side to the gunner.

He gives the bloke an evil stare: *What d'you do that for? And right in my ears!*

It's fair enough in a way. A dog's hearing is anything up to fifty times more sensitive than a human's. Intense noises – like a machine gun going off in a dog's earhole – can cause serious trauma. A dog experiences the world in a totally different way to us: our senses are dominated by what we see. But from a dog's point of view, smell is by far the more dominant way that they perceive the world around them, followed closely by sound.

As far as Treo is concerned right now, his senses are being besieged by the hot, peppery firework smell of burning cordite from the weapons going off all around him and the deafening wall of sound that's hammering in waves across us with each burst of machine-gun fire. It's hardly surprising that he's freaking out.

He keeps trying to pull away from the machine-gunner, so I drop my weapon and grab his harness. I start stroking him and talking to him: *calm down, lad, calm down, it's all going to be OK*. Gradually he settles, although he's still flashing the whites of his eyes as the bursts of the big machine gun ripple and flare, and the enemy rounds howl past us.

The Viking armoured vehicles have been shadowing our progress from the main road, and they start putting down covering fire from their big, thumping 50-cal heavy machine guns. The rounds go tearing into that compound, smashing it apart. The Bravo lads call for air power, and an Apache helicopter gunship comes buzzing in high above.

From two kilometres out the attack helicopter lines up on target and fires, the flash of the Hellfire missile leaving its stubwing blooming in front of the cockpit. Seconds later a black, needle-like object flashes through the air above and tears into the roof of the building, hurling a plume of rock and debris high into the air. Treo's got his paws over his ears, and he's not the only one who's been deafened. But for my dog's first time under fire I figure he's doing more than OK.

Once the Hellfire's gone in, the Bravo lads are up on their feet and charging down the compound. It's a full-frontal assault, before which the enemy resistance withers and dies. Treo and I go in with them, and we round up the two remaining enemy. We rendezvous with the Vikings, load up our three prisoners –

the two Taliban fighters, plus our suspect bomb maker – and head back to Sangin.

It's three o'clock in the afternoon by the time we're through the base gates, and that's it: patrol done. My main concern now is for the welfare of my dog. I get Treo back to his dingy cage and check his paws for any thorns, cuts or cracks. I'm aware that he's been thrown in at the deep end with no time to acclimatise. I give him buckets of water to drink and I chuck the rest over his back to help cool him. And I heap his bowl with scoops of Eukanuba dog food.

Eukanuba have the contract to supply the RAVC because their dried food provides exactly the kind of nutrition dogs need under such stressful and demanding conditions. We're on call 24/7 now, and I have no idea when our next patrol will go out. I need to get Treo fed, watered, rested and checked over as quickly as possible, but as far as I can tell he seems just fine.

Once he's eaten and drunk his fill, he does one of those Treo stretches, starting with his bottom up high and head down, then swinging his body forwards until his head's up high and his bottom's on the ground. *Ah, lovely.* He glances up at me, head tipped to one side and an inquiring look in his eyes: *Any chance of walkies?*

Were we back at home I'd take him for a stretch on the lush green of the Lincolnshire fens. It's as flat as a pancake and you can see for miles and walk to your heart's content. The best I can manage for Treo here is a quick mooch around the helipad – a bleak stretch of dirt that's barely enough to stroll a poodle.

After walkies, I leave Treo to get some rest and go and mingle with the Bravo Company lads. We're going to live and breathe

the Afghan heat and dust for weeks now, so they're going to become like family. They all know who I am by now: I'm Dave Dog. But I've got dozens of names to learn and I don't want to keep calling them all simply 'mate'. I share a brew and watch them open their mail. It'll be weeks before Treo and I start getting ours, and I'm not kidding myself for one moment that Treo won't get the lion's share. He always does.

One or two of the young lads ask if they can get their folks to mail out some treats for Treo. I sense that it's all good. After today's patrol we've gone from being the comic man-and-dog team who jump on and pee on warheads to being the dog whisperer with his magic-nosed hound who can sniff out the enemy's bomb factories. I just hope Treo and I can keep delivering the goods, because the lives of these lads depend upon his nose, and upon my eternal vigilance.

Late that afternoon Major Dan Cheeseman, the Officer Commanding of Bravo Company, calls me to an Orders Group. He's six foot three and whippet-thin, with close-cropped sandy hair above ice-blue eyes. He speaks with a cut-glass English accent, and there's something of the great British eccentric about him. His blokes say that he'll try just about anything to get the job done, and that he's fiercely loyal and dedicated to those under his command.

The major tells me that he wants Treo and me out on ops the following morning. It's a follow-up mission to today's highly successful patrol. I explain to the major all my concerns about Treo being out on patrol two days running during the heat of the afternoon; I explain that my dog's new into theatre, and yet to acclimatise properly; I tell him that whatever we do out here,

I won't put any more risk on my dog than is absolutely necessary.

The major's clearly not used to having someone question his orders, and especially not from the junior ranks. But whilst I may be a corporal and he a major, no one can order my dog what to do. I'm under the major's command, but my dog is only ever answerable to me.

Eventually, the major and I settle upon a compromise. Treo and I will head out early on foot, and we'll catch a ride back with the Vikings. That way Treo's not kept working during the heat of the day. All being well the vehicles won't be loaded up with wounded, so there'll be plenty of room for us. I'm good with that.

That evening I manage to log onto the internet. Along with some messages from my folks there's a typically cheeky one from Ken, up at Inkerman. It's something about how he's in Taliban Central whilst I'm sunning myself down by the river at Blackpool-on-the-water. It gives me a good laugh before bed.

That night is the third that I bed down with my dog stretched out beside me. Today's mission has exhausted us but I'm feeling pretty good about it. Treo and I have had our baptism of fire and we've done OK out there.

The following morning we muster at first light at the front gate – two dozen Bravo Company lads plus me and my dog. I've got this nasty voice banging away in my head: *Is this your day, Dave, the day that you and Treo are going to get smashed?* Right before we'd left our kennel I'd had Treo's steady, trusting amber eyes holding my own, as if to say: *What are you so scared of – I'm here with you, Dad.*

But we're heading out on the search, and each time we do I know there's a real chance that we won't come back, or we'll be brought in missing a limb. But worse than that would be me surviving and losing my best friend, Treo. That would be a scar in the mind that would never heal.

We're out on the ground by seven sharp, and Treo and I start the search. I'm scanning the terrain for the slightest sign that might reveal an IED's been hidden in the bush or buried in our path, plus I'm keeping an eye out for my dog in case he pops out of sight. I'm looking everywhere but where the enemy is going to be – up ahead with their guns zeroed in on one man and his dog.

But I've got this growing feeling of confidence in the Bravo Company lads – that every second they're doing everything in their power to safeguard Treo and me.

I've fashioned a makeshift leash out of a fifteen-metre length of paracord. I've got Treo roaming loosely on that leash, with the near end hooked over the bayonet that I've got jammed into my chest webbing. I figure this will give him the freedom to search whilst allowing me to haul him out of a river or a pond when we really need to move.

We've not rehearsed this kind of long-leash means of searching. We're learning as we go here, making it up as we go along. I sense that each patrol is going to be different, a process of trial and error to see what works best on the ground. I'll keep experimenting with different harness rigs and leads to see what suits the kind of tough and challenging conditions we're moving through.

We spend the morning clearing compounds and paths. I send

Treo down into a ditch full of broken rubble. It's a classic Taliban hiding place for explosives and bomb-making kit. He glances up at me: *Yeah, right – four paws, no great big clumping Army boots, thanks, Dad.* But he checks it out anyway.

By midday we've found pretty much nothing compared to that first day's search. We take a five-minute break by a small stream. I get hold of Treo's front paws and hold them up in my hands, gazing into his eyes. I give them a good rub.

'Are your pawsies hurting, lad, are they?' I ask him. 'I know my feet are aching like hell.'

I glance around a little sheepishly. I can feel the lads with their eyes on me. For a moment I find myself thinking *I hope no one saw me doing that.* But those that have noticed have got these indulgent smiles on their faces, as if they've seen the dog whisperer having a talk to his hound, and they figure it's all right.

I dig Treo's plastic water bowl out of my backpack, and I'm just slopping some water into it when the silence is ripped apart. Suddenly, there's a fearsome stream of rounds hammering through the bush just inches above my dog and me. There's only one way out of the fire, and that's to dive backwards into the water. I land with Treo on top of me, for I've dragged him in there by the paracord leash.

It doesn't bother Treo. He loves the wet. As for me, I've landed right on top of a nest of vicious, biting insects. I've got a thick swarm buzzing around my head and I'm getting bitten raw. I can't stand up, in part because I've got Treo on top of me, but more because the gunfire's hammering across us and I've got my body between my dog and the fire.

As the insects gnaw into my face, bullets kick up savage spurts of mud along the rim of the stream, and whine and pop angrily across the water all around my head. I just know that Treo's laughing at me.

The longer we lie there half submerged the less sympathetic my dog seems to get. It's like he's saying, *So, if you don't want me in the river what are you doing pulling me in here with you? And on top of all those insects, too! Make your mind up, won't you, Dad?*

The Bravo Company lads put down a barrage of murderous counter-fire. Their skill and aggression is unsurpassed, and they're the kind of blokes you really want on your side in the midst of a bloody great firefight. Clouds of thick cordite smoke drift across the water, and it does a little to drive the insects off. Finally, the enemy must realise they're outgunned, for they melt away into the surrounding terrain.

By the time we drag ourselves out of the water I've been bitten raw by the swarm, but otherwise I'm unharmed. Treo is completely fine, which is a huge relief because I've got this horrible feeling that a great deal of the enemy fire was targeted at my dog. Maybe I was just imagining things, but just where we'd taken cover was where the enemy fire seemed to be at its most concentrated and deadly.

It's the hottest part of the day by the time we're back on the search. I check Treo for dehydration by pulling at the scruff of his neck: when it fails to spring back into place I know that he's suffering. I check his gums and his nose: if they're not soft, glistening and moist I'll know that the heat's really getting to him.

By the time we rendezvous with the Vikings, Treo's nose is noticeably duller and drier. I reckon it's not a moment too soon

to get him out of the burning heat, into some shade, and on his
way back to base. I give my remaining water to the lads who'll
be completing the patrol on foot and go to mount up the Viking,
but it's then that the convoy commander puts out an arm to stop
me.

He tells me that there's no room in the vehicles for me and
my dog. I tell him there has to be, 'cause Treo's not walking back
to Sangin in the boiling heat of the afternoon. He's not acclimatised to the conditions yet, it's a long hike back to base, and I
am not visiting that on my dog. I tell him the major's orders
were that the dog team goes back in the Vikings.

We get into this massive argument, but eventually he half gives
in: Treo can ride in the Vikings, he tells me, but I can't. He's a
young, gobby lieutenant, and I'm fifteen years his senior. If I'd
remained in the Cheshires I'd probably have made officer by
now. In my mind and attitude I outrank him, but I don't need
to argue this one. Treo, I know, will sort it out in his own, inim-
itable fashion.

All I say to the lieutenant is: 'Fine, sir, have it your way.'

But secretly I'm laughing my head off at what's about to
happen here. I unclip Treo's harness, give him a quick 'get up',
and he leaps into the rear of the Viking.

He half turns, looking for his dad to follow him. Instead, I
give him a good ruffle around the neck and what verbal reassurance I can: 'Good laaaad – you take it easy in there while I'm
on these tired legs doing the long haul back . . .'

Then I flash him an encouraging smile and stride off to join
the rest of the patrol. I've left a less than happy-looking Treo at
the lieutenant's feet, and no sooner has the door swung shut

behind me than I hear this low, throaty growl. Treo is a one-man dog. I'm the alpha male – his pack leader and his dad. All he ever wants in life – apart from the odd bit of flirting with the likes of Sasha and Jihad – is to search for bombs and to bask in the love of his dad. And as far as he's concerned he's just lost his pack leader. *Not good news.*

On the few occasions that we've been separated in the past, Treo's got scared. The only way he knows to show fear is to growl. If you don't back off he'll show his teeth: *Listen, I'm real scared of you, so back off* . . . And if you keep coming once he's done that he'll bite you: *I warned you twice but you took no notice . . . NOW BACK RIGHT OFF!*

I can just imagine the fate awaiting that lieutenant on the drive back to Sangin, and I've no doubt who will be getting the better of that confrontation. I'm smiling inside as I think of it, but I don't keep doing so for long. There are several problems. One, I've now got no water and I've got eight miles to go during the hottest part of the day. More importantly, I can't get my mind off Treo and the fact that he's not at my side. Suddenly, I feel like some useless tourist bolted onto the patrol, like all meaning in my life has gone. I know that I've done the right thing letting Treo ride back, because he was totally whacked, but still I'm worried sick for my dog.

What happens if the Viking gets hit by an IED? What happens if Treo gets injured and I'm not at his side? What happens if I lose him? Mile after mile on that long trek back to Sangin I can't get those dark thoughts out of my mind.

I'm parched with thirst long before we're approaching base. I'm torn between my fear for Treo, the worry that I'm going to die of thirst, or that the Taliban are going to hit the patrol with an IED because we're out here bereft of our search dog. I see the Marine that I gave all my water to taking a greedy neck, and I give him the eye. *You going to share some of that with me or what?*

By the time we reach the outskirts of town, it's a fantastic morale booster to see the Afghan flags flying, and not those of the Taliban. It means that we're winning the battle for hearts and minds here but, more importantly, that we're almost there, which means me being reunited with my dog.

I stumble through the front gates exhaustedly. Immediately to one side there's one of the Bravo Company lads, with Treo held on a makeshift lead. My dog's overjoyed to see me, and vice versa, but the Bravo lad can't seem to stop laughing.

'All right, mate, out with it: what's so funny?' I ask, as I give Treo a good ruffle and a hug.

'Two things, Dave. One, there was room for you on the wagon after all.'

'What the— I did eight bloody miles in the heat of the day with no water, and there was space!'

'Yeah, once we'd taken our seats we realised there was one free. Sorry, mate.'

'And what's the other thing that's so funny?'

'Well, best of all your dog had a good pop at the convoy commander. All the way back he kept growling and biting him, like he knew he'd been left with us sweaty lot while you got to walk home.'

'Serves him bloody right.'

I glance down at Treo. He's got this look on his face like he knows he's done wrong: *I'm sorry, Dad, but he threw you out so what choice did I have but to bite him?*

At no stage do I chastise my dog. I'm glad Treo chewed out that gobby lieutenant, and in a sense I'm the one most at fault here. I should have been there to settle and control my dog. I make a decision there and then: wherever it is we're going next, they either take both of us or neither of us.

This is the last time I am ever going to be separated from my dog.

CHAPTER FIVE

The first priority for any frontline soldier once he's in off patrol is his weapon: to unload it, to make it safe, clean it, and to reload his magazines. My first priority is my dog. I have to make sure he has plenty of food and water, and he gets time for a good run around the helipad or by the river. Treo needs his down time and his playtime as an antidote to the intensity and stress of the search, not to mention being locked in a Viking without his dad.

Once he's done having his run, we return to our makeshift kennel and I set to grooming him. First I use the 'rake', a strong metal comb that can drag out the worst knots and the tangles in his hair. After that I give him a good brushing down with a softer kind of a shoe brush. It'll leave Treo's jet-black coat looking smooth and glossy like dark satin.

This is a crucial part of being a top handler. An average handler doesn't put in the extra 5 per cent to forge man and dog into an unbreakable team. Out here in Afghanistan, if Treo doesn't get regularly groomed his hair will get matted. He'll keep licking himself to try to free it, which will give him hairballs. Dogs tend to pick up burrs in the bush, which can work their way into the skin and cause infections, and I need to remove them before they can do him any harm.

Grooming is part of keeping your dog at peak performance. As opposed to all the fun stuff we do with our dogs, grooming is the more mundane side, but it's one that keeps your animal in top form. Grooming Treo is the equivalent of one of the Bravo lads maintaining his assault rifle. He's taught to care for his weapon, and to check for any damage and to remove any dirt. Likewise, Treo's weapons are his senses: his nose, ears and eyes plus, on occasion – as with the Lieutenant who locked him into that Viking – his teeth. A dog like Treo is perhaps the most highly trained animal on the planet, and he's cost tens of thousands of pounds to bring to the stage he's at now.

As I run the brush repeatedly across Treo's glossy flank, I think back over the last time that my dog chewed someone out. It was Belfast, 2007, and Treo and I were out on those mean, rain-lashed streets preparing to do yet another gruelling search. We had a Royal Engineers Search Advisor (RESA) with us, and he was guiding us as to where exactly he needed us to look.

We were just about to start the search when I realised I had forgotten a crucial piece of kit. I tied Treo to a convenient lamp-post and prepared to make the short jog back to our truck to fetch it. It was then that the RESA bloke asked me if he could stroke my dog.

'Please don't, sir,' I told him. 'He'll bite you.'

'Would he really?' he queried. He sounded like he didn't believe me.

'Oh yes, he would. So please, sir, don't go near him.'

I jogged back to the wagon and I was just reaching inside when

I heard this almighty scream. I knew instantly what had happened. I ran back to where I'd left Treo, and there was a shocked RESA officer clutching his hand. He had blood dripping between his fingers, and I fancied I could see Treo licking his lips.

'Your dog bit me!' he exclaimed.

'I can see that,' I said. 'What happened?'

'Well, I kind of went to stroke him . . .'

'And?'

'Well, he growled.'

'And?'

'I went forwards to stroke him.'

'And?'

'He showed me his teeth.'

'So what did you do?'

'Well, I tried to stroke him. I mean, I thought he was joking.'

'Well, I guess he showed you he wasn't. That's Treo. He'll only tell you twice. Two strikes and you're out.'

I took him over to the truck and bandaged up his hand. I was completely with my dog on this one. I'd warned that RESA guy. Treo had warned him repeatedly. He only had himself to blame. Whether in Northern Ireland or here in Afghanistan, Treo's a one-man dog. No one comes between us.

After those two patrols in the burning Afghan heat and dust, Major Cheeseman decides the Bravo Company lads need a couple of days' down time. The men need some space in which to chill and to sort their kit. It's time in which I can address my number one priority right now, which is making Treo a decent and safe kennel.

Whilst out on patrol I've realised just what a wild and murderous place it is here. On both occasions the enemy hit us big time, and on the second mission I was convinced they were targeting my dog. I'm certain I made the right decision getting Treo and me posted to Sangin, for who else amongst our young handler and dog teams could handle it here? But I'd sure like another dog team to deploy alongside us.

Rockets and mortar rounds keep slamming into the base. Late afternoon the previous day I'd dropped off to sleep, only to be jerked awake by the sound of a 107 mm Chinese-made rocket screaming over the top of us. The warhead ploughed into the desert some fifty metres beyond the base, throwing out a deafening blast and a cloud of dirt, and punching an angry mushroom cloud of smoke high above our heads.

A second rocket zoomed over our kennel, slamming into the dirt next to a steel shipping container. A Bravo Company lad was tanning himself on the roof. He was off it like a greased weasel, as big lumps of hot metal exploded in all directions. Treo and I dived for cover, and it served as a powerful reminder of how I needed to make my dog a safe, sandbagged kennel as an absolute priority.

At one time there had been a patrol dog team based here in Sangin, and I get one of the Bravo Company lads to show me their old quarters. They housed themselves in this little, traditional mud-domed building, one that is just about big enough for me to split into two. It's one of the few buildings on the base that remains unoccupied and I figure with a bit of work it'll do for Treo and me.

I beg, borrow and steal the materials that I need: a pile of breeze blocks, some sheets of HESCO walling, and some cage wire. I build a wall down the centre of the room, constructed from an inner layer of breeze blocks, covered in a layer of HESCO mesh. That divides the room into two, in case we do get sent the second dog team that I've asked for. I roof over both runs with wire mesh, and I provide each with a wire-mesh door.

I build a wire-mesh enclosure out the front, where I can let Treo run free. That way he can choose: he can opt either to have a doze in the shade of the hut, or he can sun himself out in the open. That completes our K9 fortress-come-home. Treo and I can sleep inside that walled and roofed semi-bunker in some degree of security. It won't survive a direct hit from an enemy mortar, but it should stop most shrapnel.

I get a broken plank of wood and make up my own official 'Kennels' sign. It reads 'Arms Explosive Search Dog Treo', below which is a sketch of a dog's paw, with '104 MWDSU' beneath that – the 104 Military Working Dog Support Unit. I also get a makeshift sign printed up on a sheet of paper, which I tack to our outer door.

It reads: *Please do not feed or touch the dog. He bites quite hard and it hurts!!*

Whilst building the inner dividing wall I've been using a lock-knife to saw through the HESCO. I'm putting the final touches to it when the knife springs back, slicing deep into my finger. It's not just any old finger that's been left half hanging off: it's my trigger finger.

I go to see the Bravo Company medic and he tells me that I need stitches. I hate needles. He injects me with the painkiller, and he's barely started to sew me up when I faint. I drop like a

That's the thing with Treo – his expression says it all. He's in his harness and ready to start the search. We became so close to the soldiers we were protecting, they got Treo to wear their regimental shamrock, which was sewn onto his harness, for luck. Little did we know that the harness would end up saving his life.

Out on patrol with Treo and taking a much-needed breather. No matter how hard I pushed him searching out the bombs, he never seemed to tire.

The battle-worn stronghold of the Sangin District Centre, the headquarters of the British forces in the region. Treo's kennel and my place of sleep alongside him is out front, marked by the MWDSU (Military Working Dog Support Unit) sign.

Treo with a bog-standard tennis ball. This wasn't just his favourite toy in the world – it was also a key part of our search routine. Treo knew if he found a bomb or some weapons, he'd get a play with his beloved ball!

Treo's laser-eyed stare says it all: *Dad, I think I'm onto something.*

Here it is! Here it is! I didn't normally get Treo to dig out a bomb or a hidden arms cache, but just occasionally there was no stopping him, he was that keen to find it!

The power supply that's used to trigger an IED. Discovering this lethal 'collapsing circuit IED' was one of the most terrifying moments of my life, and one of the many finds that won Treo the Dickin Medal.

One of the main charges that would have been triggered had Treo not sniffed it out – a 105mm shell packed with explosives.

Treo knew I had broad shoulders and many's the time I carried him up ladders and over walls when we were on the search. It was a good place to sit, especially when posing for a photo.

A happy dog with a right mouthful. Treo was trained to search for weapons, as well as bombs. Here he's unearthed a large calibre round, and come to show it proudly to his dad!

Two lifesavers in one picture. Treo eyeing up the base doctor: he's after his chocolate. No matter how many treats Treo got, he was always on the hunt for more.

Treo in his Doggles. He knew they made him look very uncool, but they were invaluable in keeping sand out of his eyes when helicopters were around.

Pretty it wasn't, but our K9 fortress did at least offer us a degree of protection. Treo seemed to sense that this was his sanctuary and he was as safe as he could be in there.

The 104 Military Working Dog Support Unit, On Tour.

That's my boy! Treo always did a good job of looking like he owned the place.

My fellow handler and gentle giant, Steve Purdy, with his infantry patrol dog, Reece.

stone onto the hard-packed dirt of the medical building and I'm out cold. Meanwhile, the medic is laughing his rocks off at this big, tough dog handler who faints at the sight of blood.

I return to the kennel with my hand swathed in bandages. I see Treo giving me the eye: *What have you done there, Dad? I leave you for five minutes to make me a kennel, and this is how you end up . . .*

Before I can declare the new kennel officially open, I need the Bravo Company padre to come and give it his blessing. I tell him that Treo and I have been out on two patrols so far, and both times we've had near misses. He finds it funny that I want a *kennel* blessed but I really do want him to give our quarters the once-over.

He throws some holy water around the walls, and as he does so he mumbles some prayers for Treo and me to be kept safe, both here and out there in the badlands. He makes the sign of the cross at various junctures, and I can hear him muttering softly.

'In the name of the Father I bless this kennel . . . In the name of the Father I bless this kennel . . . May the Lord keep all those who serve in her safe from any harm . . .'

With the kennel blessed, I move Treo in. I can tell that he's much happier in his new digs. He's got this look on his face like he can't wait to invite Jihad over for some quality face time.

I place my camp cot, my DVD player and my spare uniforms in the other half of the kennel, and that's it for me. Just across the dividing wall is Treo's domain. To the front are Treo's food bins and his meal preparation area. To one side of the kennel building I've constructed a seating and brew area – the chairs made of sandbags, the table from an upturned wooden door.

I've got Sly, my favourite Afghan terp, to go into town and buy me a tin kettle. Sly's got long, dark straggly hair, and he figures he's a real ladies' man. We tease him that he looks like Sylvester Stallone, hence the nickname. Sly loves it. It never seems to occur to him that we might be taking the piss.

I've made a fire pit in the chill-out area so I can light up some hexy fuel blocks – British Army cooking fuel very similar to firelighters – and get the kettle on. I know we're going to get a lot of visitors here in the new kennel. Soldiers love nothing more than a bit of chill time with a dog. They start talking about their dogs back home, and that reminds them that there is a normal, sane life outside the madness of war.

I decide I'm going to get each visitor to sign my makeshift table with a black marker, or to carve their name into it. It'll be the Sangin kennel tradition, and it'll help while away the hours.

Luckily, my folks have been in touch with a coffee company local to my home town, and Bob – my Dad – has convinced them to donate a job lot of their gourmet-blend coffee to my war effort. I've brought rakes of the stuff with me, and just as soon as word goes around that I've got it I know I'll get inundated with visitors.

Our makeshift kennel done, I put in a request to Sergeant Major Frank Holmes, our second-in-command at Camp Bastion, for a portable kennel system to be dropped out to us. The 104 has these steel shipping containers that have been converted into field kennels. They come complete with air conditioning, and it's the promise of the air con and the chance to cool my dog that I most want for Treo.

Whilst I've been making the kennel, the 104 has sent a new handler and dog team out to join us, but they're a patrol dog team, one trained purely to do security. Their job is to patrol a base to stop any would-be intruders. I've been so busy constructing the kennel that I've spent precious little time with them. It's only when the wound to my finger forces me to stop, that I take a moment to visit the Bravo Company OC to see what use he's been making of them.

Major Cheeseman doesn't particularly seem to want the new dog team here. He argues that he's not much in need of a patrol dog. What he does want – and what I requested – is a second AES team getting out on patrol. I arrange for John Allison, the young handler, and his dog to get returned to Bastion. I do so reluctantly, because I know young John doesn't want to go. He wants to feel that he's being used at the cutting edge of war.

I get John to carry a message for me back to the 104. I explain that we can only make use of an AES team, and how urgently in need we are of one. Bravo Company consists of four troops – over two hundred men at arms – and Treo and I have to cover for them all. Those troops are out doing back-to-back patrols, and my dog and I could be on-search 24/7 if I allowed us to be.

John's dog, Toby, is a ferocious German shepherd. Like all patrol dogs, he's been chosen for his aggression and his drive to bite. We load him into his flight cage and carry it up to the helipad so that we can get John and his dog into the helicopter and gone. But it doesn't quite work out that way. By the time we've got the cage halfway up the rear ramp, the aircrew have been ordered to get airborne and they wave us off again.

Unfortunately, John fails to dismount the aircraft in time, the ramp whirs shut, and I'm left alone on the helipad with one extremely enraged dog. I've got no option but to take the cage and Toby back to our newly built kennels.

I've trained German shepherds before, and a dog never forgets a handler, the smell of whom will always bring a sense of familiarity and companionship. Unfortunately, I've never worked with Toby, and I don't get the impression that he likes me very much. After all, why should he? I'm very much not his dad. But somehow I've got to get him out of his flight cage and into the kennel alongside Treo's.

I edge Toby's flight kennel up against the entrance, throw some doggy treats inside and ease open the door. Toby smells the treats and takes the bait. My dog is now sharing the Kingdom of Treo with this lunatic German shepherd, one who's going wild for his handler. In no time, Toby makes it clear that he needs a wee and a poo. Wherever possible the dogs are trained not to soil their own quarters. I've now got to work out how the hell we manage this one.

Somehow, I succeed in getting Toby onto a leash and his toilet stuff done without me getting bitten or losing control of him. But this is starting to get more than a little silly. More importantly, Treo and I are needed out on patrol, but instead I'm having to babysit a teeth-gnashing Toby-wolf. I head to the ops room and get a radio call put through to the 104 at Camp Bastion.

'John's on his way, but his dog's still here,' I tell them. 'I need John back to pick up his dog, or an airframe sent to lift him out.'

The boss reassures me that they'll get John on a helo flight to come and fetch Toby. 'Don't worry, Dave,' he tells me. 'We'll get it sorted.'

His 'getting it sorted' takes two full days. I can't get out on patrol because I can't leave an attack dog unsupervised. At the same time I've still got to try to wee, poo and exercise him. The only way I can get him to half behave is to bribe him with copious amounts of doggy treats, and I can tell that Treo's getting resentful and jealous. I can't say that I blame him. More to the point, both me and Treo are burning up with frustration that we're not getting out and getting used.

There's a real risk here that Toby will seriously turn on me. If he does, that'll be me out of action for a very long time. He's trained to bite and hold and not let go unless his handler orders him to. And right now his handler's hardly in yelling distance to call off his dog. You can't run from a patrol dog, either. They're trained to pursue and bring down a fleeing suspect, and a young German shepherd like Toby is far swifter than an ageing Dave Heyhoe. It would be a case of me having to take the bite and drag him back to his cage.

Treo's a lot smaller than Toby, but I've never once seen my dog back down from a fight. If he could just get at Toby – the dog that's seriously pissing off his dad – I know Treo would go for him big time. And the last thing I need is Treo getting an ear ripped off, as that would be him out of action for the rest of the tour. There's no doubt about it – we need to get Toby gone.

Finally, I get word that John's flying in to pick up his dog. It's not a moment too soon, as far as Treo and I are concerned. The helicopter touches down in a thick, broiling dust storm, and I'm waiting there with Toby in his flight crate. By the time the brown-out has cleared, I can see that it's only a Lynx that has flown in, not the big, bulky Chinook that I was expecting.

I'm familiar with the Lynx from my infantry days. It can carry up to nine fully equipped troops, but we've rarely if ever used one to transport a dog. I figure they'll just about be able to get Toby and his crate aboard, but it'll be a tight squeeze. In fact, I'm wrong. Whatever way we try it, the crate just won't go in.

Finally, John is forced to muzzle Toby and drag him aboard the aircraft minus cage. I can see how reluctant the dog is to go in, and in a way I feel for him. To Toby, this giant beast with screaming turbines and thrashing rotor blades must appear like the world's most terrifying monster. Just as soon as they've got him in and slid shut the door, the pilot piles on the collective and they're airborne.

But as the Lynx climbs into the sky it starts veering wildly and it's all over the place. Toby is visible through the Plexiglas sides and he's going insane. His head is snapping this way and that as he tries to shake off the muzzle and sink his teeth into the neck of one or other of the flight crew, just a couple of feet in front of him.

Slowly, and horribly erratically, the helicopter dwindles into a distant speck in the sky. Thank God he's gone. I return to our kennels and do a quick check on Treo. *Lunatic dog gone?* he asks me. *Yes, lad, lunatic dog gone!*

It's great being just the two of us again, for there's nothing worse than losing that bond with your dog.

CHAPTER SIX

Before deploying to Afghanistan I'd made a point of watching any TV shows I could about the war. No matter what training we did, we couldn't replicate the real-life experience – the heat, the dust, the terrain and the combat. From those films I saw what a compound looked like, the kind of paths and tracks we'd be searching over, what kind of a barrier an irrigation ditch presented and the nature of the Afghan bush. And all the time I was thinking: *how will we search to maximise our effectiveness and to safeguard the dogs?*

The majority of our handlers had been in the Army Dog Unit (ADU) in Northern Ireland, the forebears of the 104. With peace coming to Northern Ireland the ADU had been disbanded a few years back, and we handlers and dogs had gone on to form the 104. Northern Ireland had been a fine proving ground, but the tasks we'd been given were fairly limited. We'd be sent out to search a specific area, based upon a specific piece of intelligence.

Afghanistan we knew was going to be completely different. We figured it would involve long patrols searching under fire. We'd be reacting to the dog's senses, plus snippets of intelligence picked up along the way. We had new guys coming into the unit – eighteen- and nineteen-year-olds who we had to prepare to go to war. It was a big old tasking. At times I'd come across one of those young lads or lasses in floods of tears, worried sick about whether they'd make it back from Afghanistan.

I didn't blame them for being worried. There was a fierce debate going on within the RAVC regarding the training; whether we should concentrate more on classic handler-and-dog work, or more on infantry skills. Some argued that if a handler had wanted to be an infantryman, they'd have joined an infantry unit. I argued that we needed to give them both skill sets, for there was no point in being the world's greatest dog handler if you couldn't keep your dog and yourself alive.

Treo and I are barely a week into our Afghan deployment by now, and nothing could have proven more our need for infantry fighting skills. Afghanistan is like Northern Ireland, Bosnia and Iraq all rolled into one. It's all the horrors of all those wars condensed into one patch of territory. I've had the living daylights scared out of me and we've barely started. Only one hundred and eighty days to go.

The older I get the more I notice that I seem to feel fear. I'm trying to use that fear to sharpen my search procedures here in Sangin, and I'm drawing enormous strength from my dog. The fact that Treo's heading out tirelessly searching alongside me, helps give me the strength to place one boot in front of the other, when every footfall might be my last.

But at the same time I'm having to send my best buddy forwards, and the tension is eating away at me. I know Treo senses this: one glance into my eyes and he can read my mood and what I'm thinking.

Yet there's another, much deeper and more hidden layer of worry now: *it's the fear of not finding something*. If I tread on an IED and set it off, most likely I'll be dead or very seriously injured. The same for Treo. When Treo and I have moved through a search area I can tell you exactly what we *have* found. I cannot tell you how many devices we've missed. So whenever we're done with a patch of terrain I've found myself thinking, *Was it really all clear?*

If Treo misses something, everything we've done before will be as nothing. The guys coming behind us are already starting to think, *OK, the dog's been across it; we're safe to proceed*. That leaves them free to concentrate on finding the Taliban, so they can fight them man-to-man. But if we miss something and one of the blokes gets blown to pieces, all of that trust will be gone, and it'll torture me for the rest of my days.

I ask myself a hypothetical question. If either of the guys running the 104 at Camp Bastion were put out of action, would I go and take his place? I'm the next highest-ranking soldier, so it would make sense for me to do so. The answer is an emphatic 'no'. I feel part of something hugely meaningful here. Treo and I are going out every day to save lives. What could be better than this?

For years I've searched for some kind of meaning in my life, especially since I lost my father early in my childhood. Basically, he walked out on my mother, my sister and me. I was nine years old when it happened and I've spent a lot of my life trying to compensate. I never had a father figure to pat me on the back and say 'well done', and I spent years trying to seek a surrogate father's approval.

But out here I'm starting to feel as if I'm proving myself as never before. All the thanks that I'll ever need are the same number of boots – and paws – coming in off a patrol as went out. That's the best 'well done' a dog team like us could ever wish for.

My youthful need for approval was coupled with a rebellious, maverick streak. When I was twelve years old my stepfather, Bob, turned up on the scene. At first I was dead set against him and I spun pretty much out of control. It was joining the Army Cadets that sorted me out, and at a time when my mum was about to put me into a home. Bob had spent twenty-five years in the RAF and it was his guiding hand that turned me away from petty crime and absconding, towards a military career.

But because I had to be different I decided to join the Army, as opposed to Bob's arm of the services. I joined up as a private at sixteen, in the Cheshire Regiment (now 1 MERCIAN). By then Bob had become a fantastic father figure and I decided to take his surname, Heyhoe, rather than that of my birth father.

I'd first been deployed with the Cheshires to Northern Ireland at the height of the Troubles. British soldiers were being targeted mercilessly, and there was a sniper on every corner, a bomb in every vehicle. I'd been out on patrol in Crossmaglen, and we had an Arms Explosives Search dog allocated to our platoon. I was fascinated to watch the handler and his dog in action; how they worked as one fluid, unbreakable team. They were out front clearing the way, and spreading reassurance throughout the patrol.

The dog was a black Labrador similar in appearance to Treo.

I could tell that he adored his handler and that the handler had ultimate respect for his dog. I'd always been drawn to dogs. I'd been given a black and white collie puppy when I was young, but he couldn't learn his toilet habits and kept peeing on the carpet. Within days my mum had made me send him back to his original owner, and I was heartbroken.

During early days with the Cheshires I'd been sent out to Kenya to do the British Army's basic training in desert survival. We were out one night using the standard Mark One eyeball to navigate across miles of trackless Kenyan bush. At one point I spotted a glowing green cat-like eye staring at me from maybe fifty yards away. When I found the other to match its pair, I realised how far apart they were. Whatever cat-like animal was watching me it had a simply humungous head.

It was then that I heard a hoarse whisper from behind me: 'Best move on, Dave, it's a lion.'

The thrill and the fear of being face to face with nature in the raw really lit me up. But after that I made doubly sure that if only one guy in the patrol went out with live ammunition, then it was me!

I loved the Kenyan bush. The only thing that I was truly petrified of was the snakes, but every other walking crawling growling beastie had me in raptures. I was drawn to the wild and the wide-open spaces. Each night we'd hire a warrior from the local Masai tribe to sit in camp and keep watch. He'd be hunched over the fire for warmth, complete with his blood-red robe and sharpened spear.

We'd see the Masai during the daytime moving through the bush with their long easy strides, and with nothing more to protect them than their clubs and their spears. With their light sandals and their cloaks they appeared so at ease here, and we developed a strong mutual respect. One evening I sat up late chatting to the Masai on watch, conversing in his broken but usable English, which I figured he'd learned from scores of passing squaddies.

At one point he turned to me and asked: 'Dave, why is it you always light a fire at night?'

'It keeps the wild animals away, doesn't it?'

He laughed. 'You think it keeps them away, but the warmth draws them in. The heat brings them closer.'

'Yikes!' I got up and started dancing around, stamping out the flames.

That had the guy in stitches.

A few days later I was out on patrol and we spotted a herd of elephants. For me this was simply the biggest ever wow. I had to stop and take a photo, and I chose the biggest bull elephant to capture on film. I stepped forwards and framed him up, but I couldn't understand why he kept growing bigger and bigger in my viewfinder, and why I had to keep reframing the shot.

Finally I took a glance over the top of the camera, only to see an enraged elephant charging towards me, ears flapping murderously. Needless to say I turned and ran; the other lads in the patrol were already on their toes. I only managed to escape the mother of all crushings by diving down a nearby ravine. The bull elephant came skidding to a halt, stamping and trumpeting wildly. I crawled up the other side, only to be met by a row of lads laughing their socks off.

I was a member of the regimental Corps of Drums and I was also its mace carrier, more formally known as the Drum Major. The Cheshire's mace has a silver eagle mounted atop a twisted wooden shaft. One night my Masai friend asked to take a look at it. After studying it for a while he asked me if I'd like him to carve me a copy. I said that I would. He returned to camp a few days later with this replica made entirely from ebony. I was blown away by the intricacy of the thing.

After that I asked him to carve me all the elephants, lions, zebras and rhinos that he could manage. He even rustled up a couple of three-legged folding leather stools – one with a lion painted on it and the other with a rhino. I ended up with so much stuff that I had to get my Masai friend to build me a wooden trunk so I could ship it all back to the UK.

I gave each of my nephews one of the folding stools. The one with the lion stool argued that his animal was the toughest. The one with the rhino stool said no way: his would beat the lion in any fight. To settle the argument I told them that each animal was so tough that they'd hurt each other if ever they fought. As a result, they'd agreed never to come to blows. Lion and rhino knew they were each other's equals, which was just as my two nephews should be with each other.

After Kenya, I knew that I had this innate affinity with animals, but it was seeing that search dog at work in Northern Ireland that really lit my candle. I realised there was a big part of me that wanted some of that, yet I hadn't got the faintest idea how you got into K9. Still, I went ahead and got my first dog, a magnificent German shepherd called Max. And that was it – dogs became my life.

On a second tour of Northern Ireland I was posted to Ballykelly, in County Londonderry. There was a K9 unit stationed nearby, and that gave me the chance to visit their kennels. Pretty quickly I realised that this had to be the ultimate partnership between man and animal. The dog teams worked in the twilight zone where doing their duty forever put them in the line of fire and up against the bomb makers. It was only their trust and faith in each other that enabled them to overcome their fear. The dogs would give their lives for their handlers, and vice versa, and I knew that this was something I wanted to be a part of.

I was posted to the British military base on Cyprus, and one day I had to take Max to see the resident vet at the RAVC unit. I volunteered to start helping out at their kennels, and one of the first things I did was build the dogs an assault course. It was the kind of thing that they'd use to train the dogs for deployment to places like Iraq, and eventually to Afghanistan.

Eventually, I plucked up the courage to ask about how I might get to be a dog handler. The bad news was that at thirty-two years of age, I was already too old to apply. But in light of my total, burning commitment, the RAVC agreed to bend the rules a little and to make an exception.

In 2002 I left the Cheshires and joined up as the RAVC's oldest ever recruit. It was the most significant decision I'd ever made as a soldier, and the turning point in my life. I had to accept demotion from sergeant to lance corporal, as the RAVC argued that most of what I'd learned in the infantry was irrelevant to K9. I was sent to the RAVC's Defence Animal Training Centre, at Melton Mowbray, and my instructing sergeant was a good few years younger than me. I told him I was fine with that, as long as he taught me everything he knew about working with man's best friend – the dog.

I loved every minute of my K9 training. I learned how German shepherds were prized for their strength and ferocity as guard dogs. My German shepherd, Max, had epitomised that during the years that I had him. They have everything you want in a military working dog: strength, endurance, devotion, athleticism, plus the drive to learn and to work. I learned how Labradors and spaniels made the perfect search dogs, due to their boundless energy, curiosity and intelligence, coupled with their unrivalled sense of fun.

At the Defence Animal Training Centre I was put through my basic training. I started by practising how to say my commands properly, using a plastic bucket as my stand-in dog. I'd have to reward the bucket in my 'praise voice': high-pitched, squeaky and unthreatening. I'd have to chastise the bucket in my 'punish voice': low, throaty and growly, as if I was angry.

I graduated onto learning basic handling techniques with real animals. I learned I had to build a good rapport with my dog, before I could start the specialist and intensive work to turn him or her into the most highly trained animal on the planet – which Arms Explosive Search (AES) dogs are.

We trained the dogs using a Kong – an indestructible rubber ball – giving them a play with it when they responded to the right scent in the right way. From that basic foundation we built months of further specialist training, searching across fields and forests and factories and parking lots for tiny amounts of explosives hidden in the most unlikely of places – explosives which the dog had to find but never touch.

I was deployed first to Northern Ireland as a qualified K9 handler, and it was there that I first got to hear about this enigmatic search dog called Treo. Treo's reputation went before him. In RAVC circles he was this legendary black beast, one who would apparently bite your hand off as soon as look at you. He was a dog with a big personality and teeth to match. He sounded rough, tough and boisterous, and like he didn't take any prisoners. In a way he sounded a lot like me.

It's in my nature to favour the maverick and the rebel, and I simply had to get a look at him. As I walked down to the kennels I was expecting to encounter a snarling whirl of white teeth and black fur. But I told myself I wasn't going to show fear. Treo was known as a dog that loved to challenge who was boss. I decided to kneel down at his cage and get eye-to-eye with him. That way, he'd know I wasn't afraid.

I did just that, and this black beast of a dog came up and stared at me in silence for several seconds. And then the most amazing thing happened. He flicked out his tongue and licked me on the nose. That was it: it was love at first sight.

I told him there and then: 'I want you, Treo my lad, and I'm going to get you!'

I did get Treo – but it was then that he became the teacher and I the student. He had bags of Northern Ireland search experience and I had next to none. He took me through the ropes of being an AES dog handler for real, and taught me all that he knew.

I was certain that there had to be something behind Treo's nasty, rebel reputation, just as there was behind my own rebellious ways. I looked into his background, but there was nothing

I could see to account for the dark reputation that he'd earned. Treo had had a loving upbringing with the Abbott family. They'd got him when he was a tiny, cute ball of puppy fluff, and their kids had adored him. But over the months that followed they'd realised that Treo had too much energy and too sharp an intelligence to sit around being a pet.

They found they had to strap him into a protective plastic collar because the young and boisterous puppy kept leaping about, crashing into things and falling over. Without that collar he was constantly getting hurt. From the earliest days the only way to keep him still was to give him a giant bone to chew on. He exhausted the family with his non-stop hunger for play, and eventually they made the difficult decision to donate him to the Army.

Treo had been with the family for two years when they decided to give him up, and it was a tearful parting. But the Abbott parents were right: he needed more than they could give. In a way they'd done Treo a favour. He was tailor-made for being a search dog, and at the RAVC he was amongst handlers who had all the time and energy to challenge and push him.

Treo had taken to search work like a duck to water. He passed his training as an AES dog with flying colours, and it was a couple of years after that when I'd managed to get him. Over the months of training and play I'd learned that Treo never tired of his ball, and never tired of the search. To him they were both just a fantastic game. From the start I realised that Treo's favourite toy wasn't a Kong: it was a green tennis ball, the same type that I now carried with me on patrols into the Afghan badlands.

Whilst Afghanistan is Treo's first war, it's not mine. I've come here worrying if he'll deliver the goods and be able to use his nose in full-on combat. Would he stand the heat and the pressure? Was the love between us strong enough to make him go into the heart of battle time after time and keep finding the bombs? Would he do it for me? And would he do so repeatedly, day after day after day?

I figure I've pretty much got my answers by now. Treo's a rock, and there's an unshakeable, indestructible trust between us.

It's worries about my own capabilities and losing some of the Bravo Company lads that are at the forefront of my mind.

CHAPTER SEVEN

I'm called into an Orders Group with Major Cheeseman. He briefs me on our next mission, which is going out at night under cover of darkness. It's a black-light op – operating in the depths of night and with no lights. We'll be working on night vision goggles (NVG): special binocular-like aids that boost ambient light, enabling you to see in the dark.

The aim of the operation is to secure the 611, the main road leading into Sangin, so a resupply convoy can come in. But the mission's got a real sting in its tail for Treo and me. The major wants us to search and clear an old tank park to one side of the 611 – a graveyard of armour from the time the Soviet Red Army was fighting in Afghanistan, back in the eighties.

The major's got intelligence that the abandoned tank park has been sown with IEDs. I've got no problems with the mission but I tell him that I'll need my own set of NVGs (as dog handlers we're not issued with any). I'm told there are none available.

'Sir, if I've got no night vision how will I see my dog?' I ask. 'How will I know one end of him from the other when he's sniffing out what's what?'

Black-light operations weren't something we'd done much of

in Northern Ireland, for the Belfast city streets were always lit by streetlamps or by car headlights. Even so, it's obvious to me that without NVG I won't be able to see Treo work, and particularly because the only harness I have for him in Afghanistan is a black one.

'Apparently, the previous handler managed it,' the major tells me.

'His dog wasn't black, sir. It was a yellow Lab. And I'm not him.'

The major exchanges a glance with his second-in-command. He still can't seem to get his head around a mere corporal telling him he can't do what he's just been told to do. But as far as I'm concerned, Treo's got the world's most hazardous job already, without heaping added risk and trauma on his shoulders.

'Sir, if I can't have NVG you'll need to put up a light, so I can see my dog work.'

'Corporal, my men are going in under cover of darkness and showing no lights to try and catch the enemy napping. How can we put up light on a mission such as that?'

I don't see what more there is to say. I'm not taking Treo out on an operation that risks getting him killed for all of the wrong reasons. The Orders Group breaks up with the matter very much unresolved.

The Royal Marines are scheduled to rotate out of Sangin in less than two weeks. Their replacement unit is from Ranger Company, of the 1st Battalion, the Royal Irish Regiment. Over the past few days they've been trickling into Sangin on whatever flights are available, in preparation for their takeover.

I've already had the pleasure of meeting their OC, a Major Shannon. The major's reputation goes before him. He's spent years soldiering at the coalface in Northern Ireland, before working closely with US forces in the bitter and bloody Iraq conflict. He's been around the block and seen a great deal of the rougher end of war, and I can tell that he knows his onions.

I go and have a quiet word with Major Shannon about tonight's mission. He's a smartly dressed, crisp Irishman, and he looks to be in his late thirties, which makes him around the same age as me. His men act as if they would follow him into the very jaws of hell itself if he asked. He's a natural born warrior and leader of men, and I sense already that I can relate to him.

I tell him how the Bravo Company OC is trying to send my dog and me out on a night mission with no NVG and no light. I point out that my dog is jet black in colour, and how in the dead of night I'll not be able to see him work. Major Shannon offers to go and have a quiet word to get it sorted.

Via Major Shannon's good offices we settle upon a compromise that works for both parties. We'll go in using night vision equipment – although Muggins here still isn't being issued with any – and once we reach the tank park the patrol will put up an illume round (a flare suspended beneath a parachute) so that I can see Treo at work.

I return directly to the kennels to prepare for the mission. I spend a good twenty minutes talking Treo through the entire thing. The whole time he's got me fixed with this beady-eyed stare, his eyes twinkling like stars in the light of my head torch, his little stubby tail going thud-thud-thud against the frame of my cot.

By the time I'm done talking he's practically bouncing off the walls: *Oh goody! You know, Dad, I just love these night ops. The air's all cool and silky, the smells are richer and more concentrated at night, and those dumb Afghan fighting hounds are locked in their compounds. So, when can we get started?*

At midnight we gather at the base gates. Just before we'd left the kennel I'd gone through my moment of dark, clawing fear and dread. I'd had the look from Treo: *Hey, Dad, come on, there's nothing to be worried about.*

I can tell he's up for a new adventure and raring to go. He's done that half-his-body-wagging thing – wherein he shakes the whole of his rear in time to his wagging stub of a tail – just as soon as he's realised we're setting off into the brooding darkness.

I know how funny he finds it that I can't see in the dark: *So tell me, Dad, why is it you need that flashlight thing to see where you're going?* A dog's natural night vision is far superior to a human's. The canine eye is built to see at night, with a larger pupil to suck in ambient light – the kind thrown off by moon and stars – plus a concentration of rods and cones arranged to amplify it. Treo finds my night blindness almost as funny as my need to lace on my boots anytime we go walkabout.

There is a quiet nervousness and tension in the air as the lads gather in the muggy darkness. The night is black as pitch and it's boiler-room hot, even at this hour. It's especially sticky, what with all the kit we're carrying. As the Bravo lads snap their night vision goggles down over their eyes, I sense a hunger to get out there. As for me, I'm cursing under my breath, for right now I'd kill for a pair of NVG.

The gates to the base creak open. The atmosphere is electric. We are about to venture into the heart of Sangin town on foot and in pitch darkness, knowing the enemy are all around us. Bravo Company have had good men killed and injured fighting for control of this territory, and we are about to walk into the fire.

We form up and I have to place a hand on the shoulder of the guy in front, so he can guide me as I walk. I've got Treo on a short leash so he can help steer me, but all I can see of him is a pair of eyes glowing like silver coals in the faint moonlight whenever he glances my way.

I know what he's thinking: *Come on – let's get this show on the road!*

We file past the front *sangar* – the sandbagged position at the gate – and thread our way into the wall of black. We set off, the silence and the tension rippling back and forth along the patrol. As I shuffle blindly forward I'm trying not to trip over any hidden obstructions.

I'm acutely aware of how this is supposed to be a silent, covert night operation, one designed to catch the enemy unawares. If I stumble into something, that'll be our mission blown wide open. I'm also conscious that if the patrol gets hit and the lads go to ground, I'm going to be fighting blind. And then the worst of all thoughts hits me like a speeding truck. If we get hit, I'm going to be battling to save my best mate, my black dog, when I can't even see him.

No sooner have we exited the base than our radio intercepts start going wild. The Talinet – the Taliban's radio network – is buzzing big time. We have Sly, our regular terp with us, and we have the ability to listen in to what the Taliban commanders are saying.

Sly starts translating. 'Wake up! Wake up! They're coming out on foot!'

I feel a shiver of fear running up my spine. Apart from the scrunch of boot soles on gravel, and the suck and blow of our breathing, we aren't making the slightest sound. And aside from the faint fluorescent glow thrown off by each soldier's night vision, we are invisible to the naked eye. As I alone have no NVG there's no way that I can see anything, the enemy included.

We're twenty minutes into the silent night march when the patrol commander calls a halt. The dark closes in on us, predatory and menacing. A Bravo guy drops to one knee right on my shoulder, his weapon levelled at the wall of shadows. Another provides cover in the other direction, with a string of lads to the front and the rear. But I've got not the slightest idea what they're aiming in on, because I've been led in here blind.

The word gets passed along the patrol in whispers: *Dog team, this is where you start the search.* I move forwards to link up with the patrol commander, a corporal, and I ask him to put up the illume round. He gives me this look, like it just doesn't compute.

'When do me and my dog get our light?' I prompt, in a hushed whisper.

'What light? No one told me a thing about any light.'

'You're supposed to put up an illume round so we can see to do the search.'

'Well, no one told me. I haven't got any, so it's not happening.'

He's not being particularly aggressive or unhelpful. He's just telling it like it is. It's a typical SNAFU: Situation Normal All Fucked Up.

'I can't do the search if I can't see my dog working,' I tell him.

The corporal offers me a try with his NVG, but I soon realise that even via the faint fluorescent green glow of the night vision I still can't see my dog properly. I need to be able to detect his slightest change of behaviour, to know when he's onto something. Otherwise, I might let him blunder onto a pressure-plate IED and get my best buddy blown all to hell.

We're at a major impasse here. The entire *raison d'être* of this mission is to get the tank park cleared of IEDs, yet it's looking like we're going to have to abort. The corporal's all out of suggestions, and for a long moment so am I. I know we can't afford to delay. The resupply convoy is coming in at first light, and we've got to get the tank park cleared.

I'm not a can't-do kind of a person. Never have been. Treo and I are both can-do kind of blokes.

'How about this,' I suggest. 'I get a cyalume, break it in two, and pour the contents over his harness. That way it'll glow and I should be able to see it clear as day with the NVG.'

The corporal breaks into stifled laughter. 'What are you, a dog handler or Harry bloody Potter? But if it works for you, mate, it sure as hell does for me.'

I've never tried this before. I've never trained for it. I've never once even thought of it. No one's ever suggested pouring the chemical gunk that fills a cyalume light-stick over my dog, to make him night-visible. As with every patrol before, we're making it up as we go along.

Of course, my attempt to get the chemical goo onto Treo's harness alone fails dismally. In no time I've got it all over his thick hair as well. By the time I'm done my dog has been transformed from this black shadow to this giant fur ball that glows in the dark.

He glances down at his fluorescent green coat and sniffs at it: *What the hell . . . ?* In spite of our situation, which is a totally shit one, I can't help but smile. Likewise, I can hear the Bravo Company lads behind me desperately trying to stifle their own laughter.

Treo gives me this scowly look: *Ha-ha, Dad. What's so bloody funny?*

But after the initial shock of the thing, he doesn't really seem to give a shit any more: *So, I look like a giant version of my tennis ball. So what? Let's just get in there and get it on.*

The cyalume goo makes Treo stand out like a glowing beacon. Via the night vision goggles I can definitely see him work, and I can see enough of the terrain to know where he's at. But if I can see him so can a Taliban sniper, or an IED team waiting to trigger a bomb. I hate sending him in there when he's so visible and so vulnerable, but there's no other way to do this.

I show Treo his beloved tennis ball, which is worn ragged from his chewing. We step into the eerie, abandoned silence of the tank junkyard. There are the silhouettes of Soviet hulks all around us, like giant bones in some dinosaur graveyard. Needless to say, any one of them represents the ideal place to conceal an IED.

We're alone here, just me and my dog making the walk. There's this suffocating, visceral terror that's clawing at my throat: *take another step, Davey-boy, and it's sure to be your last.* But it's my fear for my dog that's got my pulse pounding through the roof of my skull, and which keeps pushing me ever onwards.

My every sense is focused on Treo as he sweeps his head this way and that at just above ground level. I can read his every movement, and I'll know the instant he's hit the 'scent cone'. At its outer limits the particles in the air will be less concentrated, and that's what he'll detect first. He'll pause and 'air up', which means his head will come up and his nose will be snorting away to check for the smell.

Then he'll 'check step' to come around to where he first detected the smell, from where he'll track the concentration of particles to the strongest point – the source. The closer he gets to the device the more frantic and fierce his snuffling will be. Finally, I'll be able to hear him snorting in the scent like a pig. That's the signal for me to call him back, before he puts a paw wrong and triggers it to blow.

If I don't, he may flop down onto a pressure-plate IED or blunder into a booby trap with a trip-wire trigger. Either way, he'll blow himself to hell, and most likely me with him. Here in Helmand, I've got to watch him like a hawk and call him off just those few instants early.

If he detects an IED we'll withdraw from the tank park and we'll call in an Explosive Ordnance Disposal (EOD) bomb-disposal team to disable it. By then the area will have been cordoned off and the patrol will have thrown a perimeter of steel around it. Treo and I will have found the thing: it's the job of the EOD boys to go in and snip the right wires to make it safe.

We creep forwards to clear the heaviest concentration of derelict hulks. In each of the shadowed relics of Soviet armour I imagine I can see the beady eyes of a Taliban watcher, waiting to punch a firing switch to incinerate me and my dog. The stench is at its worst in here. It smells as if someone's died, or at least as if the Taliban have been using this as one gigantic toilet.

We're halfway across a sheet of armour that's lying discarded on the floor, when Treo darts around the corner of an angular steel carcass. He flicks his head to the right, spies something, and an instant later he's leapt forwards and he's out of my sight completely. I lunge after him, heart beating like a machine gun, and I'm hissing: 'Get back here, now!'

Moments later there's this almighty, deafening metal-on-metal explosion: *KABOOM!*

For an instant I'm convinced that my dog has set off some kind of killer device. A voice is screaming inside my head over and over and over: *They've got my dog! They've got my dog! They've got my dog!*

The Bravo lads on security have hit the deck, weapons at the ready. They're on their belt buckles and about to open up.

I race around the corner, expecting the very worst, but there I find Treo, a sheepish grin on his features. I can see instantly what's happened. He's knocked over this rusty oil drum, one that's about half as tall as I am and three times as wide. It's cannoned into the flank of a Soviet hulk, making a noise like a massive steel drum . . . or an explosion.

I breathe out the longest sigh of relief. I realise that I've been holding my breath. I try my best to get my pulse rate under control again. I give Treo a look: *Careful where you're stepping, big lad, you almost gave me a bloody heart attack!*

His eyes meet mine with this unapologetic doggy gaze: *So I knocked it over? So what? I am pretty big and chunky for a dog . . . You send me in here covered in shiny green gunk, what d'you expect? By the way, have you smelt that stuff? It's revolting.*

I figure it's more than a fair one. My dog would have had every right to plonk down his stubby tail and go on strike, after what I've done to him and asked of him tonight. Yet even after everything – and almost getting crushed by that rusty oil drum – he remains eager to finish off the search. *That's my boy.*

I turn to the blokes somewhere to my rear. 'Sorry about that, lads,' I hiss. 'Treo just knocked over an oil drum is all.'

I hear a string of muttered curses issuing from the shadows, from a pair of Marines who were primed to unleash merry hell onto whoever it was that had just blown up my dog.

We clear the tank park in one long ghost-ride of dark, suffo-cating terror. By the end of the search I'm exhausted from the crushing tension and the fear, but at least we're done and we can declare the place clear. We've found not a single IED, or the materials used to manufacture them. I guess the intel was way off the mark. It wouldn't be the first time that we've been fed dodgy intelligence.

All I really care about is that Treo and I haven't been blown to smithereens, and neither have any of the lads. Treo is totally finished, and I'm not far behind him. We're well ready to get out of there.

We push ahead to a patch of empty bush and make camp. Treo and I curl up together on the bare dirt. There's no room in my rucksack to carry any sleeping gear, so the best we can manage is to hold each other close for warmth. After the pounding heat of the Afghan day, the temperature drops rapidly and the nights can be bitterly cold.

We'll overnight here, so we can keep watch at first light as the convoy comes in.

CHAPTER EIGHT

I wake sometime in the early hours. For a moment I stare at the brilliant night sky, which is a kaleidoscope of stars, wondering what it is that woke me. And then I can feel it: I'm stiff with the cold. I grab Treo and lift his sleepy form until he's on top of me, like a dog blanket. I feel the warmth of my boy radiating into me, and I've just found another use for my working dog: he's like one giant living breathing hot water bottle.

At dawn we get the road convoy in safely, and we head back to base. Fortunately, I'm able to scrub the worst of the fluorescent green goo from the cyalume out of Treo's fur. But there's going to be little let-up for me and my dog.

The Royal Marines are scheduled to rotate out of Sangin in just a few days, and Major Cheeseman is planning one of Bravo Company's last big operations. He wants to get a series of vehicle check points set up on the 611. The Bravo Company lads are going to stop and search any traffic, to try to intercept any bomb-making materials or ready-to-blow IEDs the enemy are bringing into town.

To make things a little safer, the major wants a sniper team in overwatch on the highest point in Sangin – up on the roof of the Red Hotel. The Red Hotel is four floors high, making it the tallest building in the area. It's a perfect vantage point from which to dominate the surrounding terrain. It's also a great place from where Major Cheeseman can show Major Shannon the lie of the land, before he takes over.

Unfortunately, the Red Hotel is also a Taliban bomber's paradise. It's a half finished, rubble-strewn shell of a building, one that's been well blasted apart. The British Army has never ventured in there and it's a complete unknown. The major says he wants the dog team – that's me and Treo – to clear a route up the stairs to the roof, so his men can break in and take the high ground.

'Sir, we'll need to search and clear every floor in the place as we go, so it doesn't get blown to pieces beneath us. Basically, if Treo and I get you in up the stairs directly, any one of the rooms below could harbour a bomb, or even a Taliban bombing team.'

When Treo and I were operating in Northern Ireland our unit motto was: *Search and Secure*. If all I do is get the major and his men onto the roof of the Red Hotel, I'll have done neither the one thing nor the other. It won't have been searched properly, or been made secure.

'In that case, you'll have to go in and get the whole of the Red Hotel cleared,' says the major. 'We'll only hit the roof once you tell us you're done.'

He makes it sound like we're going out for a Sunday afternoon stroll in the park. In reality, we'll have to painstakingly clear every room in that cavernous shell of a building. There are hundreds, each one of which is a complete unknown, and in reality this is the nightmare of all search taskings.

The major tells me that we're to go in at last light, and that it's crucial none of the Taliban spot us. He wants the sniper team on the roof and settled by first light, so no one sees them getting into their positions. The upside – if there is one – is that Treo and I have got all the hours of darkness in which to get the job done.

We end the briefing as we always do, by synchronising watches. It's vital to know that every member of the patrol is working to the exact same minute and second – crucial for coordinating all elements of the coming mission. Bravo Company's communications specialist steps forward.

'In approximately two minutes it'll be sixteen-fifty-eight Zulu,' he announces, gazing intently at his watch.

I move my watch hands to one second away from 1658. We now have two minutes to kill before the synchronisation second. My biggest worry is how we're going to see to do the search. Whatever ambient light there is – even if there's a bright moon and stars – it'll be pitch black in the heart of the Red Hotel. That means it'll be impossible to search using NVG.

'Sixteen-fifty-eight ZULU in fifteen seconds,' the comms specialist warns. 'Five, four, three, two, one. Mark!'

On his 'mark' call we each set our watches running, and we're synchronised. The comms guy will have got his time-synch from headquarters back at Camp Bastion. The British war effort encompasses most of Helmand Province, plus other parts of Afghanistan. We need to be 100 per cent certain that we're working to exactly the same local – Zulu – time as are the pilots flying missions above us, and all other units.

Cheap watches tend to lose a few seconds every day, so it's

crucial to wear a reliable timepiece. I have an Animal watch, for obvious reasons: the name reminds me of the world's greatest animal as far as I'm concerned – Treo. It was bought for me as a present when I'd first become a dog handler, because it was the nearest you could get to a 'doggy' watch.

Since then I've never once had to replace the battery and it's proven pretty much bulletproof on operations. Here in Afghanistan it's been totally reliable. I've dived onto rocks with it, dived into the sand with it, and dived into the Helmand River with it, but short of blowing the thing up it seems squaddie-proof. In fact, it's proving to be about as robust as my dog, which means it's looking pretty much indestructible right now.

I've had some extra K9 gear sent out from Camp Bastion, including a high-visibility fluorescent doggy jacket. That bit of kit is going to be crucial for tonight's mission. We'll be working on black light, and that fluorescent jacket is going to be one of the only ways that I'll be able to see Treo work when we hit the dark heart of the Red Hotel.

At all times on this one I'll need to think like the enemy. Rather than using the front door we'll go in via somewhere unexpected. I'll have a couple of security guys on my shoulder, but they'll know not to get in the way of Treo's freedom to search. We'll clear the place floor by floor, and when each is done I'll radio: 'Floor One – secure,' and so on. That'll be the signal for the Bravo Company lads to come in behind us, so the enemy can't sneak in and mess us up.

In spite of all of the preparations put in place, it's still one hell of a tasking for any dog. Clearing such a massive building, especially when many of the rooms and stairways will be heaped with rubble and other war debris, is a massive ask. To get him to do so at night and in the heart of hostile terrain, when every door may conceal a deadly threat, makes this a dog's mission impossible.

I fetch Treo from his kennel and talk him through what lies ahead. As the Bravo Company OC briefed me, so I brief Treo. I tell him that we'll need to do this whole operation in total silence, otherwise the enemy might hear us. I can't use hand signals to guide him, because it'll be pitch dark in there. We'll need to rely on whispers, and our instinctive, intuitive understanding to get it done.

I tell him that once we're on the last set of stairs leading up to the roof we'll need to get down on our belt buckles. We can't risk getting silhouetted on the roofline, 'cause the enemy might realise what we're up to up there. We'll clear the entire roof with the both of us crawling around on all fours, me and my dog.

I know I can be overheard talking to Treo, giving him his briefing, but I don't give a damn. If the Bravo Company lads conclude that I'm cracked, so be it. As far as I'm concerned Treo needs to know as much as I know about what's coming, and bugger them.

When I'm done talking Treo looks up at me, scratches his belly with one of his back legs, and has a big stretch and a yawn: *Yeah, Dad, got it. Good to go.*

We form up at eight o'clock, a good hour after last light. We've got to get the snipers up on the roof by two thirty a.m. to ensure they can get in position unseen. We've got around five hours in which to clear the entire building. We're going to have to go some to get it done. As my dog and I step out of the gates into the night, I have never in all my life felt so daunted or so scared.

We flit through the dark, deserted streets of Sangin like a troop of wraiths. Our destination is a ghostly, rubble-strewn shell of a building that stinks of piss and neglect. There are dozens of rooms to clear on the ground floor alone, the door to each of which I'll have to be first through, so Treo can get in. Any one of them may be crammed full of an enemy, or booby-trapped with a tripwire or other device.

We reach the outskirts of the hulking great building. It is a darker, empty shadow against the black of the night. It's now that I slip the search harness onto Treo. As we moved across town I had his leather collar on, and he was clipped into the paracord leash. But unless and until I clip him into his search harness, and give him the seek-on command, Treo knows he's not on the search. He can't always be in search mode, as it would exhaust him.

When Treo's in-harness, he becomes my dog soldier: out of it, he's just my dog.

By now we seem to have won the total respect of the Bravo Company lads. I've briefed my security guys that I can't have them breathing so much as a word when we enter the building. I'll only be able to whisper in there, at best, and the last thing Treo needs is other voices confusing him. I need total silence in which I can talk to my dog.

We halt at an empty window. Treo knows what's coming and everything about him has changed. The harness is the signifier, the trigger. He knows that any area I take him into he's expected to check and to clear. Just as soon as he sees the ball come out of my pocket and he hears those magic words – 'seek on' – he'll be in there, nose down, nostrils and lungs hoovering away. And he'll stay that way until I take the harness off again, God bless him.

We step towards the black void of the window. For a long moment we pause and we listen. My heart's pounding away inside my skull. There's not a sound from up ahead that I can detect – not a clink of broken glass underfoot, or the slightest murmur of voices. It's as silent as the grave in there, which makes it somehow infinitely more eerie and threatening.

I place one, reluctant hand on the window sill. 'Bup. Bup. Bup,' I whisper.

This is Dave and Treo speak for 'get up.' My throat is so constricted with fear that I can barely get the words out.

Treo glances up at me: *Come on, Dad, don't be scared. We can do this.*

He places his two front paws on the window frame, kicks with his back legs, and he's through. He lands with a barely audible plop.

He glances back at me. His eyes say it all: *You coming, or what? We'll have this wrapped up in no time. Come on.*

I've barely set foot in the place when I realise it's hopeless trying to use the NVG. It's dark as death in there, and many times spookier. I turn to the two Marines I've got as security, and with hand gestures I signal that I'm switching to using the Maglite that I've got attached to my weapon. I'll have to be first through the door with the torch beam flashed around the room, groping in the darkness for the enemy.

Of course, it'll make me a sitting target. All the bad guys have to do is aim in on my torch beam and they've got me. But there's no other way to go about getting this done. I let out a barely audible whistle, and Treo's instantly by my side. I crouch down, place the butt of my weapon on the dirty, uneven concrete, and flick on the torch. A beam of light pierces the darkness like a laser, and I let Treo see it and get used to it before we move again.

Then I'm up, butt pulled hard and tense into my shoulder, the flashlight piercing the gloom. Door one lies to the right of me, with a dozen similar doorways stretching off towards the dark corridor's end. It strikes me that this is going to be just like that game: So, what's behind Door Number One? Yes, it's Mr Taliban with his AK-47! And what's behind Door Two? Yes, it's a monster IED . . .

We move up to the first room. The door itself is made of cheap, bare plywood. The whole feel of this place is as if they'd got it 90 per cent finished just as the war began. It's been frozen in time ever since, and very likely it's been taken over by the worst of the bad guys. Or so I can't help thinking.

My pulse feels like it's pounding through the ceiling above, as I reach out a hand to grasp that first door handle. I need to open this thing painfully slowly, in case it's been rigged with a tripwire or other booby-trap device. I've just closed my fingers around the handle when I stop myself. There's another, much better way of doing this, but it's only just occurred to me.

Using silent hand gestures, I indicate to Treo I want him to sniff all around the doorframe, or at least as high as he can reach. My dog can detect explosives underground, or from incredible distances away. Sniffing out any devices hidden behind this door should be child's play. Treo understands instantly what I want of him. I see his nostrils flaring, and he's slurping in the air around the doorframe in great heaving gasps.

His intakes of breath sound deafeningly loud in the crushing quiet of this ghostly shell of a place. If there are any enemy fighters in here I can't help but think they'll hear my dog. He stops snuffling, glances up at me and I swear he does this doggy kind of a shrug: *What's the big deal? It's just a door. There's nothing there – nothing that'll get me a play with my ball, anyway.*

I twist the handle and the door swings open with a faint creak. I step inside, sweeping the room with my weapon and the flashlight. As far as I can tell, it's an empty concrete shell. I signal Treo forward, he gives the place a quick once-over and he's back at my side. He rolls his eyes at me: *See, I told you there was nothing in there, but you still had to have me check.*

We exit the room, and I close the door as softly as I can. Treo pauses for an instant, and I can tell what he's after. *Dad,* he's saying, *I'll have a bit of a drink now, if I can.* The interior of this place is filthy and dusty as hell, and it reeks to high heaven of human waste. Down at Treo height it must be even worse, and I'm not surprised that he's parched.

I've got a couple of three-litre Camelbak water carriers stuffed in my rucksack. I've got one with its drinking tube poking out and clipped through a D-ring on the shoulder strap of my pack. I crouch down, Treo opens his mouth a little, I press the end of the tube to open it, and give the backpack a good squeeze.

A fine jet of water goes spurting out and into Treo's open jaws.

That done I stand still for a moment, listening. There's a new noise about the place now, and I'm straining my ears to catch it. I hear it again – a faint, eerie, hollow wailing. I figure it's nothing more than the night breeze whistling through the empty window frames, but there's this creepy feeling about the place, as if the very essence of the building is laughing at me and my dog, and mocking us.

We check through a second and a third room, and find nothing more than we did in the first. But there's a new sound rising now, and as it grows in volume it starts to reverberate all around us. I have no idea how, but somehow the locals must have realised that we're here. They've started this weird, horrible howling, like a pack of wolves calling to each other in the darkness.

One household picks up the wolf-howl and passes it onto another, until the sound is rippling backwards and forwards all around. Those howls are one of the most unearthly sounds that I have ever heard. Usually, the enemy does them to get the village dogs barking, so as to cover any noise they make as they move around. But tonight they are doing it all for us, to freak us out.

The spine-chilling chorus goes from one place to another, on and on and on. The howls go circling around and around the darkened building, echoing ghost-like through deserted corridors. I feel the hair on the back of my neck go up, and I can only imagine how Treo is feeling. Those voices sound close, like spitting-distance close, and they must sound a whole lot louder to him.

We set out to seize the high ground here, but somehow the enemy has managed to encircle us. I feel like the hunters have become the hunted, or at least we're in danger of becoming so. We flick off our torches so as to make ourselves invisible.

There's a sudden sharp thud. It sounds deafening in the tense, suffocating darkness. It's probably just a door smashing shut in the wind on one of the floors above, but my mind can't help thinking it's the bad guys. Over all of this I can hear the deafening beat of my heart, plus my pulse thumping through my veins.

We push on. We know there's a back-up force out there, consisting of the rest of the Bravo Company platoon that brought us in. They've supposedly thrown a security cordon around the entire building to prevent anyone coming in after us.

But it doesn't exactly feel that way from inside: it feels like we've walked into a trap.

CHAPTER NINE

I lose count of the times I ease open the door to a room as dark as a cave, and Treo gets in there giving it the once-over. He's so good at this I'm all but convinced there's nothing in there by the time he's done sniffing the doorframe. But still we have to be certain.

We're an hour in by the time we're done with floor one. I pause to give my dog a cuddle and a few words of reassurance.

'Well done, lad. Good boy. Good boy. But here we go again, next floor. Are you ready?'

I glance up the first stairwell and it's a choked jumble of rubble and debris. I've got no choice but to push ahead of Treo stair-by-careful-stair, checking for obstacles that might injure my dog, or places where he might take a fall. There are parts of the stair-well that have half crumbled away, leaving a gaping hole down to the hard concrete below. In places I'm forced to physically carry my dog over the worst.

By the time we're nearing the roof itself, we're four hours into the search, and still there's no sign of Treo flagging. What a dog. I pause at the last flight, a patch of starlit sky hanging above us impossibly bright at the far end of the stairwell. I flick down my

NVG as the light's good enough here to use it, and no way can I afford to use my flashlight on the roof. That would be a dead giveaway.

We edge up those last few steps, my dog and I keeping careful pace with each other. Before we emerge, I drop onto all fours, until I'm crouched alongside Treo. For a moment his head flicks towards me and he gives me this affectionate nudge with his muzzle: *Come on, Dad, stop being silly. What you doing that for? I know you're not a dog!*

We emerge into the night. It's blinding bright after the interior of the hotel, which was like being buried alive. I scan the rooftop for craters, or any bombs or booby traps that may have been set. I see nothing obvious, and we proceed to search the entire place, me on my belt buckle and Treo on four paws. We find three further stairwells opening onto the roof, but otherwise it's as we expected and all seems clear.

We radio Major Cheeseman. We tell him we've checked the entire, ghostly building with nothing found. We describe which route we've cleared, and warn him which stairwell to use to make it up here – the one that we've just secured. That done, the Bravo lads start filtering in and silently securing the rooftop. By the time the sniper team moves into position, Treo and I are en route back to base, totally and utterly exhausted.

At first light the Bravo lads begin to stop and search every vehicle moving on the 611, but by then Treo and I are in our kennel sleeping the sleep of the dead.

Bravo Company is almost finished with Sangin now. The boys from the Royal Irish Regiment are replacing the war-weary Commandos, platoon by platoon. The guys that Treo and I have patrolled with and fought alongside will soon be gone, and we'll have five months with the newcomers. My dog and I have lost not a single Marine, and it's a great feeling to be sending them all home. No one's died on our watch: what more could we wish for?

The Ranger Company lads have heard of Treo's reputation long before they get to meet my dog in person. Many of them grew up in Northern Ireland, so they've seen what search dogs can do. They seem to have a fantastic attitude towards working dogs. I know it's going to be a busy old time we'll have with them, but it feels right with the Rangers from the very start.

No sooner has the Ranger Company OC taken over command than he calls for a proper briefing with his dog team. I can sense the difference with Major Shannon from the get-go. He makes it clear to me that not only is he a dog lover by nature, but he also recognises what a dog like Treo can do in a place like this. He explains that he doesn't want a single patrol going out without us being at the head of it, clearing the way.

'From what I hear of Treo, I want him at the front of my blokes every time,' he tells me.

I tell the major that's all well and good, but my dog needs a minimum of two hours' break between missions. The major says he's fine with that. He understands that a handler knows his dog best, and it's up to the rest to adapt. He tells me that I'm to speak up if something isn't quite right for my dog, and we'll adapt the plan accordingly. It's like a breath of fresh air.

There are four Ranger Platoons, and each has its own bomb-detection element. They have an Electronic Counter Measures (ECM) operator – a guy who carries a box of tricks designed to jam any signal the enemy might use to trigger a remote-controlled IED – plus they have an EBEX operator, the EBEX being a military-grade metal detector. Few bombs can be built without some form of metal component, and that's what the EBEX scans for.

When compared to the computerised wizardry of the EBEX and the ECM, a dog's nose tends to seem a little prehistoric and inexact. To the uninitiated. To those of us in the RAVC nothing could be further from the truth. Science has failed to design anything remotely as sophisticated as a dog's nose. No one knows for sure, but it's anything up to a thousand times more sensitive than our own. Dogs have millions more scent receptors, and the part of their brain used for analysing smells is far larger. They can literally sniff out explosives.

We get out patrolling with Ranger Company on a daily basis. The lads need to familiarise themselves with the lie of the land. There's much to be done, and often Treo and I are back-to-backing from one patrol to another. It's pretty much love at first sight between the dog team and those Ranger lads, all except for Lieutenant Wilcock, this one bloke who has yet to fall for Treo.

Late one afternoon we set out searching the 611 with the Ranger's Eight Platoon, commanded by Lieutenant Wilcock. It's last light, Treo and I are bang out front and the nearest Rangers are a good few paces behind us, doing security. We're forty minutes into the patrol when I see something that strikes me as odd. To our left there's an old car parked in a garage. The car's got a red light flashing inside it, one that looks like a car alarm warning light.

What's strange about it is that the vehicle is too old to warrant garaging, and no one in their right mind would ever want to steal it. I send Treo around the garage three or four times, but it's clear that there's nothing suspicious in there. I tell myself that maybe here in Sangin that's about as fine a motor car as ever you could wish for, and that every young Afghan car thief wants one.

Treo and I have pushed ahead a good three hundred metres when I get a call over my radio.

'Dog handler, go firm.' It's Lieutenant Wilcock. 'Have you searched this vehicle? There's a red light flashing on and off.'

'Affirmative,' I reply. 'The dog's been across it. It's clear.'

'Can you come back and search it again?'

As Treo and I do the long walk back to his position, I'm rehearsing what I'm going to say. He's going to have to learn the hard way to love and trust my dog.

'Sir, we've searched that car three or four times already,' I tell him. 'I'm not getting my dog to do so again. Like I told you over the radio, the dog's been across it and it's clear.'

'Just get him to do it again. There's this red light—'

'Are you saying you don't trust my dog? 'Cause if you are, there's no point us being on your patrol.'

I whistle for Treo and we start off as if we're making our way back to base.

'Corporal, are you disobeying my order?' he yells after me.

I turn around to face him. 'No sir, I'm not. But like I say, if you doubt the dog there's no point us being here. So my dog and me are returning to the DC.'

'That amounts to disobeying an order.'

'Sir, no one orders my dog what to do. No one. And never, ever doubt my dog's nose.'

I'm not just making a point of principle. This goes to the very heart of why we're here. If I keep sending Treo back to search what he's already done, he'll lose confidence in his own abilities. He'll think his dad is starting to doubt him. And that is courting disaster, especially in situations where every man has got to have absolute faith in my dog. If they lose that faith, they'll not be able to walk across a patch of ground with their minds crystal clear and focused.

The lieutenant and I have locked horns. The frustration and tension builds between us for the remainder of the patrol, and it's clear that something is going to have to give.

The following day Treo and I are out again with Eight Platoon. My dog and I are up front a long way from Lieutenant Wilcock and I hope to hell it stays that way. Treo's not particularly bothered by the lieutenant. I've shown him a flash of his tennis ball, made as if to hurl it up the track, and he's off, stump wagging and nostrils sucking away. I need to take the lead from my dog. I need to put everything else out of my mind and get tuned in. If not, I may get someone – even my dog – killed.

We're an hour in and we're fully exposed to the burning afternoon sun. Sangin's roasting, and the heat feels like it's melting my head and my shoulders, and the whole lot is dripping down my back in a thick slurry of sweat. My camos are a mass of dark sweat patches, and I have to keep stopping to get liquid into Treo and to spray water from my Camelbak over him. As the water evaporates in the intense heat, so it cools him.

Each time he gives me this look: *Ahhhh . . . lovely. But tell me, Dad, where's the nearest river?*

It's early May by now, and the Afghan heat is building to its summer climax. The streets are sweltering, and simmering with discontent. I've got to keep checking my dog for heat exhaustion. A dog can only sweat from the pads of its feet or its tongue – hence the way Treo has his tongue lolling out as he pants away. In the early stages of heat exhaustion a dog's tongue swells to double its size. Before it can expand enough to choke him, a dog will simply collapse from heatstroke.

It's mind-numbing trying to remain 100 per cent focused on my dog in this baking, suffocating heat. It's frying my brain. My mind drifts, and for a moment I can't help thinking about Lieutenant Wilcock and how exactly I'm going to get him to respect my dog. As I reflect upon all of this I almost forget that Treo is an animal, and not a mechanical bomb-sniffing machine.

Something – maybe that instinctive, intuitive bond between us – pulls me back to my dog. As I focus in, my blood practically runs cold. Treo is showing all the signs of being right on top of a device. He's got his nostrils glued to a patch of hard-beaten earth, and he's standing over it sucking in the scent in great, breathy gasps. He's tracked whatever it is to the heart of the scent cone, and he's about to sit at source.

I've missed all the vital signs: the change in behaviour; my dog airing up as he hit the scent cone; him checking step to come around and establish the scent cone's periphery; his direct move towards the source; his finding it, and sampling it to double check that he's there. I've caught him at the very last moment, which shows the danger of letting your mind wander for just an instant when your dog is on the search.

I yell out a warning. 'TREO! Get back here! NOW!'

I tell myself to get a bloody grip. Whatever it is he's found here, there might be a Taliban in one of the buildings nearby waiting to punch the firing tit, and eviscerate the both of us. I need to get sparking. I put out a radio call to bring the patrol to halt. I move my dog and me back a good few paces.

I crouch down and give Treo the praise that he so deserves. 'Good boy, good laaaaad. What d'you think it is you've found there? What've you got, lad, with that clever nose and those pawsies?'

I gaze into his face, reading the expression in his eyes. He's got as sombre a look as you'd ever see with my dog, who's too cool to ever take anything too seriously: *Dunno what it is exactly, but whatever, it's a big one.*

I now know that buried thirty feet ahead of us is some kind of device designed to maim and kill – and we're likely talking a monster. I radio for the patrol's bomb-detection element to come forwards – the guy with the EBEX metal-detector, and the one carrying their portable ECM kit. That box of electronic wizardry should jam any signal the enemy might use to trigger the device.

The EBEX operator goes forwards with his metal detector. It looks like a strimmer handle with a hoop-shaped sensor attached to the bottom at right angles. I watch the guy as he passes the EBEX over the spot that Treo's indicated, but there's no response. Several times he repeats the pass, but still there's not the slightest hint of a bleep.

The Ranger turns to me and gives a shrug. 'I guess, like, there's nothing there.'

I send Treo forward again, and again he's dead certain. The EBEX guy checks again, and again he gets nothing. Treo remains absolutely convinced that he's onto something. It's a stalemate. I can sense Lieutenant Wilcock watching intently, and I just know that he's itching to get the patrol under way once more. This is make-or-break time for me and my dog.

I think through our options. The ECM operator's got his box of tricks going, so there's little danger of the enemy setting off a device remotely. If it was a pressure-plate IED, it would have to be just below the surface, and the metal detector would have found it. I figure I can risk breaking all the rules here, just to prove once and for all that my dog never false-responds.

I send Treo forward and I give him the order: 'Dig, lad, dig.'

Treo starts scrabbling eagerly with his front paws, dirt flying in all directions. A few seconds later he stops quite suddenly and turns to fix me with a look: *Here it is, Dad, just like we told 'em.*

I move forwards and glance into the hole. I practically have a heart attack on the spot. Treo's unearthed three rocket-propelled grenade (RPG) warheads taped together and threaded with detonation cord. This is the main charge of an IED, one big enough to take out an entire section of our patrol. The only thing I can't tell is how the Taliban are intending to trigger it.

I drag Treo backwards and yell at the Ranger lads to get the hell away from there.

Once we're back a good distance I glance over at Lieutenant Wilcock. Treo's eyes follow my gaze. I don't have to say a word. Treo's look says it all: *Don't ever doubt what I can do with this nose.* Their metal detector guy has missed a monster IED buried well below the surface at the roadside. Treo's nose hasn't. It's game, set and match to us.

To be fair, the lieutenant starts sparking now. He's on the radio to Major Shannon, reporting what we've found and asking for the bomb-disposal guys, and he's getting the area cordoned off and made safe. I tell the lieutenant to get the EOD boys to come in on the same route that we used, for at least there's some reassurance it will be clear.

Treo and I remain on the cordon, ready to brief the EOD team when they arrive. As we stand around nattering, Lieutenant Wilcock shoots me and my dog a look: respect. From that alone I know that he's learned his lesson and that he'll never question Treo's abilities again.

It's a good three hours before the EOD boys get flown out to Sangin and patrolled to our location. For all of that time we're stationary at the bomb find. There are scores of local men watching our every move, and they're paying special attention to my dog. Their faces are a mass of dark scowls as they mutter amongst themselves. I can just imagine what they're saying: *It's that black dog again! It keeps finding stuff. We've got to get shot of that dog.*

I hate being static like this for so long. Any one of those guys could be a Taliban watcher, waiting to signal an attack force to hit us. All it would take is one good sniper on a rooftop somewhere within range, and he could put a bullet into my dog. Treo's the only one amongst us who's not wearing body armour. It's hot enough for him already in his thick coat of fur: a suit of armour on top would finish him. But it means that he's got zero defences.

I crouch down beside him and do my best to shadow him with my bulk, keeping it between him and any obvious firing points.

But it's far from easy. The Rangers have thrown a cordon of steel around the IED find, yet there are buildings to the left and right of us. Each has a flat rooftop, which offers an ideal point upon which to locate a sniper team. There's a dark and angry tension in the air, and it's a far from pleasant feeling being here.

The EOD boys arrive and get to work. Typically, they are first class at what they do. They suit up, move in and have the IED defused in what seems like a matter of minutes. The EOD officer comes to have words with me. Sure enough, it's a cellphone-triggered IED that my dog's unearthed. He figures it was only our ECM kit that's prevented the Taliban from blowing it under our very noses.

The ECM has a good range and it should protect Treo and me, but I've no idea if it could do so for the whole patrol. We can't afford to close the distance between the men, for then we could all be taken out with one well-aimed burst of gunfire. But it means that if Treo and I miss an IED, the bad guys may be able to trigger it when we've passed, so messing up those coming after us.

It's an added burden of responsibility for me and my dog.

The EOD officer briefs me that the Taliban have just started using Ammonium Nitrate Aluminium, a type of explosive that's new to theatre. With typical black humour, the EOD lot have nicknamed it 'ANAL' for short. It's a substance that's well known to anyone in the bomb-detection business. It was responsible for the deadliest non-nuclear man-made explosion in history. In 1917, during the First World War, the British military detonated nineteen ANAL mines buried beneath German lines, killing ten thousand.

The main advantage of ANAL to the Taliban is that it's made from cheap, readily available materials. In spite of its home-made, budget credentials it's a very potent killer: ANAL detonates with a velocity of 4,400 metres per second. Any shrapnel fragments with that kind of force behind them will shred human flesh and bone, and they'll certainly make short work out of a dog.

The EOD guy hands me a small lump of ANAL. It's a sample with which I can train Treo, so that he can get his nose in. I take the proffered gift and stuff it into the breast pocket of my body armour, alongside my portable camera. That in turn reminds me to take a photo of the IED when we're back at base. It's vital to document any find in as much detail as possible, so as to help identify similar devices in future.

As we start the walk back to our Sangin base, I slip my hand into my trouser pocket and pull out Treo's ball. 'Seek on, lad, seek on.'

We may be following the same route as we came in, but I'm not taking any chances. There's always a risk that the enemy will have sneaked in behind us and planted something in the hope that we'll get sloppy. I start channelling my mind into that of my dog – blocking out all external factors and stimuli – as he hoovers up the scent all around him.

There's a sudden, high-pitched snarl just inches from my head. A bullet rips past and it's followed an instant later by the bark of the weapon firing. I know immediately that it's a sniper.

A sniper's bullet travels faster than the speed of sound. When the round is that close to your head, you hear and feel it passing before the crack of the weapon firing reaches your ears. It would be utterly terrifying if the adrenalin hadn't kicked in, trans-forming me into a pumped-up, burning frenzy.

'SNIPER! SNIPER!'

Voices start screaming for us to take cover. But take cover where? I've had all of my senses focused on my dog, and I've got no idea from where the round's been fired. The gunman will likely be using a Soviet-era Dragunov sniper rifle, which packs a ten-round magazine. When the Soviets pulled out of Afghanistan they left rakes of weaponry – Dragunovs included – behind them. There's plenty more bullets where that came from.

Another round tears into the dirt, this one right at Treo's feet. He bounds back in alarm, and throws a glance my way, seeking much-needed reassurance from his Dad. I feel this red mist of rage sweep over me: they're trying to kill my dog!

I blank the voices yelling at me to take cover. I go down on one knee until I'm crouched over Treo. I've seen the direction the shots are coming from, and I've got my torso – which means the bulk of my body armour – between the gunman and him. I'll take the next round if I have to, but no Taliban sniper is shooting my dog.

I lift my Stubby and pull the angular butt into my shoulder. I jam my right eye against the smooth metal of the sight. Its four-times magnification pulls the enemy position into instant close-up focus, the smoke from his shots hanging in the air above the rooftop.

I place the diamond-sharp tip of the pointer on the heart of the smoke, and open fire, pumping round after round into the sniper's lair. With each squeeze of the trigger a gleaming brass case spews out of the assault rifle's ejector, spinning onto the dirt track beside us. With each I imagine a bullet tearing into the Taliban sniper's skull.

In a matter of seconds I've loosed off an entire magazine of ammo. I grab a second from out of my chest harness, slam it into my weapon, cock it and open fire again. But the sniper is fast becoming the least of our worries. The entire neighbour-hood seems to have turned on us, with muzzle flashes sparking from every darkened door, window and alleyway. The bad guys have decided this is the time to take us on. They're hitting us big time with all they've got.

Angry spurts of dust kick up all around my dog, each being a bullet that's hammering into the dirt surface of the road. It's like the entire highway is alive with bullet impacts, the length and breadth of it being saturated with hot lead. Behind us I can hear the Rangers putting down a withering wall of return fire, but it's only a matter of seconds before a bullet finds us.

I reach down with my one free hand, keeping the Stubby firing with the other. I clip the lead onto Treo's collar.

'LET'S GO!' I yell. 'LET'S GO! LET'S GO! LET'S GO!'

He doesn't need any second urging. Suddenly we're on our feet and surging forwards, as rounds go chasing after our heels.

'Let's go, Treo!' I scream at him. 'Let's not dawdle, big lad! LET'S GO!'

My dog and I make a dash for the nearest cover, Treo's black paws flashing across the dirt as we sprint through a hail of fire.

CHAPTER TEN

We reach the corner of a mud-walled compound and dive into its shadow. The Rangers are right on our shoulder. As I drag Treo out of the line of fire, they're down on one knee hammering rounds into the enemy positions. I can't fault those young Rangers for their aggression or their professionalism. They're kick-arse fighting Irish and it's great to have them with us.

There's a momentary lull in the battle, and one of them turns to me. 'Sure, Dog, you're a crazy fecker,' he grins. 'Next time, take cover first before you open fire!'

'Yeah, well, mate, I was thinking of my dog.'

He gives a nod of approval. 'Sure, Treo comes first. No one's getting our dog.'

I like that. I like it how he's calling Treo 'our dog'. Treo's getting to be the Ranger's four-legged friend and protector, and we've only been with them a matter of days.

'But sure, that feckin' sniper's trying to shoot Treo,' the other Ranger remarks.

'He'll have to get past fifteen stone of me before he does.'

'The rounds hit right around Treo's feet. Your dog's the target.'

I force a smile. 'Then it's lucky he can't bloody shoot straight.'

Putting down well-aimed bursts of fire, the Rangers start to win the firefight. But it's now that my dog and I have to get back out on the streets and recommence the walk.

As we inch our way onto the emptiness of that bullet-scarred highway, I feel sickeningly vulnerable and exposed. I'm struggling to hide my gut-wrenching fear from Treo, for I don't want my terror running down-leash to my dog.

'Come on, lad,' I tell him, as we regain the open. 'Only a couple of miles and we're home.'

The journey back turns into an epic. It's a good three hours of pushing forward, then going to ground and trading fire with the enemy, before we finally approach our Sangin base. I've had Treo on-leash for the entire time, and all we've been able to afford is a quick sniff of the route ahead, before taking cover from fresh bursts of enemy fire.

My dog and I have been playing a deadly game of cat and mouse with the enemy and it's largely luck, coupled with the Rangers' warrior spirit, that gets us home. But I'm not kidding myself any more: doing that search under fire was at times more terrifying than unearthing an IED. And no doubt about it, the enemy is hell-bent on nailing me and my dog.

The men of Ranger Company are known as 'The Warriors'. I was wondering how they'd measure up to the Royal Marine Commandos. From what I've seen so far they are every bit as fine a bunch of soldiers. I felt them watching over us out there in that shitfight, and that makes me even more determined to bring every man amongst them home alive.

As we step through the gates I see the young lads visibly soften and relax. A couple of them turn to Treo and me.

'How yer doin', Dave?'

'You OK? Treo OK?'

I tell them that my dog and I are good. I've never spoken to those lads before, and I don't know them from Adam. Treo doesn't either. But their expressions of concern for us are totally genuine, and testament to what a close part of Ranger Company they feel that my dog and I have become.

Although we're fine, the bomb-disposal guy who defused the IED only envisaged being out on the ground for an hour or so. As a result he only brought the one litre bottle of water with him. By the time we're back to base, he's going down with heat exhaustion. It just goes to show: never underestimate the enemy here in Sangin, or for how long they might keep you pinned down.

Whilst the medics are getting some rehydration salts into him, I grab the IED so I can take some photos. The bomb-disposal boys will do a proper study of it back at Camp Bastion, to try to discover all they can about how the enemy construct such devices, and maybe even who it is that made this one. But I want some photos myself. Next time Treo's nose nails something, I want to have the best possible chance of recognising what it is before it can blow.

I put Treo into his kennel and give him a juicy bone to gnaw on. That'll keep him busy, and Lord knows he deserves it. If he hadn't unearthed that IED, the likelihood is that the Taliban would have detonated it under the rear part of our patrol. My dog has saved a number of young lads today, and he deserves a hero-sized bone. I'll take him for a run and a swim just as soon as I'm done with my photographs.

I carry the three-RPG IED to a remote area and stop between a massive set of HESCO walls, which will shield the rest of the base from any blast. In theory, a camera flash or even a video signal can trigger an IED. This one has been disarmed, but even so I'm not taking any chances. If it goes off, it'll be only me that gets hurt.

In Northern Ireland we learned how the IRA developed a new type of roadside bomb. The IED would wait for a flashgun to go off, which was the trigger that made it fire. I've no idea if the Taliban have become that sophisticated yet, but they're obviously evolving their technology, as signified by their adoption of ANAL as one of their explosives. There's no harm in my being extra careful.

Once I'm done shooting my photos, I return the IED to the bomb-disposal bloke. Word has gone around the base like wildfire that Treo's outsmarted the EBEX metal detector on today's patrol. He's becoming like this miracle dog. Major Shannon calls me in for a chat and gives me a few heartfelt words of thanks. If Treo hadn't sniffed out that hidden bomb, the odds are that the major would be sending some of his boys home in bodybags, and he knows it.

'Dave, if you're not able to get out on patrol 'cause your dog's being used too much, I still want you in on the Orders Group,' he tells me. 'Can you manage that? That way, if you see a better way for Treo to get used, we can shift around the schedule. I want you guys out and used in the best way and as often as possible.'

I tell the major that I'm good with that.

It's nice for Treo's skills to get recognised, but it's a double-edged sword. We're being asked to up the tempo even more now.

I guess it's a case of beware of what you wish for, for you may end up getting it . . . I've always craved approval, but out here it spells added danger, stress, pressure and fear, not to mention repeated brushes with death.

Treo and I have a few hours' down time before our next patrol. The major asks me how I'm going to spend it. I tell him that I've got to get Treo out training with this new explosive that the Taliban are using. I've got to get his nose in.

'What's this new one called?' the major asks, curiously.

I give him a kind of a half smile. 'Sir, they call it ANAL.'

'You what?'

'ANAL, sir. Or Ammonium Nitrate Aluminium, to use its full name.'

I explain what it is and why the Taliban have likely started using it.

'Understood,' the major tells me. He gives me a wry grin. 'Best you get Treo out there training with this ANAL . . .'

Once I'm done with the major, I get collared by Frankie O'Connor, the Ranger Company sergeant major. Frankie is one scary-looking bloke. He looks like some Irish bare-knuckle boxing champion. He's tattooed up to the eyeballs, and he's obviously been in his fair share of street fights, and you'd not want to take him on down a darkened alleyway.

To offset his scary look he's got this quiet, lilting Irish brogue. I've never seen him once having to raise his voice, for he's not the kind of guy who'd ever have anyone question his authority. He's a natural at getting the best out of his men, and it's a given that he'd never send a Ranger out to do a job that he wouldn't do himself. He's been keeping his distance up until now, as if he's been watching Treo and me at work and withholding his judgement.

Today that's all changed. Frankie gives me a heartfelt 'well done' on the IED find. As the Royal Marines are a Navy unit, they'd given everything in Sangin these weird Navy names. In a pally kind of a way, Frankie tells me we're done with all of that.

'From now on, Dog, the cook house is going to be a feckin' cook house, and not a "galley". And the shitters are the shitters – not the feckin' "heads" . . .'

'Too right, mate,' I tell him. 'And a brew's a brew, mate, not a bleedin' "wet".'

Frankie and I have a good laugh about it. We're not exactly making eye contact yet, because his gaze is far too scary for that, but I sense that Treo and I are going to be part of Frankie's family from now on.

Frankie tells me he's keen to get Treo and me out with their Seven Platoon. They're the Ranger's bomb-search specialists, and they're the guys that he wants us working with most closely over the coming days.

After a brief rest and some food I take Treo out for a special treat. A tributary of the River Helmand runs through the base to the rear of our new kennel. The first time I took Treo down there I had to more or less force him in. I had to jump first, with the lead tied to my belt, pulling Treo into the raging torrent after me. But once he had that first dip there was no stopping him.

Now, my dog acts as if he thinks he's just another crazy soldier. He joins the other lads on the bridge a good ten feet off the water. For a moment he stares at the frothy white surge below, and then he leaps with all fours in a massive belly-flop. He hits

the surface with a mighty splash, goes under, and comes up splut-
tering – to the wild cheers of the assembled Rangers.

He's swimming alongside the lads, diving under the water with
them, then trying to float on his back, just as if he thinks he's a
human. It reminds me of the time when he and I were tasked
to clear a royal palace, in preparation for a royal tour of Northern
Ireland.

We'd just finished the main stateroom when Treo noticed the
ornate throne set aside for Her Majesty's esteemed posterior. He
gave me a look: head cocked to one side and his eyes alight with
mischief. I knew exactly what he had in mind.

'Go on then,' I told him. 'Bup! Bup! Bup!'

And that was it – Treo jumped up and plonked his backside
on the Queen's throne. He sat there, back straight, head up and
lip quivering ever so slightly, looking entirely regal and imperi-
ous. He was now King Treo, and I was some kind of grovelling
minion at his feet.

Sometimes in this relationship I swear I feel like I am the dog
and Treo the human.

After finding that three-RPG roadside IED, I decide to give
my dog an extra treat. I throw his ball – his beloved tennis ball
– into the river just a little ahead of him.

'There you go, big lad!' I yell, above the roar of the current.
'Go get your ballsy!'

Treo pops his head up and he looks about excitedly, then he's
doggy-paddling madly, his black muzzle cutting through the
water like the prow of a battleship, his nostrils blowing and his
eyes darting forwards. I've got him clipped onto a length of cord,
just to make sure he doesn't get swept away in the current.

I run along beside him keeping pace on the riverbank, and pointing out the faded green ball bobbing along. 'There you go, lad, there's your ballsy!'

An instant later he overtakes it, lunges for it, misses once, then grabs it in his triumphant jaws and turns to me proudly.

'You got it!' I tell him. 'Good laaaaaad. Good laaaaaad.'

Treo finishes his swim and his play, and I haul him up the steep bank and unclip him from his lead. He has a good shake, starting with his head and shoulders and running down to his bum and his stump of a tail. That done he finds a patch of soft sand and proceeds to roll in it, backwards and forwards a good few times. He's got grit and twigs plastered all over his fur – from wet nose down to damp stubby tail.

He gives me this happy look from out of dirt-encrusted features: *Nothing like a good dust bath after a cold swim, is there, Dad?*

Whenever I think that Treo must be exhausted from the work we're doing here, all he ever seems to need is a quick swim and a play, plus a good chat with his dad, and he's raring to go again. But some things can prove too much even for my dog, and it's the Afghan National Police lot co-located with us at Sangin who are about to prove as much.

The Royal Marines have been gone a week now, and the Rangers are determined to get the ANP out on patrol, to get their measure. There's no way of warning them what the ANP are like. I've rarely been out with them and not had one or more stoned off his face, or stumbling about drunkenly.

But nothing could prepare even my dog and me for today's nightmarish performance.

We gather with the Ranger lads by the headquarters building, awaiting the ANP to join us for a patrol. They're a good quarter of an hour late, and still there's no sign of them.

To get to the ANP part of the camp you have to cross a bridge over the river. We're mooching about trying to hide our frustration at the delay, when all of a sudden there is an almighty great explosion: *KA-BOOOOOOM!* The blast reverberates around the headquarters, and we all of us – Treo included – dive for cover. We figure we're taking incoming mortar rounds, or maybe some of those nasty 107 mm rockets.

Word reaches us that it's actually the ANP that have taken the hit. We head over at the double, only to discover a scene of absolute mayhem. One of the ANP blokes has come out of his quarters pissed up and with his RPG slung over his shoulder, pointy-end downwards. He's joined a group of fellow men, and accidentally pulled the trigger.

The RPG has rocketed into the ground, killing two of them outright. The RPG gunner is one of the dead, and he's left total, blood-soaked carnage in his wake. We take a look at the worst guys and it's clear we need stretchers to get them across the bridge and into the medical centre.

My dog can sense the panic and the trauma in the air, plus the screams of the wounded must sound horrific to his hypersensitive ears. He's never heard anything like this before. He's glancing up at me nervously, seeking some kind of reassurance from his dad. He's got an expression on his loyal and trusting features: *What in God's name has happened?*

For once I've got zero time or space to comfort my dog. In a frenzied rush we load the nearest wounded onto stretchers. The guy I'm helping carry has lost both his legs, and blood is spurting everywhere. We pound across the bridge, Treo's lead gripped in my left hand as my right carries one corner of the stretcher. We're halfway over when Treo loses his footing – or gets shoved by one of the running figures – and he half falls into the river.

Underfoot it's greasy with blood, and for a moment we're all about to go. Somehow we manage to right ourselves and we make it to the medical centre without dropping the wounded guy, who's writhing about in agony. We deliver him into the hands of the medics, and they get tourniquets onto his wounds and start to stabilise him. In no time a helicopter's inbound, and the wounded get airlifted to Camp Bastion, with its top-rate medical facilities.

By the time that's done our patrol is well and truly not going anywhere. It's over. For the Rangers fresh into theatre this is a total eye-opener. They've just been treated to a perfect bit of Afghan National Police theatrics. I can see by the looks on the guys' faces what they're thinking: *who needs feckin' enemies, with friends like these?*

Treo and I make our sodden, sticky, dejected way back to our kennel. My uniform is spattered in the Afghan's blood. As for Treo, he was at a lower level than me and he's taken a right good soaking. His fur's matted with congealed human gore, and his nose and ears are caked with the stuff. If I leave him like that he'll have to lick himself clean, and no way do I want to visit that on my dog.

I spend hours bathing and grooming him, until every last speck of that madness and horror has been expunged. But whilst you can clean a dog's body, that doesn't necessarily mean you've cleaned a dog's mind. The last few hours constitute the most gruesome thing that I have ever seen in over two decades of soldiering. It's been proven that dogs can suffer Post Traumatic

Stress Disorder (PTSD) just like humans, and I'm worried for Treo.

Troops exposed to relentless combat conditions can suffer lasting psychological damage, just as anyone who suffers intense trauma. It can hit immediately after the traumatic event, or many months later. Symptoms can include repeatedly reliving the event and the trauma that accompanied it, as if trapped in a living nightmare, and erratic and sometimes violent behaviour.

Dogs feel many of the same emotions as we humans, and here in Sangin I've been worried about a clever, perceptive animal like Treo getting PTSD. If anything's going to start messing with his head, it's what we've just lived through today.

I bed down with Treo that evening, hugging his powerful form close to me. Thankfully, he falls into a deep, deep sleep. I have him snoring away beside me, whimpering and snorting as he dreams his doggy dreams. He's probably off chasing a rat around our North Luffenham base, which is his most favourite pastime in the world.

I can feel how much weight he's lost since we arrived here. With the relentless pace of operations the fat's been falling off him, and he's a bundle of rippled muscle and honed sinew.

I just hope that all the trauma isn't going to make my dog start losing his mind as well.

CHAPTER ELEVEN

Treo and I are next due out with Seven Platoon, those with specialist training in the art of arms and explosives search. They've learned how to get on their belt buckles to do painstaking, fingertip investigations, feeling for wires or pressure plates or trigger switches amongst the vegetation and the dirt.

They've gained wide experience in Northern Ireland using their bayonets to locate buried IEDs, so that bomb-disposal teams can be called in to defuse and disarm them. If there's one team in Ranger Company that thinks it can rival my dog's nose in terms of bomb-detection work, it's the Seven Platoon boys.

The platoon is run by a Sergeant Trevor 'Speedy' Coult. He's a fiery, red-headed, rake-thin dynamo of a bloke who talks nineteen to the dozen. Speedy won the Military Cross in Iraq and his reputation goes before him. The men of his unit mean everything to him, and he'll stand up for them no matter what. He's in his early thirties, younger than me, and if I listen extra carefully I can just about understand his machine-gun-fire, thick Belfast accent.

Speedy outranks me, and he's clearly earned his stripes. But

I can sense him looking at me like he's thinking – *sure, you look like a wise old bastard*. I figure it's going to be a relationship of equals between us, but there's no knowing. I tell Speedy what Treo and I can deliver. He tells me that whatever protection we need as we search, Seven Platoon will deliver it.

Seven Platoon's corporal is Sean 'Ronnie' Corbett. He looks like he's stepped out of a Lowry stick painting, but he's got the strength and endurance of ten men. Ronnie's a plain-talking, no-nonsense bloke, and he's very serious about his job. He carries all the spare batteries and heavy kit for the platoon's ECM gizmo, plus the EBEX metal detectors.

There's something of Mater from the movie *Cars* about Ronnie. He's got one of those honest, guileless faces, and I know instinctively that he finds it very hard to lie. He's a fine soldier, and I sense he and I are going to be close.

Seven Platoon's EBEX operator is Ranger Davy Miller. Davy's a cheeky chappie from Belfast who clearly thinks he's as tough as any Royal Marine. He's thickset and built like a donkey, and I sense he's the kind of bloke who would throw himself in front of me and Treo to catch a bullet. He's got the brash self-confidence that comes with youth, and knowing he's good at what he does.

I've got an extra reason to warm to Davy. Treo has instantly taken a shine to him. Invariably, Treo tends to ignore new arrivals until he feels he's got their measure. But with Davy, he right away gave him his head-tilted-to-one-side curious, appraising look: *So, I guess it's going to be me and you out front, eh? Think you can beat my nose with that EBEX gizmo? Who are you kidding . . .*

There's one other member of Seven Platoon who really digs my dog, only this guy has really pulled one over on me the first few times we've met. Ranger Justin 'Cups' Cupples just can't seem to get enough of Treo. He's forever popping down to the kennel to share a brew and a ciggie, which is really just an excuse for a play with my dog.

He's got this soft American accent that sounds quite posh to my ears, and at first I presumed he was an officer. Accordingly, I kept calling him 'sir'. He offered me a ciggie: 'Don't mind if I do, sir.' I saw this slight grin pass fleetingly across his features, and I wondered what that was all about. I didn't say anything at the time, because he was a mature-looking officer-sounding type. I'd do my best to enjoy his company, and to let him enjoy some Treo time.

As Treo and I set out on our first patrol with Seven Platoon, I'm about to learn the truth about Justin Cupples. Our mission is to check out the old Governor's House, which is known to all as 'JDAM Central'. At some time in the past an Allied jet has dropped a JDAM – a thousand-pound Joint Direct Attack Munition smart bomb – on it, hence the name.

The wrecked building is four floors high in places, although much of it was reduced to rubble by the bomb's blast. The stairwell is more or less intact, and it's via there that access can be gained to roof level. It remains a point of high ground from which the enemy can observe, and put sniper rounds into our base. Major Shannon figures it may also be a trigger point for their IEDs.

Two days earlier a Land Rover patrol was hit on the 611. One of the vehicles was blasted by an IED, and an officer riding in it was badly wounded. He was airlifted out of Sangin and back to Camp Bastion for treatment. Major Shannon wants to know if the Taliban had a watcher positioned on the roof of JDAM Central, waiting to trigger that device. Treo and I are to check especially for any command wires, or any trigger that might still be in place.

No sooner have we set off on the patrol when I hear Speedy yell out an order: 'Cupples, get here!'

'Hold on a minute,' I object. 'You can't speak to the boss like that.'

'You what?' says Speedy.

'Cupples. He's an officer, isn't he?'

Speedy let out this short yelp of a laugh. 'Yer man's a feckin' Ranger, like the rest of 'em.'

'Cupples!' I yell. 'Get over here, now!' He saunters over to the two of us. 'Why the hell did you let me think you were an officer? Why did you let me keep calling you "sir"?'

'You know,' he drawls, 'I kinda figured it was quite funny really.'

'Did you now,' I grate. 'Ranger Cupples, you are now so completely and utterly in the shit. You're banned from the kennel, lad, and I might even get my dog to bite you.'

'Hey, come on, not that. This is between me and you, not your dog . . .'

The little sod has even allowed me to call him 'sir' in front of the other Rangers, who evidently have been having a great time with the joke. But at the end of the day it's a fabulous wind-up, and I had to love them for it.

Cupples is the radio operator for Seven Platoon. He's also fluent in Pashto, the main language spoken here. I can't for the life of me figure out how a mature-looking Yank who clearly has a gift for languages and a brain in his head has ended up being a Ranger – the equivalent rank of a private – in a Northern Irish regiment. I sense there's a tale to be told here. Once I've tortured him good and proper over his officer prank, I'm going to make a point of finding out.

We patrol out towards JDAM Central on foot, Treo clearing the way as we go. It's not exactly hard to find our way there, as the building is visible from just about any part of Sangin. En route we pass through the marketplace, and I can see the hatred in the eyes of many of the stallholders, and especially for my dog. The majority of the stalls are selling food, and I reach this one where the guy leaps up aggressively and blocks our way.

'Dog not allowed! Dog not allowed!' he keeps yelling at Treo and me. 'Dog not allowed! Dirty animal! Dirty animal! Dog unclean!'

Well that's it, as far as I'm concerned. It's the 'dog unclean' bit that's really got to me. Treo and I are going to give his stall a thorough turning over, if it's the last thing we ever do. There's no stopping fourteen stones of pissed-off Dave Heyhoe – by the way I keep having to tighten my belt, I figure I've lost a good stone already – especially when someone's insulted my dog.

'I don't give a damn what you say,' I announce. 'The dog's coming in – to find, kill or to capture!'

'Dog not allowed! Dog not allowed!' he keeps screaming.

'Mate, you've got your job to do and I've got mine,' I tell him. 'Now stand aside, 'cause my clever, handsome, devilish rebel of a dog is coming through.'

I take Treo around the entire place, the stallholder gnashing his teeth, tearing at his beard and wailing. The Labrador side of Treo makes a beeline for the nearest food – a pile of fresh-baked Afghan flat bread. Before I can stop him he's flicked his tongue out and got a loaf pinned between his jaws. He raises his head and with a look of wild abandon starts to swallow the lot more or less whole.

'No!' I yell at him. 'Treo! Put the bread down, lad!'

I'm about to try to rescue a few crumbs when I hear a voice in my radio earpiece. It's Speedy, and he's calling to check we're OK.

'Dave, what's going on in there? We heard you yelling like a madman . . .'

'Sorry, dog eating bread in shop. Repeat: dog eating bread in shop.'

I emerge from the stall with Treo licking his lips and his nose dusted with baking flour. The guys on patrol are rolling about with laughter, but if looks could kill the Afghan stallholder has just murdered us all. There's an unbridgeable gulf between us. The Afghan hates me because I'm a white-eye infidel dog-lover; I hate him because he hates my dog. It's not great for hearts and minds on either side. But it is what it is.

We move on to JDAM Central, Treo's gut doing these happy rumbles as we go. It's rare for him to get some fresh scoff – as opposed to his Eukanuba dried food – and that bread's gone down a treat. I just hope it comes out the other end the same way. After weeks of dried rations, fresh food can seriously screw with a dog's digestion, which was the main reason I wanted to stop him eating that bread. It certainly wasn't so I could return the half-chewed loaf to the Afghan stallholder.

We pause on the roadside, at the location where the IED was detonated a few days earlier underneath that Land Rover patrol. I search the crater, trying to pick up even a hint of the roadside bomb's scent so that my dog can trace it from here. But there's nothing. Either the entire device was utterly obliterated in the blast, or the Taliban have been in to remove any evidence from the scene.

I spend a while observing the wrecked JDAM building, trying to figure out how best my dog and I should approach the search. The key feature of the place is the piles of sharp rubble and war debris scattered all around. It presents no problem to the Rangers, with their heavy Army boots, but if I send Treo in there he'll get the delicate pads on the underside of his feet cut to shreds. Infection could seep into the wounds and he'll be out of action for an age.

I dig Treo's protective dog booties out of my rucksack. They look like tiny reef shoes, with a ribbed rubber sole and a Velcro strip that fastens around the ankle. It's a real struggle to get Treo to lift each paw so I can slip them on. I know how much he hates them. Treo stands there with all four paws booted up, and he gives me a dark scowl: *I feel like a kid dressed in some dumb party suit. You're making me look like a right idiot!*

Treo thinks of himself as one cool dog, and rightfully so. He's solid, dark and handsome, plus he's classy and heroic, and he's got an ego to suit. He hates being made to look uncool. His normal stance – legs together and standing tall and proud – has gone to pieces. Instead, he's got his feet splayed apart awkwardly, like he can't stop staring down at those god-awful booties.

He didn't much appreciate it when I sprayed him with that

fluorescent gunk from the light-stick, back when we searched the tank park. But as far as Treo's concerned, this is a whole different league of humiliation. I can't help myself – I start laughing at him, and that only serves to make it worse.

'Listen, big fellow, they're for your own safety,' I tell him. I gesture at the rubble all around us. 'You don't want to cut your pawsies on any of this lot, do you? You cut yourself and you'll be no use to your dad then, will you?'

But I'm still laughing fit to burst, and Treo absolutely hates it.

There's another problem with the booties. A dog releases heat by sweating via the pads of his feet. In hot weather Treo will lie belly-down on a cool surface, all four legs splayed out, to further cool himself. The booties lessen Treo's ability to release sweat via his pads, and so the heat proves doubly debilitating. It's approaching high summer, and its pushing fifty degrees or more come mid-afternoon.

I turn to JDAM Central and scrutinise it some more. I figure the only way to do this is to allow Treo to have a totally free search. That means sending him in off-leash and with no guidance from me, leaving him free to follow his nose wherever it takes him. It's such a maze, there's no way that I can methodically cover the entire building. It's better to let my dog have his head.

I release him and give him the magic command: 'Seek on, lad, seek on'. He edges forwards but he's got a real hangdog expression about him, and I can tell his heart's not in the search. He reaches the first pile of rubble and starts trying to sniffle around it, but all the time he's gazing down at his feet and trying to use one of his paws to lever free a bootie.

This isn't working. If he's more concerned about those booties than he is about the search, it's pointless us being here. Worse than that, it's dangerous. My dog might blunder into something because his mind's not on our life-or-death mission. I turn to the bloke behind me, who happens to be Ranger Cupples.

I fix him with this look. 'Hey, Cups – or should I say "Sir Cupples", you bleedin' chancer – get one of your spare mags for your SA80 and hide it under that rubble. But make sure Treo doesn't see you doing it.'

Ranger Cupples does as I've asked. I can't use one of my own mags of ammo because Treo would recognise my scent right away. I call my dog back to me and point him in the direction of the hidden magazine. He catches the scent, perks up a bit, and makes a beeline for it. He finds it and I pretend that I'm ecstatic. I give him a whole world of praise, and we have a quick play with his ball.

All of a sudden Treo's forgotten his booties, and the fact they make him look so idiotic, and he's tuned into the search. I pretend I've thrown his tennis ball into the rubble of the building and he's off, nose chuffing away like a steam train. I follow on his heels, checking everywhere for craters, or chunks of rubble waiting to fall and trap my dog.

We reach the centre of the building, and it's a blast-scarred concrete skeleton, one that reeks of human faeces. There have been people here, and recently. The central staircase rises like the backbone of some long-extinct dinosaur – battered, skeletal, and covered in dust and debris. I guide Treo up it, carefully feeling our way over each step and navigating around gaping cracks and fissures.

At one point I have to call my dog back: 'No! Back here – good lad. Not that way . . .'

I scoop him up and place him onto my shoulders, and we squeeze past a massive hole that's been blown clean through the concrete underfoot. We reach the roof to find it scattered with empty food wrappers. Treo quickly sniffs out some bullet casings, which are the calibre used by the Taliban. The enemy has been up here all right, and they've been using this space as some kind of fire platform. The only thing we can't find is anything that identifies it as a trigger point for IEDs.

It's taken three hours to clear the place, and in a sense we've found nothing. But on another level we've gained vital intel. I discuss what we've discovered with Speedy and Ronnie. They figure it makes sense to keep a permanent watch on the place. It's visible from the high points of our base, and we'll get a Ranger with a spotting scope zoomed in on it, waiting to catch the enemy next time they put in an appearance.

As we exit the building I realise we've achieved something on a deeper level too. The Seven Platoon lads have seen how my dog can do just about any search asked of him. It doesn't matter what kind of terrain or structure it is, we'll find a way. I can see a new-found sense of respect and camaraderie in the young Ranger's eyes. We're starting to build the unbreakable bond of brother warriors at war.

Major Shannon decides to adopt Treo and me as two of his own – as Rangers. He sends me down to the Ranger Company stores and I get kitted out with every piece of equipment the Rangers have, including my own set of NVG. I've worn out my British Army-issue boots during the few weeks that I've been here, what with all the leg work that I've been doing and the weight that I'm carrying. The Ranger Company storeman issues me with a brand new pair.

But more importantly, we need to score a shamrock. I've noticed that the Ranger lads have this green shamrock flash on their helmets. It's regimental tradition, and of course it's for good luck. I'm superstitious by nature, and I need one for my dog.

I score Treo a flash from the stores. It's a square of tough canvas material with a bright green shamrock – which looks similar to a four-leaf clover – set within it. I superglue it onto Treo's harness, on his left-hand side at shoulder height, which is about as near as I can get to where the Ranger lads wear theirs.

Little do I know how much we're going to need its luck in the days that lie ahead.

CHAPTER TWELVE

The Rangers have been on the ground long enough now for Major Shannon to decide it's time for a real show of force. He wants to get the entire Ranger Company out on patrol, in an effort to saturate the area and deny it to the enemy. This is a direct and deliberate provocation, and Treo and I will be embedded with Seven Platoon for the entire duration of the op.

We head out at first light, and it sure is a splendid sight to see some two-hundred-odd Rangers fanning out from the base to take possession of the whole of Sangin town. Immediately we're out the Talinet starts going crazy. We've got Sly, our regular terp, translating for us what the Taliban commanders are saying.

'They're coming out in force! Can you see them? How many are there? Can you attack?'

Word is passed from Sly down the entire length of the patrol, so that every young soldier knows exactly what the enemy is saying. Every time they up their chat and start yelling that they're 'poised to attack', the tension is raised an extra notch amongst us. For most of the lads of Seven Platoon this is only their fourth or fifth time out, and the fear is still very fresh and raw and real.

It takes a while to learn to accept that you're up against a hidden enemy, one that deliberately hides amongst the civilian population. They can hit you at any time, and that's just how it is. It takes a while to develop the state of mind to deal with it. You have to accept that the enemy will hit you when they choose to hit you, and it's only when they open fire that you can ID them as the bad guys and take the fight right back to them.

You learn to take the enemy fire when it comes, and that what matters is how you react when the bullets start to fly. But there are some kinds of attack that no amount of training or experience can ever prepare you for, or safeguard you from. The Taliban are about to hit us with something new and extra nasty today – but right now we've not got the faintest idea what's coming.

Treo and I are out front as usual. We've been here for hours, clearing a safe path for the patrol to move through, and deliberately poking the hornet's nest. It's mid-afternoon, and there's not been a sniff of enemy action for us lot. But the Talinet's still going wild, and right now the enemy commanders are urging their men to hit us now, 'before it's too late'.

We reach the limit of our patrol arc and turn to head back to base. Treo's off-leash and he's forwards of me some twenty metres. We're about an hour out from home and heading down this back road when Treo stops dead in his tracks. He airs up, checks step, and suddenly he's staring straight ahead of himself at this Afghan male, a good thirty metres to his front.

Treo's that much closer to the Afghan, and I'm unsure as to what he's sensed here that's so grabbed his attention. I see him glance my way and I can read the confusion and indecision in his clever, intensely focused gaze.

'What is it, boy?' I ask of him. 'What is it you think you've got there?'

Maybe it's an Afghan drugs dealer, and it's the smell of the opium that's got Treo stumped. He glances back at the Afghan male, then fixes him with his unmoving, laser-eyed stare. I'd know that expression anywhere. Treo knows exactly what scent he's detected here: it's explosives. But the weird thing for my dog is the source of that smell: it's a human.

The Afghan male is barely twenty metres from Treo when it clicks. With a horrible flash of realisation I know for certain what Treo's onto here: it's that Afghan male himself who's the bomb. He's a suicide bomber. And right now he's making directly for my dog.

I raise my stumpy SA80 and I start screaming at him to stop right there. Instead, he keeps coming. I guess he doesn't care any more. Either way, he knows he's a dead man. In his eyes I can read the blind hatred and the glazed look of someone on the verge of death. He slips his hand inside his robes . . .

There's no space for panic or for fear. All I'm thinking is: *My God, my God, don't let him kill my dog.*

Treo's that much closer, and he'll be that much nearer to the blast. I know I can't stop what's coming. Invariably, these human bombers are drugged to the eyeballs and no amount of body shots will stop them detonating their explosive belt. It would take a sniper achieving a perfect headshot to instantly put the guy's lights out, and I don't have the right weapon or the time to achieve it.

I dive forwards, determined to use my body to shield my dog from the blast. I land practically on top of him. I know I'm not far enough across him yet, and that I've left his right flank exposed. I scrabble wildly, ripping my nails as I claw at the dirt in an effort to drag myself between my dog and the human bomb that's about to blow. If I can just get there before he presses the detonator, maybe I can save him.

I see the Afghan's arm twitch, as he presses the firing mechanism.

I say a last farewell to my beloved dog, my son that I've failed to save. I tense myself for the bolts and ball bearings that the suicide vest will have been packed with.

There's a sudden, blinding flash.

The blast wave punches into us, smashing me in the stomach like a speeding truck and jerking my head violently backwards as I try to cling onto Treo and save him. We're engulfed in a howling gale of choking smoke and dust. A second later my world turns black.

I come back to consciousness gradually, my head full of a driving pain and a muzzy fog. As my sight returns, I realise that my eyes are swimming with blasted dust and sand. I rub one clear and spot a distinctive figure. It's Treo, and he's on his feet standing over me, his eyes wide with terror. He's searching in the smoke and dust for a sign of life from me.

If my dog could talk I know what he'd be yelling right now: *Get up, Dad! Dad, get up! Show me you're still alive!*

He sees me open my eyes and I swear he yelps and smiles in delight. An instant later he's on top of me, madly licking my face. I reach up and drag him in close and for a moment I hold him like I'm never letting go. And for that instant I'm crying tears of joy that they failed to kill my boy, my dog.

I haven't got the faintest clue how we can both still be alive. I glance up from where I'm laid on the deck, with Treo crouched over me protectively. All I can see is this mushroom-cloud of smoke where seconds before the suicide bomber was standing. The air is full of the sickening stench of burned and seared human flesh, which must be all that's left of him.

High above us, I see a tattered, bloodied Afghan robe floating down towards the earth like a mini parachute. The Afghan male has vaporised. All I can think is that whoever built that suicide vest must have smoked too much opium that morning: he'd forgotten to pack the device full of shrapnel. Nothing else can explain how Treo and I are still breathing and alive.

I hear boots pounding forwards and voices yelling: 'DOG! DAVE DOG! DAAAAVE!'

It sounds as if the cries are coming from down the end of a very long tunnel. They're faint and muffled and distorted, and there's this horrible ringing in my head. I don't doubt it's a whole world worse for Treo, with the sensitive hearing that he's got. But at least my dog's not lying beside me bleeding out his last.

Speedy, Ronnie and the other lads are beside us now. They simply can't believe that Treo and I are still with them on this earth.

With a shaky hand I point upwards at the tattered robe-cum-parachute. 'There used to be a body in that . . .'

With that the tension bursts. With the adrenalin levels pumping like they have been, we've taken on these taut, rigid expressions like a pack of ghostly skeletons. Amidst the settling dust and the deafening silence the humour forces us to relax a little, and it makes us just that tiny bit human again.

Now he knows that my dog and I are still alive, Speedy starts sparking. 'GO FIRM!' he yells over the radios. 'GO FIRM! And shoot anything that moves! Shoot anything that moves!'

Then he spots a young kid at the far end of a nearby compound and he realises what he's just said.

'Counter that! Stay firm! But don't shoot anything that moves! Don't shoot! Don't shoot! There are kids out there!'

No doubt about it, this has been a deliberate set-up – a come-on attack by a suicide bomber, one which was intended to rip me and my dog apart. Knowing how closely the lads relate to Treo, the enemy would have hoped the Rangers would react in a blind rage. They'd have charged ahead seeking to avenge their dog soldier, and they'd have blundered into the Taliban's trap.

Instead, we move back and throw a cordon of steel around the bombing scene, and Speedy calls up reinforcements. I take the opportunity to give Treo the biggest cuddle of his life, like I'm never going to let him go.

'You're OK, boy. You're all right,' I whisper in his ear. 'You're OK. And Dad's just fine, and he's not ever going to let anyone hurt you ever . . .'

I check him over, just to make doubly sure that he's not been injured. His fur is badly singed on the side that was nearest the blast, but otherwise he seems just fine. I'm acutely aware of how near we came to death here. What were the chances of that suicide vest not being packed with any shrapnel? *What were the chances?* My dog and I have had a miracle escape. It's like we've come back from death to life again.

Once the reinforcements are with us, the Seven Platoon lads start to push forward. They begin kicking in doors and doing a full cordon-and-search operation in an effort to find anyone linked to the suicide bomber. As Treo and I have just been blown up we're left to take a breather, and we remain at the scene of the bombing with Headquarters Platoon.

Frankie O'Connor, the Ranger Company sergeant major, comes to have words with me. Once he's checked that we're all right, he says he's got a favour to ask of me and my dog.

'Dave, if you can, mate, we need you to find the bloke's head.'

For a moment I'm pretty much lost for words. It strikes me as being a somewhat odd request. Normally, a suicide bomber's head is blown vertically upwards by the blast. It goes up like a missile, and can come down any distance away from the scene of the explosion. But that doesn't explain why Frankie needs my dog and me to go out and retrieve it.

'And why exactly d'you want us to do that?' I ask.

'Finding the head's the only way to ID the bomber. And from that we can glean vital intel.'

'Frankie, we're an arms explosive search dog team,' I tell him. 'We're not an arms and other-blown-off-limbs-and-bits-'n'-pieces search dog team.' I flap my arms about to better make my point. 'What you need is a cadaver search dog, not Treo. They're the ones that get sent out to search for corpses.'

Frankie gives a shrug. 'I know, Davey-boy. But right now you're all we've got.'

I figure it's a fair one.

I get Treo to shake himself down as best he can and we prepare to do the search. We move forwards until we're near the blast point. Hardly have we got there when Treo darts off into the bush. He plunges into a thick patch of reeds about six feet high, and he's gone.

I see them swaying this way and that as he weaves his way through, and I know there's not a hope in hell of me being able to follow him. I'd lose sight of him the second I went in, with the reeds waving all around my head. I'm far better off staying where I am on the path and watching the reed heads bend and shake.

All of a sudden the vegetation stops moving. It means that Treo's stopped dead.

'Right,' I announce to Frankie and the assembled Rangers. 'My dog's onto something. I'm going in.'

I push into the thick mass of reeds, making a beeline for where I last saw movement. I ease my way through, only to get there and find my dog sniffing at a dollop of something red and distinctly yucky-looking. I yell for him to get back to me and we move onto the path. I glance down and Treo's got an object gripped between his jaws.

It's the suicide bomber's head.

I tell him to drop the grizzly specimen. He does as ordered, after which he sits there pleased as punch at having found it. He's got that expression on his face that I know so well: *I am a dog, so what d'you expect?*

I hand the gruesome remains to Frankie, so he can bag it up.

'Is that it?' he queries. 'Is that all there is?'

'At least my dog found it,' I tell him. 'That's what you asked for, isn't it?'

Frankie cracks a rare hint of a smile. 'Yeah. Sorry, Dave, that's a fair one. Well done to yer dog, mate.'

That done, we set off on the track before us to make our return to base. Further remains of the bomber are gathered as we go, and we load them onto a stretcher together with the head. One thing becomes clear as we pick up the body parts. Whoever the suicide bomber was, they haven't even made the effort to shave him. Normally, they prepare a 'martyr' for his 'martyrdom' by shaving his entire body and anointing it with perfumes and fine oils. It's so the guy smells good when he goes to meet his promised seventy-two virgins in paradise.

With this poor sod they haven't even bothered. He was probably just some simple farmer, whom the Taliban drugged up and fed full of lies. There's likely a young family going to grow up without a father now, and all because the Taliban brainwashed him into blowing himself to pieces. And for what? Treo and I barely have a scratch on us, so he's hardly taken out the hated dog team. What a senseless stupid pointless waste of a life.

But Treo and I have other things to worry about right now. Frankie's told me they want to get the guy's remains back to base pronto. He's got my dog and me out front doing a rapid search of the route. We'll be following a river all the way, so I've got Treo clipped on his long leash. Otherwise, my water baby of a dog will be one step on the search, the other in the river all the way home.

Fortunately, Major Shannon gets a quad bike sent out to pick up the stretcher, which speeds things up a great deal. We're soon back at the Sangin DC gates. Treo and I wait there as we always do, just so we can make sure the last man gets counted back in. *All the boots that go out come back in again*: it's become the meaning of life for me and my dog.

There's a call of: 'Last man in! Unload your weapons, and go get some down time . . .'

Treo and I don't need telling twice.

Back at our kennel I give my dog an intensive checking over. After all, we have just been blown up. Apart from the burns to his fur, he seems just fine. As I run my hand over his powerful flank, I linger for a second on the shamrock flash that's attached to his harness. I pause and say a heartfelt thanks to lady luck, fate and the gods. I commend them all for keeping my boy safe out there.

I fetch my stethoscope, the one that I carry with me whenever Treo and I are working. It's a bog-standard type that the doctor uses to listen to your chest. My dog and I settle down together on my cot, him with his head resting on my shoulder. I put the amplifier end of the stethoscope against Treo's ribcage and tune into the rhythm of my dog's heart.

Thum-thuump. Thum-thuump. Thum-thuump . . .

It sounds strong, unhurried and regular as clockwork. It sounds like it always does. The Taliban may have blown him up, but they don't seem to have unsettled him unduly. I leave the stethoscope where it is and keep listening. I find it comforting. Reassuring. It's not fast and anxious. It's not irregular. It's not messed up. Unbelievably, it seems to be just like it always is.

My father, Bob Heyhoe, always used to tell me that dogs are the greatest stress reliever. I lie there for several minutes, listening to the rhythm of my dog's life force. It does seem to help calm and de-stress me, being this close to Treo and tuning into his heart and soul. This is quality Treo time, and connecting to my dog like this really does seem to settle me.

As for Treo, he keeps eyeing the stethoscope and glancing at me with a bemused expression: *What are you doing, Dad? Am I sick or something?*

Yet he doesn't once try to interfere or stop me. I can manipulate Treo into any position that I want, and he's good with it – the trust between us is so deep, unspoken and intuitive. 'Trust your dog' is one of the mottos of the RAVC's dog teams, and that trust goes both ways – from handler to dog and back again.

I give Treo a look: 'Listen, lad, I trust you one hundred per cent to know what you're capable of.'

He returns my gaze: *Dad, I trust you to know you'd never put me into any needless danger.*

We're a team of equals, me and my dog, and that's the key. We've put our lives in each other's hands day after day after day here, and I've never once doubted him. I'm sure he's never once doubted his dad, either. Out here, it's that trust between us that's keeping the both of us alive.

But the thing is, however watchful I'm being of Treo, however much I'm trying to think like the enemy and to second-guess them, there's not much that I can do about a suicide bomber. I wonder how on earth I'm supposed to act next time my dog comes nose-to-nose with a would-be martyr, one who's hell-bent on blowing us all to paradise or to hell.

We've never rehearsed this. We've never planned for it. We've never trained the dogs with a dummy suicide bomber strapped with explosives, because no one ever imagined that this was what might happen to us here. It's beyond our wildest dreams and our worst nightmares, but here in Sangin it's become our reality. And, like most things in terms of what our response should be, my dog and I are going to have to make it up as we go along.

I try to think about what we can do in an effort to mitigate the threat. The trouble is, whilst Treo may detect the explosive scent, he's never been trained to search for a moving target. He's trained to track a scent to its heart and to mark it. Under normal circumstances I know him well enough to be able to read all the signs, and to pull him back just before it goes lethal. But how can he mark a moving suicide bomber – one who's hell-bent on killing him?

There are no easy answers to this one. We'll just have to hope and pray, and keep saying our thank-yous to lady luck and the shamrock.

I delve into my left breast pocket for my camera. I want a shot of my dog on the day that we survived a suicide bombing. My hand comes out with the camera smashed in two. There's a big jagged crack through the body, and when I turn it around I can see that the lens is shattered. I must have smashed it when diving onto Treo. There's no point in even attempting to turn it on. It's clearly very finished.

Tonight is yet another night when I lie awake thinking about my dog. So far he's been shot at too many times to mention. He's been soaked in a dying Afghan soldier's blood and gore. And now he's been blown up by an Afghan suicide bomber.

Treo's a miracle dog, a combat veteran, a survivor, a hero and the morale-booster extraordinaire. He's my saviour, my best friend, my brother warrior and he's the son that I never had. And I'm worried half to death for him.

They say a cat has nine lives. Well, maybe a dog does too. But for sure Treo's burning through them super fast.

CHAPTER THIRTEEN

The following morning I manage to get some face time with one of the Sangin computers. There's a bank of them in the DC building and the queues are normally horrendous. This time I'm lucky. I send an email to my sister, Pam. She and I are close, and she's got this fantastic, warped, way out, left-field sense of humour that has me in stitches.

In the past I've always been her rock whenever she's been going through hard times. Now that I'm out here in the hell of Sangin, there's been something of a role reversal. I email her and tell her I need a new camera. I ask her to find me one that won't cost the earth, but might stand up to the punishment. I tell her to burn it on her credit card and to post it out to me as soon as.

I hate not being able to keep a visual record of what Treo and I are going through, plus it's a real problem not being able to document our finds. Those images provide vital intel – both to us and to other search teams that may take over from us here in Sangin. I tell Pam that I'll pay her back for the camera just as soon as I get home. It's always *when* I get home, not *if*.

By mid-morning a whocka-whocka has made it into the helipad and there's some good news – a mail delivery. We're five weeks in now and this is our first news from home. It provides a huge lift. There's a heap of letters and parcels from friends and family, but once I've divided it into two piles – one for Treo and one for me – my dog's got about four times the amount of mail that I have.

It's bloody typical.

The first thing I do is tear open the letters, as I'm desperate for some news of home. But most of those who've written seem more worried about Treo than they are about me.

'How's Treo managing in the heat?' my mum writes. 'Is he getting his doggy treats?'

Is he getting his doggy treats? As if she needs to ask! To a man the Rangers seem to have written home and asked their folks to send something special for my dog. Already I've had a Ranger lad pop down to the kennel with a 'little something' for Treo that was posted out in the mail.

'Hey, Dave, something for Treo!' the Ranger announced, whilst holding out this choice doggy snack.

Treo snapped his head around and gave me the eye: *Hey, it's for me, not for you!* He had his ball jammed in the side of his mouth, as always, but I knew it would soon be replaced by some delicious snack or other.

'He loves his ball, eh?' the Ranger lad remarked.

'Yeah, he loves it, and when he's got it in his mouth like that it means he won't be biting you!' I retorted, somewhat meanly.

In addition to the letters, there are four big parcels all done up in brown paper. It turns out that one is for me and the other three are addressed to Treo, 'c/o Dave Heyhoe'. He comes over, sniffs at the parcels, shoves the one that's for me aside, and pulls the other three in the direction of his side of the kennel.

I can't believe how possessive my dog can be. I give him the evil eye. *You little so-and-so. You don't even know you're at war. I do. It's me who needs the treats.*

I reckon I know what my parcel contains without even opening it. By the sound of it, it's got to be a cake tin, and it'll be full of my favourite home-baked cakes. My nan makes these amazing Eccles cakes, the best you can get. After five weeks on Army rations I can't wait to get at them.

I open the tin and sure enough Nan's done me proud. It's a bumper lot. I put on the kettle, make myself a brew and settle down to demolish a good number. There is something my nan does with her Eccles cakes that is this close to alchemy. But no sooner have I put the first delicious specimen to my lips than Treo's at my side. He's abandoned whatever doggy treat he was chomping on and come to bug me.

I see him raise his head to sniff at the tin: *Ah, lovely, that's your nan's Eccles cakes, isn't it, Dad?*

He sits there, bum glued to the deck and head following my every move, as I demolish a good half a dozen of them. I can't believe my dog. He's got more treats than I could ever dream of, yet here he is bugging me. He's slobbering and drooling, and giving me that gooey-eyed stare: *Dad, I know I don't deserve one, but couldn't you just . . .*

Who could resist that look? Not me, that's for sure. I reach out and drop a morsel of Nan's Delight into Treo's open jaws. He gives a couple of ecstatic chomps and it's gone: *Just as I thought! Nan's Eccles cakes – delicious!*

I reach out and grab another. Treo's leaning with all his weight against my leg, and nudging me with his shoulder: *Hey, don't forget your best buddy!*

This dog – he knows no shame.

Before they're all gone I take the tin to the Rangers' quarters and offer one to Ronnie, Speedy, Davey and Cupples-the-chancer. Ronnie takes a bite and his face is a picture.

'That is feckin' gorgeous!' he exclaims. 'Can I have another?'

'No, you've had the one,' I tell him. 'I am very protective of my nan's Eccles cakes.'

It's true. The thought of Nan doing that baking and sending them all the way to Sangin has really touched me.

The base is getting horribly crowded, and the Rangers are desperate for space. A couple of the blokes suggest that they move into Treo's and my domain – into *our* kennel. I don't object to the human company, it's just that it won't work. We need our own space, Treo and me, and it's got to be inviolable. If I'm away and someone else pitches up in Treo's dad's kennel, he's going to freak out big time.

The answer is the shipping container kennel, the one that comes complete with its own air conditioning. True to his word, the 104's sergeant major gets it shipped out on a flatbed wagon, as part of a convoy that comes in on the 611. The kennel gets dropped on a stretch of waste ground near the helipad.

I look it over proudly. I see this as the start of our new dog section, one that will have some proper facilities to keep the dogs in tip-top condition. Or so I think. I swing open the steel door and a tidal wave of sand comes chugging out, engulfing me in a choking cloud of dust. During the long road move the convoy must have thrown up a real dust storm, and most of it seems to have blown into our kennel.

Not a bother, I tell myself. I set to work sweeping it out, then giving it a good scrubbing and thoroughly disinfecting it. By sundown I've got it pretty much back to tip-top condition, and it promises to be a palace fit even for a Treo. But first, we've got to get it moved somewhere liveable and hooked up to the electric. The kennel can't remain where it is, or every time a helicopter flies in we'll get engulfed in a dust storm. I need the Royal Engineers to move it into a more habitable location. But their officer seems to think it's more important getting creature comforts installed in his fellow officers' quarters than getting Treo's kennel sorted and the power plugged in.

He tries telling me that my dog's not a priority, compared with his other taskings. I tell him that Treo's the biggest lifesaver here in Sangin. I point out that the officers sit in air-conditioned luxury controlling ops from base, whilst Treo's out on the ground in the heat and dust dodging bullets and saving lives. I tell him to make Treo a priority. It's coming up to the hottest part of the year, and the time of the opium poppy harvest. It's soon going to be the silly season, when the opium farmers revert to being Taliban. We know the enemy is poised to up the ante. Treo and I are going to get busier still, and all I'm asking is for the kennel to be installed in a usable location, where I can run the air con.

As a bonus, I'd like to get it positioned somewhere a little more sheltered from flying chunks of shrapnel, for the enemy's mortars and rockets keep hitting us. Being right next to the helipad, the kennel is in the open and it's a prime target. The

Engineer officer is adamant he's not going to get it moved. He's got more pressing priorities, or so he claims.

Finally, I lose it. 'You're bang out of bloody order!' We're nose-to-nose and we start having a screaming match. 'I put my search dog in front of the blokes every single time, which makes his welfare a bloody lifesaver!'

Still he refuses to get the kennel moved.

I put a call through to Captain Martin Thompson, my boss back at Camp Bastion. I tell him what's what, and I explain that I'm going to have to make the ultimate threat – to pull Treo out of Sangin. I explain that this is the last thing I want to do: Treo and I are here doing the mission of a lifetime. But this has become a game of brinkmanship, and making that threat is the only way that I can see to make him understand that my dog's welfare comes before anyone's luxury.

Martin Thompson is a great bloke. He's a late-entry officer, and he made his way through the ranks by hard graft and good soldiering. He hears me out, and when I've finished making my case he backs me to the hilt. He tells me that the dog's welfare comes first. If I have to threaten to pull Treo, so be it.

That conversation done, I go to find Major Shannon in the ops room. I ask to have a quiet word and explain that all my requests regarding our kennel have been refused.

'Sir, the kennel's sat there on the helipad like a big, useless oven,' I tell him. 'I can't put Treo in there until it's moved and hooked up to the electric, or he'll roast. I've asked repeatedly, but the Engineer officer keeps finding excuses.'

'Go on,' Major Shannon tells me. 'I'm listening.'

'Sir, I know how important the dog is to your men, and I don't say this lightly . . . But, sir, if nothing is done to get that kennel sorted, I will be forced to pull the dog team out of Sangin. I've got the backing of my bosses to do it.'

I have his absolute attention now. 'Dave, don't pull the dog.' His expression is deadly serious. 'I repeat: do not pull the dog. I'll go and have a word.'

The next morning the Engineer officer comes over and he's ready to move the kennel into place. *Result*. I tell him I want it near the Ranger Company quarters, so we can better ready ourselves to get out on patrol with the lads. He tells me that he can't move it there because Treo's barking might wake the officers.

I can't believe what I'm hearing. I ask him if he's being serious. 'Listen, mate, are we at war, or what?'

I finally get my way, but not before having to threaten to pull out Treo for a second time. He orders his blokes to drop our kennel just where I want it – next to the Rangers and close by the river, so Treo can take a dip whenever we're in off patrols.

To be fair, the Engineer blokes allocated to do the job are a great bunch. In order to get the kennel into place the forklift driver has to disconnect the base's main satellite TV feed. He tries to do it relatively quickly, because there's forty lads watching at the time. But by the time it's been reconnected the feed has been lost. It turns out that they'll need to get a specialist engineer flown out from Camp Bastion to get it tuned back in. So that's no watching BFBS (British Forces Broadcasting Service – the Army's TV channel) for some time to come.

The Engineer lads pitch in good and proper, using their mini-diggers to construct HESCO blast walls around our new location. I roll out the metal fencing that comes with the kennel, to make a run for Treo, and I get some warning signs printed up so the ANA lot don't come blundering in here. The Afghan soldiers – like Afghan males in general – don't seem to take too kindly to my dog.

Each time a bit of new kit gets rolled out of the kennel, Treo is striding about like a site foreman and checking on progress: *Over a bit that way; a bit more; right, drop it just there.* He glances over at me happily: *You know, Dad, there's nothing better than getting the kennel sorted and making it like home . . .*

I cobble together a seating and table area, so I can have the Ranger lads over for a brew, and we're done. I give Treo the rear-most kennel, which provides maximum protection from any shrapnel or blast. That's his domain, where he can have some quality Treo time. I take the kennel next to it, and bung my cot in there.

At last we've got a half-decent dog section established here in Sangin. It's nothing like what we'd have in the UK, or what the dog teams have in Camp Bastion, Kabul or Kandahar. But it'll do. It's got the air con, it's reasonably comfortable and Treo's pretty safe in there from anything but a direct hit.

As soon as the air con is switched on Treo heads inside and plonks himself down in the cool blast of air. By the time the Engineer officer comes to check on things, Treo's gazing about himself contentedly, like he's in doggy heaven.

'Erm, getting it all sorted?' he remarks. 'I see the dog's happy, then?'

'He is,' I smile. 'He's like a little pig in shit is my Treo.'

He's not a bad bloke. In fact, other than this one major

confrontation we've got on pretty well. It's just that he hasn't appreciated the importance of a search dog's welfare. I figure he can see how happy Treo is now, and maybe he's starting to understand that a well-rested and happy dog means an optimum search dog.

We've not long had the air con going when a mortar round howls in and slams into the dirt on the far side of the HESCO walling that we've erected. Treo and I hit the deck, and it's proof positive how easily we could get zapped without such protection. We get up and dust ourselves down, and Treo gives me a look: *Now this place is a little more like it, isn't it, Dad?*

That evening he jumps onto my bed. He leans his whole body against me, a happy grin on his doggy features. He's gazing up at me, his expression one of bliss and contentment. As for me, I am hugely relieved at getting this kennel thing sorted. I don't like strife, and I don't go looking for arguments – it's just that no one ever gets to disrespect my dog.

The last thing I want is to get Treo and me pulled out of here. This is where we need to be. Shitty and hellish though it is, it's in sniffing out the bombs here at Sangin that Treo and I have found ourselves.

Now that the new kennel is up and running, Jihad and Sandbag come to have a good sniff around. Ever since they became honorary members of the team, they've been getting their fair share of the Eukanuba rations. I'm feeding them up good and proper, and the new kennels are now their honorary home too.

They don't have name-boards up, as Treo does. They won't be sleeping here – not unless Treo can sneak Jihad in, and I wouldn't put it past the randy old goat. But they'll be hanging out here during the day, and getting their meals here, plus it'll be the base from where Jihad will join us as we set out on patrol.

My folks got those bone-shaped nametags that I asked for, and they came out with our mail delivery. Jihad and Sandbag have them proudly displayed on their collars, and day-by-day they're looking happier and more healthy. The only problem is Jihad's lingering infection – the hangover from her pregnancy – and I've yet to receive the drugs that I need to treat her.

Jihad's infection doesn't seem to lessen her enthusiasm for going out on missions. The day after getting our kennel sorted, Treo, Jihad and I get out on a foot patrol with the Ranger's Nine Platoon, one of their standard Rifle Companies. It's long, baking hot and frustratingly tense, but ultimately uneventful.

Just as soon as we're in through the base gates Major Shannon says he needs us out again, this time with Seven Platoon. I point out that Treo needs a break, and I remind him of the two-hours-rest-between-patrols rule.

'Sir, I've just been out and the dog's knackered. You know he needs a rest – he's not a machine.'

He tries to argue the case with me. 'Dave, it's the Seven Platoon lads on a major search tasking, and they need you on this one.'

'Sir, you know your men, I know my dog. You control your men, I'll control my dog.'

The major's not entirely happy, but he accepts it. I rate him. He's a down-to-earth Irishman and he's tireless: he won't rest for a minute when his men are in danger. He's by the radio listening in whenever they're out on ops, and he's ready to push out reinforcements if they hit trouble. He's driven purely by the welfare of his men, and that's why he keeps pushing Treo and me. But I'm driven by the safety of my dog, and sometimes I've just got to push right back again.

Whenever we're having one of our little confrontations, I get the sense that the major's analysing my every word, and stashing it all away in his head. It's like he's got this photographic memory, and he uses that to argue for his men's safety in a relentless way. It's not often that he'll have a corporal saying 'no' to him, but he knows I know the capabilities of my dog.

I take Treo down to our kennel and into the air-conditioned cool and shade. I check his paws for cuts, scratches and thorns, and get a load of water into him. I also take the liberty of sticking a thermometer up his bum, to check on his core temperature. I know the major's going to keep trying to push us, and I've got to check whether my dog's in a fit state to go.

I'm giving Treo and Jihad a quick feed, when Ronnie and Speedy from Seven Platoon pitch up. Both men are looking uncharacteristically serious.

'Listen, Dave, we really need you on this one,' says Speedy. 'It's a heavy search tasking that could go badly wrong for us.'

'Dave, just tell us how long you need,' says Ronnie. 'We'll hold off until you're ready.'

I ask them for two hours. They're happy with that. It's going to be a night mission, so the delay doesn't matter much.

It'll be dark, whatever time we hit bandit country.

CHAPTER FOURTEEN

We pack our gear for the coming mission. I've been told it's a company-level op and we might be out for as long as three days. The major's received intel that a crack IED-laying team has been at work, and we're going out to hunt for the bombs before they can kill any of us, or any Afghan civilians.

We set out an hour after last light, all moving on night vision goggles. Eight and Nine Platoon are with us, one force moving forwards on our left flank and one on our right. We patrol for two days, scouring the ground for IEDs and sleeping out in the bush. We're pushing the enemy ever backwards, but the non-stop pressure and tension is exhausting, not to mention the ferocious firefights.

We're searching for our third night running, and my eyes are aching and bloodshot from staring into the artificial glow of the NVG, plus trying to keep a close eye on my dog. He comes and nuzzles his nose into my hand. His muzzle feels dusty and dry, which is a sure sign that he's flagging. I signal we need to stop, because Treo's close to finished. We need to go firm for a quarter of an hour to rest him.

Treo and I take time out slumped in the bush by the roadside.

In the darkness and the eerie silence I give him a good cuddle and a bit of Dave 'n' Treo time to help revive him. Just that physical and verbal comfort can make all the difference with my dog, reinjecting some vitality into him. Oftentimes, it's that which he needs, as much as he does a good long drink from my water carrier.

Davy, the EBEX operator, has been patrolling right behind us, using his metal detector to help verify finds. As we lie at rest, Davy asks me who I had with me in my kennel on our last night at the base.

'So, who were you talking to all that time?' he asks. 'Who's Tippy-Toes?'

It's true, I did have Tippy-Toes in my kennel. Tippy-Toes is my new nickname for Treo. I've watched him trying to walk around on the metal floor of the new kennel, his claws scrabbling for grip, and that's what made me think *Tippy-Toes*. When it's just the two of us alone that's what I've been calling him.

I tell Davy it was Treo that I was speaking to. Davy can't understand how I can spend hours talking to a dog (let alone give him such ridiculous nicknames). But the thing is with Treo he's the perfect listener. He can't reply verbally, but I can see in his eyes that he's hearing my every word.

To show Davy what I mean, I turn to Treo: 'Tippy-Toes, are your pawsies hurting?' He holds one paw up for me and I give it a good rub. 'I'm not surprised, lad, my feet ache like hell.'

I get my Camelbak out of my backpack, take a sip, then Treo opens his mouth so I can squirt some in. I hold out my hand and Treo places his paw into it.

'Little bit higher, lad,' I tell him.

I raise mine and turn the palm towards him, and Treo gives me a high-five. I do a twisting motion in the air with my hand, and Treo flips over and does a few rolls.

Then I freeze the hand: 'Steady . . .'

Treo freezes in mid-roll. He's lying on his back with his four legs limp as if he's just died. I go over and start to pump his chest with my hands, like I'm doing resuscitation. He springs up into my arms.

'You're alive!' I exclaim. 'You're alive!'

Davy laughs quietly to himself. He's forced to admit that my dog understands me on a level that goes far deeper than purely verbal communication.

A figure appears beside us in the darkness. It's Ranger Cupples. 'Mind if I give Treo a little something?' he asks, speaking in that soft, classy American way of his.

Since the Ranger lads got their mail delivery, Treo's never been without a doggy treat whenever we're out on patrol. Each of the Rangers is carrying a shedload of kit on their back, but they still find space for a little something for Treo. And Cupples is proving one of the biggest treat-carriers of the lot of them.

'Yeah, go for it,' I tell him. 'But best move your hand away quickly, or I'll get Treo to bite you. I've still not forgotten your "officer" wind up.'

Cupples laughs good-naturedly. 'Bite me? Not Treo . . . No one bites the hand that feeds them, eh?'

I let out a snort of derision. 'Treo bloody does!'

Cupples reaches out his hand a little nervously. As with the rest of the Rangers, he's still a bit wary of Treo. If they can get just a passing feel of my dog without him nailing them, then they're mostly happy. It's like they're thinking: *Yes! Got a touch of the dog without him biting me . . . Fantastic . . .*

Cupples offers him the doggy chew. Treo glances over at me for an instant, and gets the look that tells him he can have it: *Yes, lad, go on – you've earned it.* He opens his mouth ever so slightly and gently takes the treat.

'Ah, he's just one big soft pussycat,' Cupples purrs.

'No one ever calls my dog a cat,' I tell him. 'And the way you're carrying on, Treo will be thirty-two bloody stone by the end of this tour.'

I'm curious about Ranger Cupples, and how on earth he got into the Irish Rangers. I've found out he was originally in the US Navy, and moving from there to a British infantry regiment recruited from Ireland is one hell of a journey. I ask him what happened.

Cupples tells me that he served with the US Navy in Iraq during the 2003 conflict. Before that he'd grown up in Florida, in the southern US, but the family also had a home in County Cavan, in Ireland. The family was of Irish origin, and eventually they moved to live there. That's where Cupples met his young wife, a Lithuanian girl called Vilma.

Living in Ireland, he'd been drawn to the Irish camaraderie and fighting spirit. He'd decided to join up with the Royal Irish Regiment, and that's how he'd ended up deploying with them to Afghanistan. He'd learned to speak Pashto with the Army, and as a result he's often employed as an interpreter when out on patrols.

Here in Sangin, his gift for languages brings him closer than most to the locals, which means he has a more in-depth and nuanced understanding of the impact the war is having upon them. I can tell that, at times, it has him really troubled.

As with so many of the Rangers, I've warmed to Cupples. He's a real thinking-man's soldier, and he's just one more guy that my dog and I have to safeguard out here, and bring home alive.

We're ready to move again, and I slip the ball out of my pocket. I show it to Treo and he's transformed. I pretend to throw it down the path ahead of us, and then sneak it back into hiding. Treo's up instantly and raring to go. I fall back to Speedy's position and have a quick word. My dog's not got much left, I tell him. We'll need to get some proper kip somewhere soon.

Speedy adjusts the pace of march accordingly. We're back out front and we've been clearing terrain for an hour or more, when I hear a message go out over the radio.

'Get the dog handler over to Eight Platoon.' I recognise Major Shannon's voice instantly. It's crackling with tension. 'They've found a pressure plate.'

I press my send switch and come back instantly, and before anyone else can reply: 'Not a chance, sir. No way. Not with a pressure plate.'

He tells us to go firm and that he's sending a runner over. A few minutes later this figure emerges from the darkness. He proceeds to tell me that the major hasn't much appreciated my remark. He tells me that it's actually a pressure cooker that they've found, not a pressure plate. Somehow, it's been lost in translation over the radio.

'Well, you lot should get your comms sorted,' I tell him. 'There is one huge difference between a pressure *plate* and a pressure *cooker*.'

I explain to the runner that a pressure plate IED will go off with as little as a touch of a dog's paw. That's why I refused to send Treo. A pressure plate's a job for the bomb-disposal boys, not a K9 team. If it's a pressure *cooker* device, then it's most likely packed with explosives to form a very crude but effective shrapnel bomb. Either way, it's still a job for the EOD bomb-disposal lot, and that's whom the major should have called.

A few hours later we're back at base. No sooner have I got Treo into the kennel than Major Shannon sends for me. Barely have I stepped into his room when he unloads on me.

'Dave, I didn't much like what you said over the radio. How about explaining to me why you reacted like you did when I called for your assistance.'

'Sir, it's like I've said – it's about what we're here for. We're an AES team – Arms Explosives Search. My dog and I find arms and explosives, and just as soon as we suspect there's something there it's a job for the bomb-disposal lot. We're not here to verify the nature of a find, or to disarm it or make it safe.'

'So if my men find something suspect?'

'You get 'em to call out EOD. We do what it says on the tin, sir. We find devices – we don't defuse them.'

Once the major's heard me out, he's fine with it. He's not the type to pull rank or to insist that orders are orders, or that his way is the only way. In any case, I sense he's got my measure by now. He realises that to try to overrule me would only serve to ruin his relationship with one of his most vital assets – his dog team.

The major goes on to mention a problem that he's been having on base. We've had intruders come over the wall at night, and it's only been the alertness of the sentries that's saved the day. In both cases they opened fire but missed, which means the intruders got away. The major asks me if there's maybe a dog-based solution to the threat.

I explain how we had a patrol dog team out here – in the form of John and Toby – but the previous base commander sent them back to Bastion. I suggest getting a replacement team in. A patrol dog goes in fast and silent and brings down an intruder. It grabs and holds by the arm, or any body part that comes to its jaws.

It does so using forty-two razor-sharp teeth, with jaws exerting one hundred and twenty pounds of biting pressure per square inch. To put that in context, it would be like having a car fall off a jack and land on your arm. Having such a dog patrol at night would reduce the need for sentries, and increase the amount of rest they could get – all crucial factors when spending months at war.

The major asks me to get him a team as soon as. I speak to the 104, and I'm told they'll send us young Harry McKnight with his patrol dog Leo. The following morning they get jetted out to us on a Chinook. Harry comes off the ramp with his German shepherd muzzled, and looking like he's raring to go.

We take them down to the kennel, which can house as many as six dogs. Leo gets his own slot allocated to him, and Harry gets a space for his cot next to mine. I've got the place right beneath the air-con unit, because I am king of the castle here. Otherwise, we treat each other pretty much as equals.

Harry's a gobby little Scouser who not so long ago wanted nothing less than to be in the Army. He had serious problems at home and was going well off the rails. But I'd been through much of what he's been through as a kid, and he and I can relate. I got him through his K9 and his Afghan training, and he and his dog are shaping up to be a fine team.

Harry's going to be under the Ranger Company sergeant major's control. Frankie O'Connor will give him his duties and tell him where he most needs him doing security. There's an added advantage to having Harry around. He wants to be a search dog handler, and he's keen to learn as much as he can from the old dogs – Treo and me. Harry goes out and hides some explosive samples around the base, and I set Treo to find them. It's great for training.

I put the word around that Harry and Leo need volunteers. As with any patrol dog, Leo needs to train with live targets. As Treo needs to keep finding explosives in order to keep his nose in, so Leo needs to bite to keep his teeth ready. Each night we'll need a volunteer to put on the 'bite suit' – a thick, impenetrable Michelin Man outfit, which comes complete with a bite sleeve. I sense we can have some real fun here, as taking Leo's bite becomes something of a ritual.

That night, Harry and Leo do their first security patrol. They spend two hours on alert, walking the base perimeter, followed by an hour off to rest the dog. They do so until first light. Harry returns to the kennel so that he and his dog can get some rest with the air con on full blast. During daylight hours it'll be the Kingdom of Leo and Harry in there, for Treo and I will be out on patrol.

That morning I'm called into an Orders Group with Major Shannon. We go through the usual planning for the operation, but at the end there's something missing. Normally, the major lists the 'atts and dets' – those assets attached to the patrol. Invariably, the 'atts and dets' include the dog team – that's us. Today, there's no mention of us being attached to the mission. I wonder why.

I'm waiting for the major to say, 'Oh hold on, Dog, I forgot – you're on it.' But it doesn't come. Instead, he finishes the briefing by asking for any questions.

I raise the obvious: 'Sir, you haven't mentioned me or my dog.'

'That's right. That's because we have good intel that they're placing black gunpowder around the IEDs, so as to throw your dog off the scent.'

'And?' I query.

He gives me a confused look. 'What d'you mean, "and"? We figure there's no point you going out . . .'

'Hold on a minute, sir. That's all the more reason to send us. Treo's an Arms and Explosives Search dog. He's trained to search for gunpowder. We can use this to our advantage.'

'Like how?'

'Just like we used to in Northern Ireland, sir. They used to play a similar trick. All we do is when we find any gunpowder, I'll use Treo to demarcate where they've spread it, and we'll box off the entire area. We'll know that somewhere inside that box they've likely placed an IED.'

The major nods enthusiastically. 'Come forward and show us on the map, will you?'

I go up to the map board and demonstrate how we'll use Treo to box around a suspect area, cordon the entire thing off, then call in the EOD lot to search it and disarm any devices.

'Sir, let's use this to our advantage. Rather than not taking the dog out, let's use this to outfox 'em.'

After the briefing the major takes me to one side. 'I like the way you're thinking here, Dave.'

'You know, sir, it's not rocket science: like I said, it's exactly what Treo and I did when the IRA tried the same trick in Belfast.'

'Understood,' says the major. There's a slight uncomfortable pause. 'But there's one thing, Dave. We're getting very credible intel that the Taliban are directly targeting you and your dog. This gunpowder thing is only part of a bigger picture. I want you to be aware of that, and doubly careful.'

Major Shannon goes on to explain what lies behind his evident concern. Since shortly after our arrival, the control room at Sangin has been intercepting some very interesting communications on the Talinet. Each time we set out on patrol it starts going wild: 'The black dog is coming out! The black dog is coming out!'

Apparently, the Taliban commanders keep banging on about the need to kill or capture the black dog – 'the one that sniffs out the bombs'. They've been saying this for an age now, just no one felt it would do much for our peace of mind if they told us.

'Sir, if we weren't getting under their skin and up their noses, we wouldn't be doing our job properly,' I tell the major. 'The more they target us, the more a thumbs up it is that we're doing right to beat their bastard bomb teams.'

'I know.' The OC places a reassuring hand on my shoulder. 'But just take extra care, OK? We need you and Treo with us, on every patrol. Having you there makes all the difference to the lads.'

Mostly, I'm pleased that Treo and I have got to the enemy in this way. It confirms that we're the threat, and that we're defeating their bombing teams.

In truth, the intel changes nothing.

Knowing that they're out to get my dog doesn't change the level of danger we've been facing on each and every one of our patrols.

CHAPTER FIFTEEN

Treo and I set out on the search, knowing that we're target number one for the Taliban. As I give him a flash of his chewed-up green tennis ball, I can't help but flinch at the thought of the enemy getting my dog.

Treo sees me flinch. Even as I've tried to say the magic words – 'seek-on' – with as firm and steady a voice as possible, he's seen my hand twitch. It's betrayed my nervousness, and how I'm feeling inside. I'm all torn up with fear for my dog, and if the truth be told I don't particularly want myself getting blown up either.

Normally, when shown his ball and given the command, Treo is off like a flash. But not today. He pauses for a second, then plonks his butt down right beside me, his gaze fixed on mine. His hazel eyes are speckled with golden sunlight, but right now they're a mass of worry and concern: *There's something you haven't told me, isn't there? Come on, out with it . . .*

I crouch down beside him. I grab his shaggy neck in my hands and gaze into his eyes. 'You're right, lad,' I whisper. 'We've had it confirmed by the intercepts. We're their number one target, confirmed, lad. They're calling you "the black dog", and they're out to get you and me both, big time.'

I hold his gaze for a few seconds, as I read what he's thinking. I know I've got the whole of the patrol at our backs, and they're most likely having a good old stare. But they must have got pretty accustomed to the way that Treo and I carry on by now, or if not, there's no teaching them.

Treo's eyes speak volumes: *We pretty much knew that, Dad. You've got me with you, by your side, and I'm unbeatable. Don't worry – no one ever outdoes this nose . . .*

Sure enough, my dog proves what he's saying on this very patrol. We've gone barely five hundred metres when he shows an unmistakable change in behaviour. This one is so immediate and so obvious I know it can't be a standard IED or even an arms cache. He gets this laser-eyed look, his gaze glued to one spot in the road up ahead, and without even having to check step he's homed in on the source of the scent.

He's about to plonk his butt down when he sniffs to his left and his right, and he starts getting confused. Whatever it is he's found here, it seems to stretch in a linear fashion to either side. I'm pretty certain what it must be. I call him back, go forwards myself, crouch down and check in the dust. Sure enough, there are tiny grains of black gunpowder scattered in a line across our path.

I get Treo to trace it, and we box off the area. Somewhere inside that box I figure there's an IED. The bomb-disposal boys get called in, and they unearth a hidden bomb at the centre of that box. The Taliban's gunpowder trick has actually helped my dog to find it. At the end of that mission it's Black Dog 1–Taliban 0.

As we come in through the gates, one of the guards doing

sangar duty collars us. 'Dave, did you hear, your dog guy, Harry, he got a bite last night.'

I figure Harry and Leo must have caught an intruder, in which case the dog teams are coming up trumps on all sides. I wander down to the kennel area to congratulate Harry. But when I see him he doesn't look particularly pleased with himself. I can tell that he wants to talk.

'I'll be there in a moment, Harry. I'll just get Treo into his kennel.'

The first thing Harry asks me is if I want a brew. Being a gobby little Scouser, he doesn't normally bother to make the coffee. This has to mean that somehow he's in the shit. It turns out that Harry was doing some loose obedience exercises – training with his dog off-leash – and one of the Afghan bottle washers from the kitchens went running past. In a flash, Leo had attached himself very forcefully to that Afghan bloke's arm.

'Don't worry about it too much,' I try to reassure him. 'You were doing extra obedience work with your dog in your free time, and that's good. You were caring for your dog and keeping up his obedience. It's just that Afghans have zero awareness of how to behave around working dogs, that's all.'

I ask Harry if the Ranger Company sergeant major knows.

'Everyone on base seems to know,' Harry replies, morosely. 'They all think it's bloody hilarious, 'n' all.'

I can't help but laugh.

I go to see Frankie, and of course he sees the funny side of it too. But we agree we can't have Harry doing any more off-leash training. Instead, we'll up the intensity of the evening bite exercises, in the hope that will satisfy Leo's needs.

I tell Frankie that whenever we've asked for volunteers to get bitten, it's always 'Private Snodgrass' who's got pushed forwards. I figure the officers should get bitten just as much as the ranks. Frankie loves the idea. He reckons it'll be great for the lads' morale seeing the officers getting chomped. He tells me to clear it with Major Shannon, and we'll start that very evening.

I find the major and explain my thinking. 'Sir, wouldn't it be better to see the platoon commanders getting bitten? Wouldn't the men appreciate that more?'

The major gives an evil smile. 'Sure, that's a very fine idea. I'll send around a directive asking for volunteers.'

'Might I suggest, sir, we started with your good self?'

The major's smile disappears. 'All in good time,' he grates, 'all in good time.'

At eight o'clock that evening a large crowd of Rangers has gathered by the kennel. I kick things off by getting them all properly wound up. I tell them the dog will go for anything that moves, which has them standing still like statues. It's nice to see that Lieutenant Wilcock – Treo's old adversary – has been volunteered to take tonight's bite.

Truth be told, over recent days the lieutenant has proven himself to be as fine a soldier as you could wish for, and a real convert to my dog. He and I have become good mates as well. Still, for old times' sake it'll be nice to see him getting bitten.

The lads have just about got used to having Treo, the dog with attitude, around. Now they've got Leo the war dog with jaws to match. This is going to be a great bit of theatre: *Let's see which officer's getting mauled today.*

I help Lieutenant Wilcock on with the bite sleeve, which is

made of thick, impenetrable jute. It's a natural vegetable fibre, which can be spun into strong, coarse threads; doormats are commonly made of it. The sleeve is designed to take a dog's bite whilst preventing the wearer from coming to any harm.

Lieutenant Wilcock's got to be the highest-ranking person that Leo will ever have bitten, so this had better go entirely to plan. I send him off a good few paces, whilst Harry readies Leo. We call the guy we send the dog after the 'intruder'. The dog has to bite and hold and bring the intruder to a halt – to 'apprehend' him, and ideally you want the dog to go for the arm wearing the bite sleeve.

I coach the lieutenant on how to present the bite sleeve to Leo. Harry's got his dog held firmly by the collar, and he shows him the 'intruder'. Leo knows what's coming and he's looking at Wilcock with an expression like he can't wait to get him.

Harry gives the command 'Get him!' And Leo's gone, like a bullet from a gun.

He streaks across the ground, launches himself into the air and his jaws clamp shut on the lieutenant's arm. Thank God he's bitten the bite sleeve, and not ripped Lieutenant Wilcock's head off. He knocks him a good few feet backwards, and all the while the Rangers are cheering wildly. Leo keeps a good chomp on the bite sleeve, until Harry calls for him to let go.

That done, a couple of the young Rangers volunteer to take a bite. Just as I thought it would be, this is great therapy for guys who've been at war for weeks on end.

A couple of days later we're briefed on a second three-day mission that we'll be joining. We're heading for a notorious patch of Taliban territory, which the lads have nicknamed 'Wombat Wood'. We are to clear the area, establish a presence and try to capture some senior Taliban figures. There's one huge difference to all of our previous patrols. This time the major briefs us on what exactly he's got in store for us – for Treo and me.

With the poppy harvest more or less done, the enemy is gearing up for battle big time. Until now we've found a good deal of bombs, and we've not lost a single soul. Treo and I are right in the flow of things, and we're forging a great bond with the Ranger Company lads. We're keeping them safe, and the Taliban don't like it.

Major Shannon mentions using some 'bait' to lure out the enemy. Often I'm half switched off during briefings, my mind scanning the chat for the word 'dog'. This grabs my attention by the throat, and largely because the bait Major Shannon intends to use is myself and my dog.

He wants us out on a long and high-visibility patrol, one designed to really get the Talinet buzzing. Then he'll find out their location, and send in a snatch patrol to lift the bad guys.

When he's finished outlining his plan I let out a half chuckle: 'Tell you what, sir, how about I carry Treo on my shoulders and you can pin a target on my back 'n' all?'

At first light Treo and I set out with the Ranger lads, acting as the bait in Major Shannon's trap. We're going in to take a known Taliban stronghold and we're to prove we can hold it for several days. We've got a quad bike with us to carry all the extra supplies. Treo and I are going to sit there, waiting for the Taliban to hit us. Nothing like this has been tried before.

I show my dog a flash of the ball, and we take the lead on an open dirt path winding through the bush. I'm scouring the way ahead for even the slightest sign of a disturbance. In the back of my mind I know how hard they're trying to kill us now, so I'm doubly nervous and hyper-aware.

The Taliban have a technique wherein they dig in an IED, smooth the mud and sand over, and pour water onto the disturbed ground. The fierce sun bakes it hard as concrete, so it ends up looking like the rest of the path. I'm scanning for raised areas roughly the size of an IED, or any other tell-tale signs of disturbance.

As Treo and I push onwards I can't shake off this creepy feeling like I *have* got a target on my back, and that Treo's got one too. I do a quick check, just to make sure his Shamrock is securely attached to his harness. I'm relieved to see that it is. But still I can't shake off this conviction that this time, they're going to get us.

We're forced to navigate our way through several irrigation ditches, over each of which we have to build a makeshift bridge to get the quad across. It's painstaking and exhausting work. Although we set out at first light, it's the height of the day and furnace-hot by the time we're visual with the target compound.

We take cover fifty metres back, in a position from where we have eyes on the target. It's a straggle of dun-coloured, dome-roofed buildings, surrounded by a high mud wall. The surface of that wall is spattered with bullet and shrapnel holes, testifying to the ferocity of the fighting that's gone on here.

Treo and I will go in first, using a scaling ladder to get across the wall, and with a couple of security Rangers on our shoulder.

The scaling ladder is a dozen rungs high and it's made of a tough but light aluminium. I glance down at Treo, where he's slumped on the ground in the shade of a wall. He stares at the ladder for a second, sniffs at it, then gives me a look, like he knows exactly what's coming.

Whoa . . . Just hold on a minute. If you think you're getting me on that . . . I see him glance down at his feet, then back at me: *These paws can do a lot, but they're just not made for ladders . . .*

I crouch down so I'm eye-level with him. I talk him through what we're about to do; that we're going to go up and over that wall. We can't go through the main door, because that's the route the bad guys will expect us to take. This way, we go in with maximum surprise. Then we've got to clear the place of threats, and for that I need him right there with me on the search.

On the patrol commander's word we scuttle forwards. I'm half bent-double so as to present less of a target to the enemy, and with me are the two Rangers carrying the ladder. We reach the cover of the base of the wall without a shot being fired, and the Rangers raise the ladder to just past vertical. In spite of its height, it still barely reaches the apex of the wall.

I squat down, eye Treo and present my shoulders to him. I whisper: 'Bup! Bup! Bup!'

Get up lad, only this time I mean onto my shoulders.

Back at the 104's base, in Leicestershire, we have a doggy obstacle course. It includes a tunnel, a catwalk, hurdles, a window frame and a six-foot wall. But there's a big difference between a six-foot wooden wall and a scaling ladder twelve feet high – and especially when all around us there's an enemy hell-bent on killing or capturing my dog.

Treo steps forwards and nuzzles at me, nervously. I murmur some reassuring words, then take his front and rear legs and raise him into a fireman's lift. I can feel the weight of him up there, and how any residual fat my dog may have had has been honed into toughened muscle and sinew. Muscle weighs more than fat, and as I turn to face the wall he's the heaviest that I've ever felt him.

I put one foot on the lowest rung, and I can feel my dog's heart pounding in my ears. He doesn't like this at all. I flick my eyes left, and there's Treo's head on my shoulder, his eyes wide with what almost looks like fright. I've rarely seen Treo show real fear. He's not the biggest of dogs, but he's solid and hard as nails.

I whisper a few words of reassurance, raise my head and take the first step. I've got one hand gripping Treo's paws, my stubby SA80 in the other, a heavy dog on my shoulders, plus a pack weighing a good fifty pounds on my back. I feel like I'm carrying a mountain. But worst is that I can't get a proper grip on the ladder with my hands holding my weapon.

Either I get rid of it, which means I'll be going over the top unarmed, or I'm going to lose my grip and Treo and I will fall. I take a step backwards and turn to face the Ranger on my shoulder.

'Here, take this.' I pass over my weapon. 'I've got the dog. I'll have it back when we're on the far side . . .'

I'm half tempted to go up with a grenade or a knife gripped in my teeth, so at least I've got something to fight with and defend my dog. But it's a bit too dagger-between-the-teeth Rambo-esque for my liking. Still, with the enemy out to get us, I figure this has to be their golden chance to blow our heads clean away.

The Stubby gone, I go up the ladder like a rat up a drainpipe. We're horribly exposed, and I'm not armed, so we're doubly vulnerable. By the time I reach the apex of the wall I'm sweating buckets and gasping for breath. Somehow, I manage to swing myself and Treo off the ladder and onto the wall, which means we're halfway done getting into the compound.

For several seconds I'm forced to sit there, with Treo perched on my shoulders, as the Ranger lads scale the ladder then haul it up after them, so they can drop it down the far side. I feel this river of steaming sweat cascading down my back. I can just imagine a Taliban sniper's cross-hairs nailing my head, or worse still that of my dog. If they're going to get us, now's the perfect chance. I'm tensing myself for gunshots, and practically shitting myself with fear.

With the ladder finally up and over we're off the wall like greased weasels, and never have I felt so relieved to make it into the heart of an enemy stronghold. I drop Treo off my shoulders, reclaim my Stubby, and we take cover as best we can. Behind us, Rangers come pouring over the wall. As they do, I'm glancing all around, searching for signs of movement or the enemy.

But as far as I can tell the place appears to be utterly deserted. The Taliban must have got word that we were coming, and made themselves scarce. The interior of the compound is pockmarked with craters, so there's clearly been heavy fighting here. With the Rangers over the wall, it's time to start the search. I pause for an instant, giving Treo the praise that he needs.

'Go on, good lad,' I tell him, in my whispered high-pitched

praise voice. 'Fantastic, get on then.'

I rise to my feet and indicate where I want Treo to search, my raised arm sweeping left, to show him I want him to start with those buildings. I flash him a glimpse of his ball, go as if to throw it, then slip it back into the pocket off my combats. And he's off, stubby tail wagging furiously, nostrils flaring and nose going like a suction pump as he hoovers up the scent.

It takes a good twenty minutes to search the place, with Treo going in and out of every doorway and me dogging his every footstep. Once we've declared the place clear we take possession of the best room, one that we recced as we were searching the place. There's a pile of wood in one corner, and I figure we can have a fire to cheer us in the evening, and warm us through the night.

Treo and I may be the bait in a trap, but there's no point not making ourselves comfortable.

CHAPTER SIXTEEN

We're two days into the mission, and we've spent our time getting out on a series of high-visibility patrols. The point we're making to the enemy is, 'Look, we've taken your stronghold, and the black dog is out clearing the area. How d'you like that, Talitubbies?' As provocations go, it's a fine one. As for making ourselves a target, we couldn't be more visible if we tried.

We're out early clearing a path that winds through a patch of scrubby woodland, when to the west of us there's an almighty boom. It sounds like the signature blast of an IED, and a big one. I can hear the noise of the explosion echoing off the high ground, even as the worry flashes across my mind: *Have Treo and I missed something? Have they got one of the lads?*

We go pounding back to the compound, and I can't help wondering if some of the Rangers were out on one of the paths to the west of us – ones that Treo and I supposedly cleared – and that they've stumbled onto an IED. If they have, and my dog and I have missed it, I'll never forgive myself for as long as I live.

Radio reports are coming in fast and furious. It turns out that a pair of Viking armoured vehicles have been ambushed on the 611. In the ensuing gun battle they were forced into a gully, where they were hit by an IED. One of the Vikings has been abandoned. The other's made it back to base, but there's one guy dead and another seriously injured.

I feel bloody awful that we've lost at least the one bloke, but in reality there's absolutely nothing Treo and I could have done about it. We're set a good way back from the 611, and that's not the area where we've been searching. I feel this odd mixture of relief that it's not my dog and me that have failed here, and a deep sadness that we've lost a life.

The abandoned Viking is within range of our snipers, and they proceed to put down fire to try to stop the Taliban looting the vehicle. It's full of top-secret and sensitive kit. But no matter how many rounds they rattle into the Viking's armoured flanks, the Taliban keep creeping closer and closer.

As we've got eyes on the ambush site, our JTAC – the Joint Terminal Attack Controller, the guy on our patrol who calls in the air strikes – guides in a bombing mission to hit the wounded vehicle. Treo and I listen in on the frenzied radio chatter, as a French Mirage screams in to lay waste to the target.

The pilot announces: 'Standby, round in!'

A 500-pound bomb is in the air. There are a few seconds' delay as we tense for the blast, but all we hear is a dull thud. The bomb hasn't exploded. It's a dud. The Mirage comes around in a screaming turn as the pilot prepares to drop a second 500-pounder. He does just that, but again all we hear is a dull thud. It's a second dud.

An American A10 'Warthog' ground attack aircraft is also in the battle space. He's been listening in on the air chatter, and he offers to do a strafing run with his seven-barrel 30 mm Gatling gun. The cannon shells will saturate the area with leaden death, which should set off the two 500-pounders in one almighty great explosion.

The squat, piggy-looking Tankbuster aircraft comes thundering in over our heads, its twin jet engines howling like giant, overworked hairdryers. It's not been nicknamed the Warthog for nothing. It's neither graceful nor pretty, but as a ground attack aircraft it has no equal.

The A10 seems almost to stall in mid-air as the Gatling gun opens up. The thick, stubby gun barrel is clearly visible spitting out a tongue of fire. There's a long, thunderous *brrrrrrrrrrrrrrrrrrr*, as the roar of the seven-barrel cannon echoes around the valley. For every second the pilot keeps his finger on the trigger, sixty-five 30 mm cannon rounds tear into the target.

Shredded branches and jagged chunks of metal are thrown into the air all around the spot where the Viking lies. By the time the pilot has bottomed out of his dive, he's raked the entire area from end to end. The aircraft's cannon has chewed the vehicle into a twisted hulk, and it's more than scared the Taliban looters away. But it's not done a thing to set off those two 500-pound bombs.

The trouble is this. We know the Taliban dig out unexploded bombs and use the contents to manufacture IEDs. Come hell or high water, we've got to take out those 500-pounders. An order comes through on the radio that Treo and I are to make our way to the ambush sight and 'locate' the dud munitions.

I send a message back, which is about as blunt as I can make it: 'Dog handler here. I'd rather eat my own eyeballs than get my dog to dig out a couple of unexploded 500-pound bombs in the midst of a Taliban ambush. If you're going to deny the bombs, deny them: don't deny me and my dog.'

I offer for Treo and me to clear a path into the attack site, so that an EOD team can go in. But I'm not sending Treo into the heart of darkness, especially now we know it's my dog that the enemy most want to kill. I can accept making us the bait: I draw the line at making us a pointless sacrifice.

The order for us to sniff out those two unexploded 500-pound bombs has come right from the top, so it's not Major Shannon who's had the dumbest of dumb ideas. But I don't care if it's Her Majesty herself who's given the order: no one, but no one, tells my dog what to do, or sends him to his death.

Finally, a Harrier ground-attack aircraft comes screaming in and blows whatever remains of the Viking, plus those two 500-pounders, sky high, in the most almighty of blasts. It's like a mini-atom bomb going off, and it's bravo to the Royal Air Force yet again. That's one thousand pounds of high explosives the Taliban won't be recycling into their murderous IEDs.

Major Shannon gives us the call that it's mission accomplished for us lot too. We're to abandon the compound that we've been holding and make our way back to base. We decide to vary our route, to try to avoid any Taliban lying in wait for us, or any IEDs they may have planted in our path.

We're going to pass via a village where we've been searching for a High Value Target (HVT). We've actually seen the guy we're after, an incredibly tall Taliban commander. We were just a fraction too slow getting after him, which meant he got away. The journey back is a chance to have a second crack at him.

I show Treo the guy's photo. He's not a tracker dog as such, but I don't see why he shouldn't be in on the hunt.

'That's the geezer we're after, lad. Ugly-looking brute, isn't he? If you see him, give us a good bark and go grab him by the trouser leg, will you?'

Treo gives me a look: *What're you on about? You know the Taliban don't wear trousers.*

We set off, my dog and me bang out front doing the walk. It would make every sense for the Taliban to have sown all routes back to base with IEDs. They know we have to move on foot, and there are only a limited number of pathways we can follow. I can sense the tension simmering, as every man on the patrol feels the threat.

My dog and I pause before an irrigation ditch so we can take a view on the best route across. One of the Rangers comes over to offer Treo a treat. That done, he turns to have words with me, his nervousness clearly showing.

'So, Dave, is the dog, like, OK today?' he asks. 'Is the dog one hundred per cent?'

'How about this?' I tell him. 'Take a spare magazine and go hide it over there, but make sure Treo doesn't see you do it.'

The Ranger does as I've asked of him. I give Treo a quick flash of his ball, point him in the general direction and give him the 'seek' command. He wanders over, pushes his nose into the bush, and comes out with his jaws gripping the SA80 magazine. He returns to my side and I give him the usual praise.

I turn to the Rangers who've been watching the whole thing. 'Yep, I'd say the dog's on it today.'

We push onwards, the lads behind us feeling this deep sense of reassurance that Treo's sparking. We hit the village where we know our HVT is based. I recognise the narrow track as being where we first spotted the tall Taliban geezer that we're after. Treo is approaching pretty much the spot where we last saw him, when his head snaps right and he's staring through an open doorway.

I try calling him back, but an instant later he's dived into the compound and he's gone. I start sprinting down the path and I'm totally freaking out. I've lost sight of my dog, the one that the Taliban are determined to capture or to kill.

I'm yelling: 'TREO! GET BACK HERE NOW! NOW!'

I've got the Ranger lads pounding on my heels. I've got images in my head of that tall bastard and his henchmen stuffing Treo into a black sack and disappearing out the back entrance to the compound. I'm going wild.

I'm about to hit the doorway when there's a crazed burst of squawking from inside the building. All of a sudden there are chickens flying everywhere, and the air is thick with feathers. A cheeky black head pops around the doorframe. It's Treo.

Check this out, Dad! He shows me what he's got in his jaws. It's the severed head of a chicken.

Behind me I can hear the Ranger lads roaring with laughter. Treo's safe and sound, and we're only one Afghan chicken down. I have to agree with them – it is bloody hysterical. I'm cracking up myself now, but it's more with the relief of knowing that they didn't get my dog.

Treo's done everything I've ever asked of him out here, and much, much more. Like the rest of us, at times he needs to vent his anger and his frustration. I go for a run, or I shout and swear on the phone at my loved ones. Treo gets to munch on an Afghan chicken.

It's a bit unfair on the chook, but sometimes life's like that. And the aggravation and angst that he's just got out of his system – well, in my book that more than makes up for one dead chicken. Sometimes, I have to allow him just to be a dog.

He plonks himself down on his stump of a tail and gazes up at me. I know that look so well: it's half pride, half a rebellious so-what-you-going-to-do-about-it?

I say: 'So what've you got there, lad?'

He wags his stump excitedly: *What d'you think it is – it's a chicken head.* I tell him to drop it. *Not a chance*, he's telling me with those eyes of his that sparkle with mischief. *Not a chance – not this dog.*

I reach down and remove the head from his jaws. He looks up at me: *Spoilsport*. I tell him to heel and give him the 'seek on' command, but he can't stop glancing in the direction of the chicken shed. The chooks are still going crazy in there, and that's the only place he wants to be.

I give him a rest and a drink to wash the taste of the chicken blood out of his mouth, and we push on. I've clipped him on the leash now, just in case he's got any more chicken mayhem in mind. But I don't ever want to stop Treo from being a dog.

I need him to be a free-spirited, curious doggy dog. And hell, yes, at times I need him to be wilful and badly behaved. I need him to be free and wild, and out there eagerly chasing down the bombs. And for Treo to keep doing that, it's got to be *fun*.

In the past there have been those who've accused me of being a lazy handler, because I'm not always barking orders at my dog. But that's not the way you get the best out of your dog. Treo knows me and I know him instinctively, so I don't need to harangue and harass him. You win a dog's loyalty and camaraderie not through yelling or hitting him: you win it through love.

If I was always out front yelling orders, how long would it be before the Taliban heard me, and got either me or Treo or the both of us? We know they want to do violence to us or capture us. They're saying so every day on the Talinet. Treo's wild, free doggy ways mean a Sangin chicken's met its maker. Rather that than have the two of us get kidnapped or blown to pieces.

We push on towards Sangin and there's no sign of the HVT we're looking for. But en route Treo pauses before a patch of dense bush. His nose is glued to the ground, and I figure he may be onto something. I see his paws going pad, pad, pad, right up to the base of a bush. He's got to be tracking the scent cone to its source, and I'm on the verge of yanking him back from whatever killer device it is that he's found here.

He inches forward and sticks his head inside the nearest clump of leaves. The bush is thick and impenetrable and it's impossible for me to see through it. If there is an IED hidden in there I can't see a thing, and my stomach's knotted tight with fear. I have rarely seen my dog like this before: his stumpy tail's gone rigid and his head's inside that bush snuffling and snorting real hard.

I turn to the Rangers on my shoulder: 'Treo's onto something! Get ready!'

They've seen how my dog's behaving, and they know enough by now to realise what he's about. I can see the fear written large in their eyes. I turn back to Treo and still he's got his head stuffed in that bush. All of a sudden his stumpy tail starts wagging furiously. I've never seen anything like it. Why on earth is he doing all this tail-wagging, if he's just found a bomb?

'What is it, my lad?' I whisper. 'What're you onto there?'

I'm just about to step forward and investigate when I see his back end reversing out of the bush. He emerges, and turns his head towards me, a delighted grin on his doggy features. There's something gripped in his jaws. I peer at it, anxiously.

What Treo's found here is a little rubber duck.

It's yellow, and it's the kind you used to play with in the bath as a kid. Treo carries it proudly in his mouth all the way back to the base. I figure it's his surrogate chicken head. First thing he does once we're in through the gates is toss the duck around with Jihad.

'Where's your ducky, lad?' I keep asking him. 'Where's your ducky?'

He grabs it off Jihad and trots around triumphantly. The Rangers are in stitches at the dogs' antics, and what could be better for those young lads' morale than watching the Treo and Jihad rubber-duck show?

We head down to the kennel, Treo with his rubber duck gripped tightly in his jaws. I'm trying not to make too much noise, for I'm expecting to find Harry and Leo still asleep. I'm surprised when I find no sign of man or dog, and even their kit seems to be gone.

Harry's left me a hurriedly scribbled note. Apparently, he's got a young wife back in the UK who was heavily pregnant when we deployed to Afghanistan. She's just given birth, and Harry's been flown out of Sangin so he can be with the mother and baby. So now it's just the two of us, Treo and me, holding the line once more.

Shortly after Harry leaves Treo and I get a surprise visit. Captain Martin 'Tommo' Thompson, my boss from the 104, flies out from Camp Bastion. He's come here to see how we're bearing up, and to get himself some Sangin-time. Barely have I grabbed his bags off the helicopter when Ronnie asks me if Treo and I are ready. I tell the OC I'll see him later. My dog and I have got some searching to do.

I'm back two hours later, after a pretty standard patrol. Just as I'm getting Treo sorted we're asked to join a more unusual kind of mission. There's a small British Army team stationed at Sangin whose role it is to train the Afghan National Army. I wouldn't want their job for all the tea in China, but I guess someone has to do it.

They've just secured credible intel about the location of a Taliban bomb-making factory. It's situated a few kilometres south of Sangin on the 611. They're heading down there in a vehicle patrol, before moving in on the IED-factory on foot. They want me and my dog on the mission, so we can sniff out the bombs.

I tell them to give me twenty minutes to sort and rest my dog, and we'll be with them. I can see my boss staring at me with this odd expression. I can tell what he's thinking: *Dave, you just got in off a patrol.* A part of me feels like telling him to get with the programme: this is what life is like down here in Sangin.

But I say nothing, ready my dog, and head over to join the patrol.

CHAPTER SEVENTEEN

I sit in the wagon as we head south. I've grown to hate doing road moves by vehicle. We've got no one out front checking the route for IEDs. It's a twenty-minute drive, and I'm hugely relieved when it's over. We regroup at an isolated ANA base, where there are about a hundred Afghan soldiers readying themselves for the mission.

Just as soon as they set eyes on Treo, the ANA stop gaggling about like a bunch of teenage groupies. We jump down from the rear of the Land Rover, and they know that they've got 'the black dog' with them for this one. To the Afghans, this signifies that things are getting serious.

They're supposedly on the same side as us, but they really don't like my dog. Not a man amongst them is willing to come anywhere near him. Yet, like Treo or not, his reputation goes before him, and every one of them knows just exactly what he's here for.

Via the interpreter, the mission commander outlines the coming tasking. We form up and prepare to move out on foot. There are a dozen British soldiers and ten times that number of Afghans, so it's a big old force. But I feel little safety in numbers. From what I've seen the ANA aren't a great deal more effective than the Afghan National Police – the lot who blew themselves up with their own grenade.

The British commander lets his Afghan counterpart take the lead. The ANA aren't exactly renowned for their tactical abilities, and it's no surprise when he leads us up over a hill and gets us marching along the ridgeline. Below us are a series of compounds like a giant rabbit warren. We're sky-lined on the ridge, and if there are enemy down there they can hit us from any number of angles.

Being up here is like asking to get annihilated, and I can't wait to get off the high ground. Instead, the ANA commander chooses a spot halfway along the ridgeline for us to go firm. I get myself and Treo into what little cover I can find. We're static for twenty minutes, and God only knows what they're pissing around at here. As the minutes drag by, my soldier's sixth sense is screaming at me that we're about to get hit.

I turn to one of the Brits who's lying beside me. 'Does it feel to you like we're being set up here?'

No sooner are the words out of my mouth than the first rounds come howling in. In an instant, the ridgeline has been transformed into a terrifying killing ground, and the terrain all around us is alive with burning-hot lead. Not only are we getting hammered from the direction of the compounds, but bullets are ricocheting and whining off the rocks in all directions.

I bring my Stumpy to bear, and I start slamming rounds back at them. I'm taking steady, aimed shots at enemy muzzle flashes, and the hot shell cases go tumbling down onto my dog. He's getting used to this by now and just shrugs them off with a quick flick of his hind leg.

The ANA lot are unleashing entire magazines at the enemy, but making little attempt to aim. They get top marks for making a whole lot of noise, but that's about as much use as an ashtray on a motorcycle. In any case, no amount of return fire is going to cut it here. There's bugger all cover, and we need to get ourselves gone.

'MOVE! MOVE! MOVE!' the British commander starts yelling. 'MOOOOOOVE!'

He's on his feet charging down the ridge, and screaming for his blokes to follow. Treo and I need no second urging. For a good five minutes we're running and fighting our way out of there, and it's a miracle that no one gets hit.

We reach a patch of cover and go firm. The British commander is seething. He proceeds to give the ANA lot the biggest bollocking they've ever had, though I figure the interpreter is having problems translating some of the more colourful phrases.

Once it's calmed down a little, we move off with our guys leading and keeping to good cover. In that fashion we arrive at the target – the suspect IED factory. We reach the outskirts of the place and go firm. With all the noise from that almighty great firefight up on the ridge, I doubt if there are any enemy remaining here right now. But even if they have managed to scarper, there's likely to be the bulk of their bomb-making kit left behind.

The British commander turns to me. 'So, how d'you want to do this?'

'Sir, I'll need to go in first with my dog. Have your men and the ANA lot hold back until we've declared a room clear, and then they can move in after us. Plus I'll need a couple of your guys – *not* the ANA – on our shoulder, standing security.'

He gives me a grim smile – *not the ANA indeed* – and tells me that he's good with the plan. He asks his interpreter to explain to the Afghans exactly what I've just said, paying special attention to the need to keep back until the dog team declares an area clear. That done, Treo and I are on our feet moving down a rocky slope towards the building.

As we creep towards the high walls, I try to figure out the best – and therefore the least expected – route in. But before I can make any decision, a group of ANA soldiers barges past us, and they're kicking in the front door. Nice one. The entire element of surprise has been blown, so I move forward with my dog and we go through the front door.

Luckily, the place seems to be deserted, which is why the Afghan soldiers' entry hasn't been met with a hail of gunfire. Treo and I move left, heading for the nearest room. I reach out for the door handle, whilst at the same time getting Treo to sniff all around the frame, just as we did when clearing the Red Hotel.

I'm just about to twist the handle, when I sense a figure at my side. It's one of the ANA lot. I'm about to order him back, when, with the dumbest of smiles on his face, he boots the door open right in front of us. He barges past my dog, and Treo gives him a disgusted look: *Some humans are just so dumb . . .*

As for me, I'm thinking: *You touch my dog again and you've going to have it – I'll twat you.*

The search turns into a farce. All around us ANA blokes charge into rooms, in some kind of messed-up race to find the 'bomb factory'. The silly sods want to somehow prove that they don't need the dog. They resent Treo to such a degree they want to prove they're better at sniffing out the bombs.

I seek out the British Commander and make my feelings plain to him. Either he gets the ANA out of the place, or Treo and I are calling off the search. He manages to get the Afghans to back off, and they hang around the walls, glaring at my dog and me resentfully.

Treo and I move methodically through the place, whilst doing our best to ignore the Afghan soldiers' sulky looks.

We reach the shadowed recesses of the compound, where the rear doorway exits onto a narrow alleyway. It's so dark that I have to use the torch on my Stubby to search. We enter one of the last remaining rooms. Something strikes me as being odd. At first I can't put my finger on what it is. Then I glance at where Treo's padded across the floor, and I realise that each of his steps has left a distinct paw-print.

Normally, the mud floors of these Afghan compounds are hard-beaten and solid, almost like concrete. By contrast, this one's covered in a thick film of dust. I shine my flashlight all around the room. To the right of the doorway I spot something, glinting in my torch beam. There's an electrical flex sticking out of the floor, and it's the copper wire inside that's caught the light.

An alarm triggers inside my head. Recently, the EOD boys briefed me on a new type of trigger device that the Taliban have started using. They've developed this means of setting wire nails or flex into the floor, to form a trip-switch. As soon as you brush a foot or a paw against it, that moves the nail or wire, so triggering the device. I fear that's exactly what we've got here.

In an instant I'm going apeshit. I'm roaring for Treo to get back by my side. But if he returns to me direct, he may brush past the trigger, and that means my dog and I are going to get obliterated. As he trots towards me, I start yelling and using arm gestures to keep him to the opposite side of the doorway.

'Get over that way! Get over that way! Don't come back to me straight, lad, or you'll tilt it!'

No sooner is he by my side and I've grabbed him by the collar, than several ANA blokes come charging through the doorway. They must have heard me yelling, and they've just not been able to resist. Like a bunch of kids with a candy jar they've just got to plunge their hands in, although they've been warned they've got to wait.

I grab Treo, lift him up and throw the two of us back out the doorway, and we scrabble for some cover. I have visions in my head of when the ANA lot blew themselves up with their own RPG, back at our base. There's going to be blood and guts and blown-up limbs plastered all over the walls, but all I really care about is that my dog and I survive.

For a second I'm clawing at the ground as I try to regain my feet, and then Treo and I are charging away from that booby-trapped room as fast as we can go. We make a beeline for the British Commander, and as I'm running towards him I start yelling.

'Tilt-switch IED! In that room full of ANA!'

I see the interpreter cry out a warning in the local language. All of a sudden the same bunch of ANA soldiers who piled into that room come tearing back out again. Only this time, rather than eager kids in a toyshop they look like they've just seen a ghost. The lot of them have gone as white as a sheet.

I can't for the life of me explain how none of them triggered that IED. Things settle down a little now. We get the area cordoned off and call in the bomb-disposal boys. Once they're with us, I sketch out as best I can what we've got here. They suit-up and move in.

Whilst they're doing their stuff, I have a good chat with my dog. There's one thing that's got me stumped: if it is a tilt-switch IED, why didn't Treo manage to sniff it out?

For a second I wonder if he's losing his edge. But as I gaze into those eyes, and see his steady, confident expression, I know that he's as good as ever. Still, I can't figure out how the Taliban managed to plant a tilt-switch IED that Treo wasn't able to sniff out. It's a mystery.

The answer turns out to be as simple as it's surprising to me. After twenty minutes or so the EOD guys return. What they've found is nothing more than an old electrical wire sticking out of the floor. They figure the owners of the compound intended to rig up some light fittings at some stage but they never actlly got around to it – hence the bare wire poking out of the floor.

For a while there I actually doubted my dog's nose. But in fact, it's me – Dave Heyhoe – who's messed up. Treo found nothing because there were no explosives to be found. So maybe it's me who's losing it? Maybe I'm starting to lose my nerve, not to mention my objectivity? Maybe the pressure and the strain is starting to crack me up?

I have a word with the EOD bloke, together with the British commander: 'Listen, it's me who's messed up here and me only. I saw the wire and made the call, not Treo. So don't ever lose faith in my dog. I've got broad shoulders and I can take it. It's me who's to blame.'

'Listen, Dave, don't worry,' the patrol commander tells me. 'You went off the information you had to hand. This place was believed to be a bomb factory. It was a good call.'

The EOD guy gives an easy-natured shrug. 'It's not an issue, Dave. It's just the way it goes. We'll always come out to you if you need us, and we don't give a shit it's a false alarm. Better that, than have you guys get yourselves blown up.'

Two hours later the mission's done, and Treo and I are delivered back to our Sangin base. I sort my dog's food and water and get him settled into his kennel. Finally I can try and get a bite to eat myself. I'm six foot two and I'm down to thirteen stone, and still the weight's dropping off me. Trouble is, things like the false call I just made don't tend to do wonders for your appetite.

I decide to settle for a brew and a ciggie instead. My boss, Captain Thompson, is still with us, and he asks me if I'd like a coffee. I tell him that I would. He hands me a steaming mug.

'Dave,' he says, 'when you kept going on about needing a second search dog team, I just thought you wanted an easy time of things. I've been proven wrong already, and I've only been here a matter of hours. Is it always like this?'

'What, Tommo, you mean Treo and me back-to-backing patrols? Yeah, I'd say pretty much from day one it's been like this. That's our daily routine. Sometimes nights as well.' I pause for a sip of coffee. 'And you know what, Tommo, I asked for an extra team 'cause we need one.'

Tommo tells me I need to get some proper food into me. I guess it's the nearest I'll get to an apology.

He's a great bloke, but he's based at slipper city and he doesn't have a clue what it's like here on the front line. I figure the other handler lads are having it just as tough as me. I tell him it's best he gets on the next Chinook flight out of here and goes to see Dan and Sean, plus Ken up at Inkerman. They're a whole lot younger and I'm sure they're being pushed to the limits.

They say that owners and their pets grow to resemble each other. That saying is never truer with handlers and their dogs. Tommo asks me how the 'grumpy bastard' is doing. I ask him if he means Treo or me, though I know he's actually referring to my dog. In a way, it's a fair one. Treo is grumpy with Tommo, as he is with most officers. And at times like these – with Treo and me left to cover the whole of Sangin – I can't say that I blame him.

Tommo promises to get a second dog team sent out to Sangin. The only trouble is finding one free to join us. The 104's search teams are stretched painfully thinly across the areas of Afghanistan where we're at war. If we can't get a second search team in, I ask Tommo to send us an Infantry Patrol dog team. At least they can get out on patrols.

They wouldn't be able to sniff out the bombs – an IP dog is trained to sense where the enemy is located – but it'll be great for the lads' morale. And as far as the Taliban are concerned, they wouldn't know the difference. They'll see another dog and handler out on missions, and they'll presume that we've just upped our game against their bomb makers. It's a case of pile on enough pressure and hope we make them crack.

Sangin is utterly relentless. We're approaching three months in now, and we're patrolling seven days a week. Treo and I are going out on patrols lasting many hours, only to get through the gates to be told by Major Shannon: 'Dog, I need you out again in thirty minutes' time.'

The two hours' rest rule has well and truly gone out the window. Fortunately, I'm blessed with a miracle dog, and the more I ask of him the more he delivers. It would be much easier doing these back-to-back missions if we could roll with the vehicles. It would save Treo's legs, not to mention my back from all the weight I'm carrying. My dog could lounge next to the air-conditioning unit, or at least he could in those wagons fitted with air con.

But the trouble with vehicle patrols is that they're actually a lot less safe than moving on foot. Having an armoured skin around you might give the impression of security, but it's a false one. Unless you've got a man and a dog out front searching the route ahead, inch by inch and on foot, there's no way of knowing what bombs or booby traps may have been set for you. And a lot of the devices the Taliban are now building are big enough and mean enough to blow even our most well-protected vehicles to pieces.

The only safe way to move is dismounted, and that leaves the entire patrol vulnerable to small arms, RPG and machine-gun fire. And with Treo and me out front a good fifteen metres ahead of our security guys, if anyone's going to get hit it's the two of us. At the very tip of the spear there's a fluffy black dog who can't wear any body armour, and one dog soldier carrying a stubby SA80, whose every sense has to be focused on his dog.

And that's just the way it is.

CHAPTER EIGHTEEN

The tempo of operations is relentless, and the pressure's really starting to show. I'm smoking forty ciggies a day, maybe more, and in truth I'm feeling like shit. But what is really killing me is the fear of knowing that the enemy is hell-bent on getting my dog.

In a way I'd hate it more if they captured Treo, as opposed to killing him. The official British Army line on working dogs is that if a local mistreats one, we're not allowed to react with violence. The Army views Treo like it does an EBEX metal detector; just another piece of kit. Treo is Military Working Dog number 5840, and he's got a chip inserted under the skin to say so.

In theory, I'm not allowed to retaliate if I catch someone hurting my dog. Ha-ha. Funny one. Treo is like a living, breathing part of me. He's becoming like that with some of the Ranger lads too. Ask any one of them what they'd do if they saw someone mistreating Treo, and you'll get this thick northern-Irish-accented reply: 'I'd feckin' kill 'em.'

Treo's an Army number to the Army. To us he's a fully-fledged team member – our dog soldier – and the most distinctive and popular bloke in the unit. And to me, it runs deeper than that: not only is he my best buddy, he's like the son that I never had.

The Army don't see the five years of love and fear and laughter and shared experience that unite Treo and me. Anyone who thinks I could lose a friend like that and just get another – they need to get their head read. Never for one moment could I ever think of Treo as expendable. Someone hurts my dog, bugger the rules: I'll hurt them back very, very bad.

It's funny, we English are supposed to have this unique relationship with dogs – 'a nation of dog lovers' and all that. But in military circles it's actually the Americans that have the right attitude to their working dogs, as I'm just about to find out.

A unit from the mighty US Marine Corps gets flown into Sangin. They've come to bolster the force of Rangers based here, and as Sangin is IED Central, so the US Marines have brought with them an entire platoon of EOD specialists.

The commander of their EOD unit is Master Sergeant Chavez, a massive, chunky, larger-than-life Hispanic Marine. He heads up a twelve-man team, complete with every type of jamming equipment, metal detector and excavating kit known to man.

The Marine Corps has lost several of their people to IEDs in Afghanistan, and they hate the bomb makers as much as we do. They're ultra-determined to get out there and start defeating them. Chavez tells me he and his team are ready to come to our aid and defuse any devices 24/7. They'll be based alongside us, and they'll be out just as soon as they get the call.

Ronnie asks us to join a patrol heading out with Seven Platoon, plus Chavez and his Marine Corps team (and a couple of the ANA's more capable soldiers). As we're leaving the base Speedy lets Master Sergeant Chavez have a listen in on the Talinet, which he's got patched into his radio.

The Taliban are going wild: 'Get ready! They're coming out with the black dog! They're coming out with the black dog!'

Chavez gives me a 'you sure you want to be out here, buddy?' look. I shrug. It's what we've been doing for pushing ninety days now. It is what it is.

I get chatting with Chavez, and he's fascinated to learn what Treo and I can do. I ask him what the rules of engagement are concerning US working dogs. He stares at me like he doesn't understand the question. I tell him how the British Army sees Treo as just another bit of kit, as a number. I explain how we're not supposed to shoot to defend my dog.

Chavez shakes his head in utter amazement. 'No, man, no way! Your dog Treo – he's a dog soldier. He's one of us.'

I brief Chavez and his Marines on how we'll approach any compound we need to search. If there's a dog tethered in there then it's sure to be an Afghan fighting hound. I need it moved out of the space before Treo can search. My dog can defend himself, but if he faces up to one of those monsters and gets injured that's the end of Afghanistan for him.

Those Afghan dogs are a mixture of every breed you can imagine. They rear them specifically to get the most vicious and aggressive animals with which to hold their dogfights. The very fact that they get those dogs to rip each other to pieces makes my blood boil. Forcing dogs to fight each other so humans can enjoy it is, quite simply, evil.

It's in a dog's nature to give a human the ultimate in love, loyalty and companionship. That is what Treo offers me, putting his life on the line day after day after day. Keeping a dog chained up, and only releasing it so it can tear a rival apart, is sickening. I've walked past Afghan fighting hounds that have half of their face missing, ears torn off, or gross misshapen chunks of flesh growing back again.

Every time I've felt a mixture of physical revulsion and pity for that dog. My reaction is: *I wish I could put a bullet in you, just to put you out of your misery.*

Treo and I push ahead of this joint Ranger-Marine Corps patrol, and my dog's happy to be out on the search. Within twenty minutes we've reached the door of a compound that we've been tasked to search. I can hear loud and ferocious barking coming from inside. There's a fighting dog in there, and it sounds like a big old boy.

Next thing I know the Marines are piling inside the building, and I hear a single shot ring out. In an instant the fierce barking stops. One of Chavez's men pokes his head out.

'Sir, the compound's clear for your dog to go in, sir!' he announces.

'What was the shot I just heard?' I ask him.

'Sir, we've made sure no one's getting near your search dog.'

I take Treo inside, but I've got a bad feeling about this one. Sure enough, one of the Marines has shot the Afghan fighting hound dead.

'I said move the dog out, not take it out,' I remark to the Marine Corps guys.

'Ooo-rah, sir,' the Marines respond.

'Next time, just move it out or tie it up, but don't shoot it, OK?'

'Ooo-rah, sir,' the Marines say again.

For a moment I stand there thinking how bizarre Americans can be. It's weird hearing them making that 'ooo-rah' sound, as if an elephant's just sat on their chest. It's US Marine Corps' speak for which the very British equivalent would be 'understood' or something similar.

I show Treo his ball and we start the search. The compound owners are far from happy that their fighting dog's been shot. We're halfway around the place when one of the ANA guys remarks that their dog was killed to protect Treo. As he says it, he takes a swipe at Treo with his boot. Before I can react, one of the US Marines has whipped off his helmet and cracked the Afghan soldier around the head.

'Don't touch the search dog!' he snarls. He points at the dead Afghan fighting hound. 'Do that again, and you'll face the same fate as that one.'

My feeling right now is that I only briefed these guys twenty minutes ago, and now there's one dead Afghan fighting dog, and one ANA guy has been given the mother of all beatings around the head. It might be a bit over the top, but at least these Marine Corps guys get the importance of the search dogs, and the vital role they play out here.

En route back to base I get chatting with Chavez. He explains to me that in the US Marine Corps they're drilled to treat the dogs as another soldier, and to view him or her as being one rank higher than their own. So in the eyes of his Marines, Treo is a corporal at the very least. In fact, because I'm a corporal and my dog is a rank higher, that makes Treo something like a sergeant.

He's Sergeant Treo to them, and that in part explains how they've reacted to any aggression or threat shown to my dog. For them, it's akin to someone abusing a Marine Corps sergeant, and that of course would never happen without instant and significant retaliation. When explained that way, it makes every sense to me. I can't fault them on the respect and protection they show towards 'their' dog.

But shooting that Afghan fighting hound has got to me. A dog's still a dog, no matter the crass stupidity or cruelty of its owners. It's been shown time and again that a dog only becomes aggressive if its owner makes it so. Even an Afghan fighting hound might still be turned around, if lavished with affection and love. I resolve to give the Marines more specific directions in future: I'll ask them to move any dogs out the way, but please not to hurt or to shoot them.

Bizarrely, the shooting of that Afghan dog is going to come back to haunt me, and in the most horrible of ways. We're not long in off the patrol when Frankie O'Connor, the Ranger's sergeant major, comes to have a brew and a chat. It's rare for Frankie to pay me a visit at the kennel, and I can tell that something's on his mind. It doesn't take him long to work his way around to it.

He tells me that his Rangers are going down with diarrhoea and vomiting. He's been trying to figure out the source of the sickness. He reckons he's cracked it: it's Jihad. Her infection has worsened, and every time she's out on patrol the Rangers keep feeding her treats from their ration packs. Frankie reckons that's how the D & V is spreading.

I know that D & V is a big issue here in the base. Even Treo's had it, and for a couple of days I had to stop him going out on patrol. But I ask Frankie why he's sharing all of this with me. D & V is a medical issue, not a K9 one. He tells me that I'm the only guy he can think of who may know how to get rid of Jihad and Sandbag.

Maybe we can dump them somewhere, he suggests, and they'll not be able to find their way back to base. I tell Frankie there's no way we can take Jihad out and lose her, because she knows the terrain here far better than we do. The same probably goes for Sandbag. In that case, Frankie says, we've got no choice: Jihad and Sandbag are going to have to be killed.

'Sir, I'm a dog lover,' I tell him. 'I'm the last person you should ever be talking to about killing dogs.'

'Sure, Dave, I know it's a big ask, but will you see if you can't get it done? There's no one else can do it, or I wouldn't be doing the asking.'

On the one hand I'm horrified. For me, this is close to asking Frankie to put down two of his Ranger lads. But at the same time Jihad and Sandbag are members of my team, and I know in my heart that if anyone's going to have to do this, then it should by rights be me. We certainly can't expect any of the Rangers to do it. They love Jihad and Sandbag almost as much as they do Treo. It's the comfort factor. It's the familiarity. It makes them think of their dogs back home.

I go and have words with the base medic. He's the same guy who sewed me up after I half chopped off my finger, when constructing our first kennel. He's seen me faint at the sight of blood, and we've had a good laugh about it. He's not like your average doctor. He's a down-to-earth, tough-looking geezer, and he's blessed with having a big heart and great sense of humour.

Even so, it's a difficult subject to broach. I explain what Frankie's told me, and I tell him that he wants the two strays put down. I ask the medic how much morphine it would take to knock them out painlessly. He tells me a good fifteen shots per dog, but he points out that morphine is expensive, and he needs all he has in case he gets a load of wounded. We can't go using it on the dogs.

'So what's the alternative?' I ask, my gaze roving around the shelves stacked with drugs, syringes and other medical equipment.

'Dave, there's only the one quick, simple and cheap way to do this,' he says, 'and that's a bullet. The most instant and painless death is a bullet to the heart.'

I do not want to do this. This is the very last thing I have ever wanted to do. I'm a lover of dogs, not a killer of dogs. I don't know if Jihad's the source of all the D & V, but Frankie remains adamant: he needs Jihad and Sandbag gone. I tell myself that Jihad's going to die a long, lingering death from her infection anyway, so maybe this is the best way to end it.

I take the dogs down to the fire pit area, where no one can see what I am about to do. I measure out a bowl of food for both of them. That way they'll be concentrating on their meal, and not the coming bullet. I put the bowls down and Jihad and

Sandbag tuck right in. They don't seem to have the slightest idea what's coming.

I cock my pistol. I raise it until it's against Jihad's heart. My hand is shaking, but I close my eyes, say sorry and pull the trigger.

There's the sharp crack of the gunshot, but at the last minute I must have flinched and pulled away. I expected to hear a whimper and a thud, as Jihad keeled over dead. Instead, I hear this terrible, spine-chilling yelping, and when I open my eyes Jihad's trying desperately to limp away from me. By flinching just as I made the shot I've managed to shoot her in the leg not the heart.

It's the worst outcome I could ever imagine. The last thing I ever wanted was this dog to go through any pain or distress. I've made such a bloody hash of it all I feel like reversing the gun and shooting myself in the head.

Somehow, I get my lead around Jihad to hold her still again, and I pull up my pistol once more. With tears streaming down my face I try to level it at her heart. But my hand is shaking so much I just can't seem to hold the aim, plus my vision's gone blurry with tears.

Suddenly, I hear sharp shots ring out: *Bang! Bang! Bang! Bang! Bang!*

There are five in quick succession, all into Jihad's heart. An instant later she's lying before me, stone cold dead. I'm aware that I haven't once pulled my trigger. I turn to find Frankie on my shoulder, a smoking pistol gripped in his right hand.

'She's gone now, Davey-boy, she's gone.' He slips an arm around my heaving shoulders. 'I'm sorry. I didn't know how hard this was going to be for you . . . I'm sorry, Davey, I really am.'

Seeing Jihad lying there in a pool of her own blood makes me feel so awful. I feel torn up inside. I can't help but think of Treo lying there with a bullet in his heart, and wondering how I would feel then. What has Jihad ever done to us, but shown blind loyalty, courage and her fine protective instincts?

We were her pack, we were her life, and maybe in Treo we'd also become her love. And now we – her pack leaders – have turned on her and shot her down. And for what? For no reason that she would ever know or understand.

As for Sandbag, she's taken one look at Jihad's lifeless form and she's done a runner, going as fast as her stubby little legs can carry her. I couldn't have killed her anyway. I'd rather have taken on every Taliban in Sangin than do what I've just done. I've gone completely cold. Frozen. I've got to get out of there.

I walk up the hill like a zombie, tears streaming down my face uncontrollably. Everyone's heard the shots. They all know what I've done.

I go hide in my kennel. I sit there for what feels like an age, cold and empty. This is one of the few times in my life when I don't feel able to go to Treo, seeking comfort from my boy. How can I, when I've just put an end to his favourite dog here in Sangin? Jihad and Treo had grown really close. Out on patrol they'd become a class act, and I just know that Treo was dying to show his girl around his super-duper new kennel.

If Treo knew, he'd feel so betrayed by me. I feel like I'm unde-serving of the incredible love of my dog.

Then a thought strikes me. I realise that Jihad deserves a proper burial. She's looked after and safeguarded the lads on many a patrol, and she was truly one of my team. I get one of the Engineer blokes over and we use his mini-digger to excavate a hole large enough so that that no animal will ever be able to get to her body.

We bury Jihad, and I fashion a small wooden cross to go on her grave. I hang her alloy nametag on it. *In memoriam.*

But still, there's a darkness hanging over me like a storm cloud.

CHAPTER NINETEEN

It takes a few days for all of this to sink in and really to take effect. I feel totally shit, both physically and mentally. My throat starts to swell up. I go to see the base doctor. I tell him I've got this horrible pain. He takes a look and he doesn't like what he sees. He fears it might be the early stages of throat cancer.

There's a dentist who's recently flown into the base to see to the Ranger lads' teeth. The doc wants her to take a look, to get a second opinion. She keeps shoving this wooden spatula down my neck, so as to get eyes on whatever is the problem. She confirms what the doc's said. There's something badly wrong, and to both of them it looks like it might be the c-word.

My granddad died of cancer, so there is a history of it in the family. They want to get me to Camp Bastion, so the specialists there can check me out. They have words with Major Shannon, and the order comes back that I'm to leave on the next available helicopter. I tell them that I'll go, but only when we've got a second dog team into Sangin.

The K9 team that is flown in is the next best thing to a search dog outfit. Dan Barron is a plucky Scouser who'll stand up to anyone in a fight. His dog, Leon, is a simply fantastic-looking animal. He's a jet-black German shepherd, so he looks like a dark and sinister wolf. In fact, Leon's a lovely dog with a really kindly nature. I know him well, for I've trained both of them extensively.

Dan and Leon are an Infantry Patrol dog team. They're trained to go out into bandit country and for Leon to seek out the bad guys. He's trained to lie in a hidden observation post for hours on end, keeping alert for the enemy. Or he'll go out on patrol, his senses thrown forward of the troops, scanning for any threat. He can detect a hostile force from some considerable distance, which will make him an invaluable asset here at Sangin.

No one knows quite how an IP dog can do what it does. They use a mixture of senses – smell and hearing foremost – to pinpoint the enemy. But there's more to it than that. The dogs are trained to ignore humans who aren't a threat, which means they can sense intent as well as simply presence. In other words, they can sense when a human is intending to unleash aggression and violence, or when it's just some old grandma doing the shopping.

There's another great advantage to having Leon here, although it's one that only I will likely be aware of. Leon's a black dog about the same size as Treo. The Taliban won't be able to tell the difference between one 'black dog' and another. It'll keep up the pressure, and it'll provide the perfect cover for the fact that, for a few days at least, Treo and I are going to have to get ourselves gone.

Dan and Leon get flown in, and we get man and dog settled into the kennel. Treo and I are scheduled to fly out the next day, and I get Dan doing the rounds – meeting Frankie, Major

Shannon and the Seven Platoon lads. No one says as much, but they're looking for Dan and Leon to be the surrogate black dog team whilst Treo and I are away. Dan's rarely been outside the wire, but he's raring to go, and I've got every confidence in him.

That night Dan and I stay awake nattering. I catch up on news from the 104, and about the lads in the other frontline postings. Dan's talking nineteen-to-the-dozen as usual, and it's good to hear that the lads are doing great work up at Kajaki, Musa Qala and Inkerman. At one stage Dan tells me he needs to use the toilet. His torch is broken, so he asks to borrow mine.

I've got a brand new head-torch that was given me by the US Marine Corps. I pass it over to Dan, but I warn him to look after it, because it's a peachy American one. He puts it on and sets off to the latrines. He's gone a long time, and I figure he must have the shits bad. Finally, there's the creak of the door opening and Dan returns.

We can't have the main lights on in the kennel, for at night it would make us a target. Dan stumbles about in the darkness as he tries to find his cot.

'Dan, why aren't you using the head-torch?' I ask.

'Erm . . . Erm . . .' He's sounding sheepish as hell.

'Dan, where's my head-torch?'

'Well, I was wiping my ass as you do, and I looked down to see where the toilet paper was going – you know what I mean, Dave?'

'Yes, Dan, I know how you sometimes have to look where your bog paper's gone. But what's it got to do with my head-torch, Dan?'

'Well, at that moment the torch slipped off my head and landed down where all the crap is. Come on, Dave, I'll show you.'

Dan takes me outside. We don't have to take a step towards the latrines. From where we're standing I can see this bright light shining out of them, and clearly visible from a good hundred metres away. Dan offers to pay me for it. I pluck a figure out of the air – one hundred dollars. I tell Dan to buy two slabs of ice cold pop from one of the Afghan shops in Sangin, and I'll call it quits.

Dan does just that, and I've polished off all of the Coca-Cola by the time the helicopter's inbound to collect Treo and me. But the cold pop has done little to soothe my throat. It still feels like it's chock-full of razor blades. It's achingly painful, and covered in small white pustules, which the doc thinks are the tumours.

As we load up the Chinook and pull away from the base, there's a swirling mixture of emotions whirling through my head. On the one hand, the last thing I want to be doing is leaving Ranger Company. They need us. How will I feel if I'm out getting seen to, and one of those lads gets smashed by an IED? On the other hand, I'm worried shitless about my throat. Any which way I look at it, it's a mess.

We touch down at Bastion and I'm met by Sergeant Major Frank Holmes, the 104's second-in-command. Frank and I go way back, to the start of my time with the RAVC. He's a fellow lover of dogs, and he's had to fight for every rank he's ever got. He's also known as being a workaholic. Many a night he'd sleep on the floor of our base back in the UK, he'd been at it so late into the evening.

I have all the time in the world for Frank, but I'm surprised he's not been out to pay a visit to Treo and me in Sangin. As far as I know he's not got out to see the other lads in their murder postings, either. But he's the sergeant major of the unit, and he'll be a busy old boy, that's for sure, and I'm certain he'll have his reasons.

I'm expecting to get rushed in for my throat test, so I'm more than a little surprised when Frank tells me that Treo and I have to stand gate duty at Camp Bastion. He wants me running a Vehicle Check Point on one of the main gates. I've just been through three months of hell in Sangin. I've come out to get my throat checked for cancer, and Frank seems to want me to take over gate duty to give one of the guys here in slipper city 'a break'.

I'm at an incredibly low ebb right now and on the very edge of exhaustion. It crosses my mind that maybe Frank doesn't know what I've been through or about how sick I may be, but I'm feeling too low and too ill to argue about the gate duty. Treo and I stand a few shifts, before I'm told I'll have to get flown to the base at Kandahar Airfield to get my throat checked. No one seems to know when a flight might be available.

In the meantime, Frank tells all handlers to join him for an early morning run around the base perimeter. We set off and all I can feel is my throat getting tighter and tighter, and a rake of needles digging further and further in. Finally, it's like I can't breathe. I stop, doubled over and gasping for air. Frank runs past and gives me this look, like he's shocked at the state of me.

I walk around the rest of the course. I reckon I should have refused to do the run, and explained to Frank just how ill I'm feeling. Frank meets me at the finish. He asks me if I'm not fit enough to handle a run in Bastion, how am I fit enough to handle

Sangin? That's it. I turn to leave before things can get any worse between us.

It's Dodsy, the 104's admin sergeant, who finally comes to tell me that they've got me my flight to Kandahar. Dodsy's an acting sergeant and I am a corporal, but we have a mutual respect for each other. He knows I've been an infantry soldier and took a big drop in rank to get K9, and that I'm working my way up again. Dodsy tells me my flight's going out the next morning.

My first priority now is Treo. I've got to get him housed in the kennel and comfortable, because who knows how long I'm going to be away. I give strict instructions to the kennel staff: only limited air con, and one meal a day. After three months on the go Treo's a lean, mean, bomb-detecting machine. I don't want him getting fat or too accustomed to the luxury, or he'll de-acclimatise.

It's a female handler who's agreed to look after Treo. He always latches onto the ladies. Just before my flight leaves I nip in and say goodbye to him. I give him a kiss and I stroke his paws.

'You've done well, lad, you've done well,' I tell him. 'You have a good rest now. You wait, big lad, I'll be back in no time. There's work for us to do, my boy, just as soon as we get back to Sangin.'

I touch down at Kandahar Airfield, this massive allied airbase. I'm taken to see a Canadian throat specialist who works at the hospital. As I sit in the waiting room I know something is badly wrong. I can feel it. I just pray it's not the c-word. What will I say to my family if I have to phone home and tell them that I didn't take a bullet or a bomb, but I am dying of throat cancer? More importantly, I'll not be able to take Treo back to Sangin, so we can finish the job that we started.

The specialist takes some throat swabs and disappears so he can run some tests. I've got a pretty, soft-skinned Canadian nurse comforting me as I wait for the results. She's got her hand on my hand, and all I've been used to for the last few months are the rough claws of Tippy-Toes Treo.

The specialist calls me in to see him. I've got badly inflamed glands, he tells me, but he doesn't think it's cancerous. He would, however, like me to get it double-checked in the UK. I catch a flight to RAF Brize Norton. My UK medical tests confirm what the Canadian doctor suspected. It's a nasty infection, and I need a monster dose of antibiotics, but at least it's not the c-word.

I'm hugely relieved, but all the time I'm in the UK I'm glued to Sky News. All hell seems to have been let loose in Helmand. The poppy harvest is well and truly done now, and lads are getting injured and killed on what seems like a daily basis. I'm dreading hearing a report that a Ranger has been hit by an IED in Sangin. That'll rip me up and destroy me.

I'm done with the medical tests, so I pack my kit and head for the nearest pet shop. Pets At Home stocks massive vacuum-packed dog bones.

'Right, how many of these have you got?' I ask the shop assistant.

'We've got fifty, sir, in stock,' she replies, having checked her computer. 'How many d'you want?'

'I'll take the lot,' I tell her. 'I'm taking them out to Afghan, for the dogs out there.'

I pay for the lot, box them up, put a big sign on the crate saying 'War Dog Bones', and I get it onto the RAF flight as part of my luggage. Twenty-four hours later, I'm back at Camp

Bastion and dying to see Treo. And there, waiting for me on the flight line, is Ken, fresh out of Inkerman.

Ken strikes me as having aged a year for each of the months that he's been at war. He looks older and wiser beyond his years. But being a typical Geordie he has a good old moan and a whinge on the drive back to our quarters. Ken knows he can talk to me like a dad and unload his deepest frustrations, and boy does he have them.

Ken's been pulled back to Bastion to do some extra training with his dog, but he's been ordered to stand gate duty whilst he's here, just like Treo and I were. He absolutely hates it, and all he wants is to get back to Inkerman. He's worried shitless that he'll lose someone whilst he's away, and he'll have that on his conscience for life. I tell Ken that Treo and I were also put through this gate-duty crap, and he'll just have to grin and bear it.

'So, what's Inkerman like?' I ask.

'More firefights than a night out on Moss Side,' he tells me. 'Not a lot of IEDs. Whatever we do we're setting patterns when we patrol, 'cause it's such a small area. The Taliban lie in wait for us. That means lots and lots of firefights. What about Sangin?'

'IED Central it is, mate. We're finding stuff more or less every day.'

'You know what worries me most? We're not doing as many searches as we want. We're sat on patrols that keep getting hit, so there's no chance for us to properly search. I keep thinking what the hell are Sasha and me there for, if we're not on the search?'

'Trust me, whether you're searching or not the lads will love having you and your dog there. And if you find just the one IED or arms cache, that makes it all the more worthwhile. That's a load of lives you've just gone and saved.'

Ken goes on to tell me that he's just become a father to a little baby girl, and he can't wait to get home to see her. Ken's become a dad whilst here in Afghanistan, and he's more than grown to be a mature-sounding father figure. That's a privilege and a blessing that I will never have, which reminds me in turn how I'm dying to see my boy, my dog.

Ken and I natter away for a while longer, and it's fantastic to have him with me and to see him alive and well. There's less piss-taking and cheek from him now: there's more of the shared brotherhood of having taken ourselves, and our dogs, through the heart of the fire.

Ken drops me at the kennels, so I can go see my boy. I can hear Treo whimpering in excitement before I've even walked in. A dog knows the scent of his owner or handler, and Treo can smell that I'm back long before he sees me. I listen to his excited cries: *Dad, I'm here! I'm here! Come and see me!*

I walk in, switch on the light and I'm met by this fat, pudgy-looking hound bouncing about excitedly, and with the aircon on full blast. Nice one. I can hardly recognise him. No way is he getting one of those dog bones until I've got some of the weight off him. Treo's had the aircon running 24/7 and all the Eukanuba he could wish for. The little git. But still, I can't help but love him. My boy is getting the biggest ever cuddle, fat and rolly though he may be.

I get him out for a run so I can start getting him acclimatised again. We're waiting for a helicopter flight to Sangin, so we can re-join the Ranger lads. I'm desperate to get back on the search.

But whilst we're killing time at Bastion, we are asked to do a special operation with an elite forces unit. They're planning a dawn raid on a Taliban stronghold, and they want a dog team on it.

The mission is going out from the Kandahar Airfield base. One of our handlers, Angie, and her dog were supposed to be on it, but she's just taken a bad bite. Angie was doing some training with some specialist dog handlers, and one of their hounds has bitten her right on the face. It's torn a gash from her nostril up to the bridge of her nose, and it's needed more than a few stitches.

Angie's a good-looking lass, but when she meets Treo and me off the helo flight to Kandahar, she looks like she's got a Franken-stein nose plastered across her face. She doesn't make a great deal of fuss about it. Every handler knows that sooner or later they'll take a bite from a dog, especially in training. It goes with the territory. If you're not up for it, you're not up for working in K9.

Having housed Treo in a kennel, Angie takes me down to the elite forces Orders Group. Inside this hangar they've built a scale model of the target area. It replicates the exact ground that they'll be covering, in miniature detail. I stand back thinking about how different this is from operating in Sangin, where we know the ground intimately, and most times don't even carry a map.

The unit's commanding officer talks through the mission, which is designed to hit an area of mountainous terrain right on the Pakistan border, one that is pretty much unknown to coalition forces. In fact, the mission sounds so 'warry' that Angie decides she just has to be on it, injured nose and all.

The officer says that's great, for he can certainly use two dog teams. We're to be at the helipad for three o'clock the following morning.

We pitch up at the helipad to be met by ranks of elite warriors loaded with thousands of rounds of ammo and their weaponry. This is a major heli-borne op that we're now a part of, and the air's thick with avgas fumes and tension as they work themselves up to the coming air-assault. Treo and I are used to walking out the camp gates right into bandit country. This feels very different.

There's a massive adrenalin buzz as the Chinooks take to the air and the soldiers start going wild, bashing their helmets against the sides and psyching themselves up for battle. It's like *Apocalypse Now*, minus the music. We hit the ground hard off the back of the aircraft, and within minutes we've captured the first prisoner – a Taliban leader who was caught off guard as we descended from the dawn skies.

All that morning we search through knife-cut valleys that snake between towering mountains. Angie and her spaniel are clearing one side of the terrain, whilst Treo and I are doing the other, and we're rounding up scores of prisoners and their weaponry.

Angie's dog looks smart, intense and focused, and hugely on the ball as she goes about the search. By contrast, Treo's got a half-chewed maize cob in one side of his gob, and he looks distinctly unimpressed. It's like he's been there, done it all and got the T-shirt. I know how he's feeling. Somehow, this all feels like a dress rehearsal, and it won't be real again until we get back with our boys in Sangin.

After seven hours of continuous search work we mount up the helos to return to Kandahar. It felt great to be back on the ground with my dog, but every other minute my mind was on Sangin. We touch down at Kandahar, and pretty much immediately Treo and I get our orders. We're flying out to Sangin at first light the following morning.

Major Shannon's planning a massive operation, the biggest yet of the Rangers' tour, and he can't get going until he's got his dog team back again.

I can't wait to get boots on the ground at IED Central once more.

As for Treo, he can sense my excitement, and he's keen to get his paws on the territory that he knows best.

CHAPTER TWENTY

We catch a Chinook ride out to Sangin, and we're met on the airstrip by the Seven Troop lads.

'It's great to have you back,' Ronnie tells me.

'It's great to see you guys still alive,' I reply.

Our fellow handler, Dan, and his dog Leon are just doing their last-minute preparations to depart. Dan's going out on the same flight that brought us in, so there's little time for hanging around. I see Treo's rubber duck lying on the ground with the head bitten off. I pick it up and ask Dan what the hell happened.

He's got tears of laughter in his eyes: 'Sorry, Dave, but Leon just couldn't resist it.'

'Dan, you bastard, that was Treo's prized rubber duck,' I tell him. But I'm howling with laughter myself now.

No sooner have we got handler and rubber-duck-killer Leon loaded aboard the Chinook, than Speedy starts banging on about the coming mission. I ask him what kind of job it's going to be.

'Don't you know?' Speedy asks. 'We're moving into this compound in the Green Zone for two months to live there and to hold it.'

'Are we now,' I say. 'How nice of someone to warn us. And when exactly are we going?'

'Now you and Treo are back . . .' Speedy glances at his watch, 'I'd say in about a couple of hours' time.'

The Green Zone is the vegetated belt of terrain that runs along the Helmand River. It's also the term we use for Taliban territory. Apparently, we're going to set up home in the heart of bandit country, and we're not due back again for some weeks. I run around trying to pack enough kit for Treo and me to live on for two months, but there's no way that I can carry it all.

An hour before departure Speedy comes over again and asks me where all my kit is for the quad. I ask him what quad?

'We're taking all your dog kit in on a quad bike,' he tells me.

I take one look at the giant, bulging rucksack that I've just finished packing and glare at Speedy. 'Nice of you to tell me, mate.'

I now have to unpack the world's largest rucksack so I can load half of the kit onto the quad. Needless to say, the Seven Troop lads are laughing their socks off as I run around like Treo's headless rubber duck trying to get everything sorted.

Major Shannon's plan for the coming mission is simplicity itself. There's a compound near the 611 that he's identified as the enemy's headquarters. It's from there that they keep hitting us. We're going in to take it. Once we've done that, we'll establish a permanent base there, to control what was once a major Taliban stronghold.

We move out at last light and locate the compound in the darkness. I'm first up the scaling ladder with Treo on my shoulders, and we start to search the place. The first thing we realise is that it's crammed full of medical kit, and there are rooms laid out with beds, and drips and drugs galore. This is clearly where the Taliban have been treating their wounded. But I guess they must have seen us coming, because they've made themselves very scarce.

Treo comes bounding up to me excitedly and he's got something held triumphantly in his jaws. He jumps onto a solid stone seat so he's more or less at my eye-level, and he holds it up as proud as punch: *Hey, Dad! Look what I've got! And we've only just got started!*

I take a closer look. It's an unused .50-calibre heavy-machine-gun round. It's a fine find. Not only have the Taliban been treating their wounded here but they've also been scavenging our weaponry. The 50-cal is a NATO round. They've likely built up a stash of such material somewhere, with a view to emptying out the explosives and building some nice little IEDs.

Treo bounds about like Tigger and plonks his butt down next to a humungous find. It's the tail fin from some kind of massive air-launched bomb. It was once painted a sky-blue colour, but it's now stained and blotched with rust. He squats beside it excitedly and the find is actually bigger than he is. Lying on its side as it is, it's as tall as Treo and about three times his length.

It looks ancient, and I figure it's a throwback to the days when the Soviet Red Army was fighting here. Treo's proud as can be with his find. He's like a puppy beside it, his tongue hanging out pink and droopy, his eyes bright and fixed on the prize. It's the single biggest thing that he's ever found, and there's no way that he's grabbing that and giving it a good chew with his jaws.

It's made of thick plating, and it must be half a tonne or more of steel, which makes it prime IED-building material. We radio base and tell them exactly what we've got here: we've taken the Taliban stronghold. Major Shannon tells us to go firm and to secure the place. This is exactly what he's been looking for. It's here that we'll set up our permanent base in the Green Zone, bang in the Taliban's back yard.

For the next couple of days we're busy constructing sand-bagged defences. We get the Engineer blokes to blow up the odd tree and wall so we can clear our arcs of fire. By the time we're done we can see the enemy coming from just about any direction, and hit them hard. The Rangers give the place a fitting name, considering their regiment's Northern Irish pedigree: PB Armagh. PB stands for Patrol Base: Armagh is a name synonymous with the Troubles in Northern Ireland.

There are stairs leading up to the flat roof, which makes for a great defensive position. The trouble is if you run up too quickly, you're in danger of knocking yourself out on an arch over the stairs. The Ranger lads and I decide the arch has to go. We get some sledgehammers and spend hours trying to bring it down. It's only made of mud, but in the harsh Afghan sun it's set hard as concrete.

Treo's lying in the shade of a little garden area watching the show, and he's loving it. The greenery's set to one side of the compound and it's been declared 'Treo Turf'. No one else is allowed in there, apart from Treo and me. It's his chill-out area, and also his poop and pee patch. He and I have taken over the room next to it as our makeshift kennel. It's got a door leading directly onto that shady orchard and Treo clearly thinks it's great here at PB Armagh.

We know from the radio intercepts that the Taliban are enraged at what we've done. Seizing 'their' compound has really pissed them off, and they're just itching to have a go. They keep boasting about how many men they're readying to attack us, and how they're sowing the surrounding paths with IEDs. Their plan appears to be to cut us off from our Sangin base, surround the place and annihilate us. The only way to stop them is to get out and start patrolling, and to dominate the ground.

The strategic importance of what we're doing here can't be overstated. By choking off the 611 as we've been doing, Major Shannon has made it all but impossible for the Taliban to use that as their main IED transit route. Basically, as they can't ship IEDs in via the road they have to do so on foot, and via the cover of the Green Zone. But with us lot having set up a perman-ent base here, we've pretty much choked off that route too – hence their desire to wipe us out.

It's the early hours of day three when we send out our first patrol. It's four o'clock in the morning and we push out a dozen lads into the pitch dark, with my dog and me in the lead. I flash Treo a hint of his ball, make as if to throw it, and whisper 'seek on'. As he sets off, nose-a-slurping, I glance backwards, and I can see a snake of heavily armed fighters all on night vision.

Apart from the clink of gun metal on body armour, all around us is utterly silent and still. But we know that the enemy is out there somewhere, watching and waiting for their time to strike. We are going hunting; I only hope that on this patrol we don't become the hunted.

We're an hour into the mission and we've advanced a good five hundred metres from the base. We're deep into uncharted territory and still there's been not a sniff of the enemy. We're moving ahead at a dead slow, making a dozen paces before the whispered order to halt is passed along the line. The entire column becomes motionless, listening intently in the hollow, ringing silence.

Then Treo and I move off again, the snake of Rangers following silently after. We're making painfully slow progress, but this is the only way to get in amongst them and to get the terrain cleared. We push ahead for a good twenty minutes before a cry rings out in the darkness. It comes from a way to our front, and it sounds like some kind of a verbal alert yelled out in Arabic.

There's an answering cry from somewhere to our rear, and I figure they've got us surrounded. I feel Treo's nervousness, and that he can sense the hostility all around us. I glance upwards. The sky to the east is glimmering with the first rays of dawn. The terrain is lightening as the sun claws its way over the hidden horizon. We're losing the cover of darkness.

We push onwards into the building heat of the Afghan day. We've been out for six hours or more and the sun's beating down on one boiling hot dog. But Treo just keeps his paws padding tirelessly along, and his nose huffing and puffing away.

We move into an area where there's a far greater density of buildings. Each mud-walled compound seems to come with its own concrete telegraph pole, complete with a green metal junction box.

We join a track that leads directly back to PB Armagh, and we're on the last leg before home. I'm aware that as fast as my dog and I clear a path, the enemy can come in behind us and plant something, so we're just going to have to keep repeating what we've been doing all today. My thoughts are wandering, and I'm pondering on just how many tracks there must be threading through this maze of compounds, when something draws my mind back to Treo.

I see him lift his head from ground level, and his muzzle starts bobbing this way and that as he airs up, sampling the atmosphere all around him. He's detected a scent at around about waist height, which is not where I'd expect him to pick up on a buried IED. It's not something that we've experienced before, and instinct tells me to halt the patrol.

'Slow things down,' I whisper to the two Rangers behind me. 'He's onto something.'

Treo's standing stock-still now. There's something that has really caught his attention, and it's all around his head.

My eyes dart to left and right. There are compounds to either side of us, so it could be cooking smells. Maybe there's an Afghan woman preparing an early evening meal. But the way Treo's dragging in the air in great gasps, it doesn't appear like food to me. It looks as if he's sifted the airborne molecules well, and he's detected those that will earn him a play with his ball.

A moment later he takes a few steps forwards and to the right. He stops before a telegraph pole. He hasn't even bothered to look back at me for any reassurance. Whatever it is that he's onto my dog's absolutely certain, which means that it's scary as hell to be standing just a couple of metres behind him.

'What is it, boy?' I whisper. 'Show your dad. Show me then, lad.'

I see him lift his two front paws and get them either side of the telegraph pole. He keeps sniffing all around it. Then he drops his paws, has a good snuffle as he circles around and returns to where he was, front paws up on the pole. He does this several times, as if he can't work out how to signal to me exactly what he's found.

Finally, he plonks his paws to either side of the pole and gets his nose glued to the junction box. With a sideways flick of his eyes he indicates to me that he's not moving: *Come on, Dad, I can't exactly sit on it, can I? It's in here!*

I call him, sharply: 'Treo, get here!'

I move the lot of us rapidly backwards, and tell Speedy that he'll need to get the path sealed off at both ends. Whatever my dog has found, it's on that telegraph pole.

As soon as we're in some cover, I give Treo a play with his ball. I'm not sure what he's got here. It's an odd place to have sited an IED. I'm not even sure if that little green junction box is big enough to hold one. But Treo's dead certain, and I have never doubted my dog.

Speedy puts a call through to the bomb-disposal boys. Twenty minutes later the familiar figure of Master Sergeant Chavez appears jogging along the track, with his EOD team. I'm acutely aware that this is our first call-out with the US Marine Corps boys. I hope to hell that my dog's found more than just a rubber duck in that green box on the telegraph pole.

Chavez is dark, crew-cut and swarthy, and he's got eyes that can burn right through you. One look from them and you can tell he's defused a lot of IEDs in his time. He's almost the exact opposite of the British EOD types, who seem to want to spend hours easing their way into a location and deciphering what-ever device has been set.

Chavez just wants to get in there, cut it off from its detonator, and blow it sky high. He suits up, calls forward his ECM guys to jam any trigger signal, and he's ready.

He brandishes a pair of tinsnips at me: 'OK, where is it?'

I describe the green junction box on the telegraph pole.

'Got it,' he confirms. 'Now, get the hell out of the way with your guys.'

Not five minutes later Chavez is back, a big grin on his square-cut features.

'Jackpot, dude!' he remarks, speaking more to Treo than to me. He holds up a small green object, about the size and shape of a Kiwi fruit. 'Anti-personnel mine, laid with a complex little trigger. Never seen the likes of it before, man, but it sure could've done some real harm . . . if it weren't for your dog.'

I stare into Treo's eyes. He stares back at me, ears pricked up proudly: *See, Dad, aren't I good? I knew that was there and you didn't, did you?*

'You clever little bastard,' I tell him. 'Come here! Come right here for a cuddle.'

I'm well aware of what Treo's achieved here. That mine may be small, but it's designed to maim and to kill. Normally, it'd be laid in the ground, waiting for someone to step on it. But positioned as it was, it would have exploded at shoulder height, turning that junction box into a thousand shards of blasted, shredded metal. Had Treo gone past it, it could have taken my head off, or more likely a few of the lads positioned further back along the patrol.

The ECM might have kept my dog and me safe, by jamming the trigger signal, but would it have done so for the rest of the patrol? I'd rather have got my own head blown off, than have the life of one of those young lads forever on my conscience. Yet again, it's Treo's nose that has prevented untold bloodshed and carnage. But how many more times can my dog prove the lifesaver here?

The bomb makers have to get lucky just the one time. Treo – he has to be lucky every time.

CHAPTER TWENTY-ONE

A couple of days later I'm helping burn out a massive tree stump at PB Armagh. It's blocking one of the key defensive points of the compound. A resupply convoy is due in, but the vehicles can't get in right to our walls for the terrain is impassable, so we have to walk the supplies the last few hundred metres.

Word comes in that Frankie, the Ranger CSM, wants to see me, and that he doesn't need my dog. It's an odd request to be called out minus Treo, and I wonder what it means.

I put Treo into his room and give him one of the bones I brought out from the UK. After weeks on dried rations there's a danger that all the calcium from the gnawing will give Treo the runs, but he loves his bones so much and I can't resist giving a treat to my dog.

I pull on my body armour, grab my rifle and head out. I catch sight of Frankie at the far end of the track that leads down to the base. He's not looking too happy. Just as soon as I'm close enough, he puts one hand on my shoulder and he half pulls me towards him.

'I've got some bad news for you, Dave.'

I'm thinking my kennel must've taken a direct hit from a mortar back at base. Or something.

'Dave, one of your handlers and his dog has been killed.'

My heart practically stops dead. 'Sir, where?'

'Inkerman.'

Inkerman. That means Ken. That means Sasha and Ken.

I know Ken wouldn't want me to break down in tears. He'd want me to stay strong.

'Sir, thanks for coming all this way to give me the news,' I tell him. 'It's appreciated. Very much.'

I walk back to the compound desperately trying to keep it together. But it's hit me so hard. I feel like my legs have gone all to jelly, and like my heart's breaking apart. I'm thinking of Ken and all the bollockings I ever gave him when he was a trainee. I'm full of this burning, raging anger, coupled with this deep and empty sadness. It's like a dark and angry hole has been torn in my soul.

I think of Ken's dog, Sasha, the only one that could ever rival Treo; the one dog that earned Treo's respect and his everlasting love. First he's lost Jihad, and partly at my own hand. And now he's lost his first love, Sasha, and at the hands of the murderous bastard Taliban.

By the time I reach the compound the word is already out. The Ranger lads are staring at me in a shocked silence. No one knows what to say. I go to my room to hide. I sit down and I glance at Treo, but he won't meet my eye. Somehow, he knows. It's incredible, but somehow, instinctively my dog knows.

There's a knock, and Speedy puts his head around the door. 'Dave, you OK?'

I nod. Bite my lip. 'I'll be all right.'

I sit there for hours lost in this formless darkness. I wonder how he died. I wonder if he suffered. I wonder if his dog did too. I've got no more details than what the sergeant major has told me. I think of Ken's kid that was born just two months ago, the child that he's never going to get to see. I think of the joy of fatherhood that he'll never get to know. I think of what a bloody pointless tragic waste of a life it all is.

There's another knock at the door. It's Ronnie. 'Dave, I've just heard. Are you OK, mate?'

I've forged a bond with Ronnie. There's something in his genuine, easy-going nature that touches me. The tears start to flow now. I can't stop them. Ronnie sits with me for a while in companionable silence. Then he places one arm around my shoulder, tells me it's going to be OK, gets up and quietly leaves.

He knows I need time alone to grieve.

I figure they'll be getting Ken and Sasha's remains back to Bastion, to repatriate them to the UK. On the one hand I want more than anything to be there for him, to say goodbye. On the other, I know he'd want me to stay here, in the heart of Taliban territory, denying them the ability to hit and kill our lads. I'm torn. I want to be there for Ken, and here for the Rangers. I don't know what to do.

That night Treo and I are out on patrol. But somehow, instinctively, Treo knows that it's all gone horribly wrong. Somehow, he knows that Sasha's gone, and like me he's in pieces. He's lethargic, unfocused and he doesn't want to search. I've never known him like this, not in five years together. And it's because of this that I decide we've got to get to Camp Bastion, so we can send Ken and Sasha home.

We join a patrol heading back to our Sangin base. Once there, I put Treo in his kennel. He curls up in one corner. He gives me a fleeting look, his eyes full of a deep sadness and grief. I get on the radiophone to Bastion. I've got to know what happened to Ken. I get hold of Tommo and I can tell that he's in tatters. He can't say very much because the picture's still not clear. All he can tell me is that Ken's body is in the morgue, and that he needs me back at Bastion.

I put a call through to my folks. Inkerman is in the Sangin Valley, north of Sangin and south of Kajaki, but that's a geographical distinction that'll be lost on my family back home. If the news has broken about a dog and handler getting killed in the Sangin Valley, as far as they're concerned it could well be me and Treo.

After several false starts, I finally get through to my mum. 'Hi, Mum, it's me.'

All I can hear is this tidal wave of hysterical sobbing, before she passes me directly to Bob. Bob explains what's happened. Sure enough, they'd heard on the news that a dog team had been hit in the Sangin Valley, and for hours they'd believed it was us.

My mum had been waiting for the knock on the door from the guy in the dark suit. So when she heard my voice on the phone, it was as if I had come back from the dead. I put her through so much hell in my adolescent years, but this has been like the day of days. My sister's there with her, and the two of them just can't stop crying, even though they know that Treo and I are alive.

Bob and I have a long talk. Bob spent twenty-seven years in the military, so he knows the score.

'How are you, son?' he asks me.

I tell him I'm OK.

He repeats the question, with emphasis: 'No, son, *how are you*?'

I proceed to tell Bob everything. I unload on him how I feel like I've let Ken down, in the sense that we weren't there with him to hold the line in Inkerman. I share with him my fears that I hadn't given Ken enough of myself, of the infantryman, which in a volatile place like Inkerman could have made the difference between his and Sasha's life and their death. I could have given them more and it could have been a lifesaver. I'll just never know.

Ken always used to say to me: 'I can do it – I'm just as good as you.' But maybe if I'd gone the extra mile in the training I could have saved him, and saved Sasha too. Ken was a cheeky, gobby, lovely little bastard, and now I'll never know.

I come off the phone and return to the kennel. I'm torn apart, and so is Treo. It's at times like these that we really need each other. He curls up on my cot with me. Normally, Treo's not a kissy kind of bloke, but tonight he is. He leans his head across to me, flicks his tongue out and licks my face a few good times.

He's got a look in his eyes: *Dad, we've both lost someone, but I'm still here for you. Don't be so down. We've got each other, and that's what matters.*

That very look, those few unspoken words – they break my heart.

It just so happens that the entire RAF Chinook fleet is getting serviced right now. As a result, the RAF are only doing emergency flights with the big twin-rotor helos. But they are aware of what a tiny unit the 104 is, and so they lay on a special flight to get us all back to Bastion. I know how dark this is going to be – it's going to be days of anger and tears and rage.

I get Treo ready and we're up waiting on the flight line. I hear the noise of the whocka-whocka coming over the hills and it lands tailgate-down. Treo and I load up. Two of the 104's handlers, Ali Sutherland and Cat Baker, are sitting there with tears in their eyes. They're up front close by the cockpit and I figure they've just been collected from where they're based at Kandahar.

I position myself and Treo close to the open ramp. The noise there is deafening, but even so I figure I can hear Ali sobbing. Or maybe it's just my imagination playing tricks on me. It's Ali that I'm worried for. She's a sweet, blond-haired, blue-eyed Scottish lassie with a heart of gold. She'd cry at the drop of a hat, but as a soldier and a dog handler she's as hard as nails. I'd prefer to take a punch off a Para than one off her.

As the aircraft takes to the skies I can feel both girls' eyes boring into me. They're looking to me for the strength that they need. I'm trying to think of ways I can help them get through this, but all I seem able to think about is Ken. I manage a wink – *we'll get through this, girls*. Then I rest my head on the butt of my rifle and that's where it stays.

As for Treo, he's devastated. Normally, he'd be perched on the Chinook's open ramp, trying to get a glimpse of where he's going. Now, he's lying at my feet with his ears drooping and his head well down. He can feel my grief, on top of his own. I know that

Treo will need his own comfort time. He'll need walks with his dad – without having to search every inch of the terrain before him – and he'll need to play and relax and to recover.

We touch down at Bastion, but we're not allowed to dismount until the rotors have come to a complete standstill. As Treo and I go down the ramp, I turn to the aircraft's load master, the guy in charge of passengers and cargo in the hold.

'I can't thank you enough,' I tell him. 'Say the same to the aircrew. It means a lot to us what you've done today.'

He touches me on the shoulder. 'Thanks for that, mate. I will.'

I walk across the helipad ahead of Cat and Ali, trying to muster my strength as I go. I keep telling myself that I have to be strong. I can't show my emotions. I've got to set the right kind of example, one that will help get us back into the field and to war. I keep thinking what it would be like if Treo and I had died. How would I want the handlers to behave if my dog and I were being sent home?

I look around for a vehicle to collect us, but all I can see is an Army ambulance. Then I see an arm waving out the window and I realise it's Frank, our sergeant major. I move over to the wagon and he tells me to put my dog in the back, as the front's going to be crowded. I do as instructed, but when I open the rear door I feel like I've just had a right kick in the face.

Lying before me is a coffin. I can only presume that it's Ken's. I wonder how Frank can be so insensitive. I'm just in off the front line, and he picks me up with Ken's coffin in the rear. But I'm too down, and too shell-shocked, to say anything much about it now.

On the drive to the dog unit he fills me in on what he knows.

Ken and Sasha were out on a routine patrol. Sasha was shot by a Taliban sniper, and she was thrown back ten metres. But she got back on her feet again and raced over to be with Ken. Nothing could ever stop Sasha, not even a high velocity bullet. The Taliban followed her in, and that's how they managed to put an RPG round into the two of them.

It reminds me of a time in Northern Ireland a way back. Sasha was out on patrol and she got hit by a speeding car. The IRA tended to hate the dogs almost as much as do the Taliban, and they'd driven into her deliberately. But they'd only managed to hit her a glancing blow, and she got back up again and carried on with the patrol. That's the kind of dog Sasha was.

She was every bit the equal of Treo. If there were ten dogs in the pen back at camp, Treo and Sasha would only ever be found playing with one another. They respected each other, and they shared a real bond. They had the same incredible drive to work and to search, and nothing ever seemed to faze them.

The one upside to losing Sasha and Ken is that they died pretty much the instant the RPG round hit them. Frank finishes with this: 'Dave, you're older and more experienced than the rest. The youngsters need you strong now.'

I know that Frank's right. He needs me to hold the unit together, whilst he and Tommo prepare to get Ken and Sasha home. After that, I've got to ensure the handlers are strong enough to go back into the field and into the fire. Frank's words hit home. In spite of our recent differences, he and I are as one now, united in our loss and our grief.

Frank asks if I want to see Ken one last time, in the morgue. Ken was a young, punchy Geordie from the hard streets of

Newcastle, and a laugh-a-minute bloke. He was liked by all, and loved by me.

'D'you know, I don't want to see him,' I say. 'I want to remember him as I knew him.'

By saying that I've given the others a way out of having to go and see his body. In turn, they all decline. I feel most sorry for Frank and Tommo, for they had to positively identify the young lad's remains, plus that of his dog.

We rehearse the repatriation parade over and over. We have to carry Ken's coffin from the ambulance to the C130 and load it up the ramp. They fill the practice coffin with sandbags, to replicate young Ken's weight. We take a load of them out, for no way was Ken that heavy. Frank keeps drilling us over and over on how to lift the coffin, to turn, to plant it on our shoulders and go.

The coffin feels like it weighs a tonne. But it's the grief that weighs upon us most heavily. This is a nightmare for these youngsters, to be carrying one of their own. It's only the way that Frank keeps making us rehearse the funeral drill that keeps our minds off our loss.

We line up for the evening ceremony, and there's a sombre, heavy mood. The C130 pulls to a halt and the ramp goes down. I glance around and I'm expecting the runway to be packed, but apart from the tiny contingent from the 104 there's practically no one there.

I feel this cold rage welling up inside me: why aren't there more people here to honour this young lad and his dog's sacrifice?

I glance around again, and from out of nowhere there's a massive phalanx of soldiers marching towards us. They're four ranks deep and they stretch back hundreds of metres along the runway. They're wearing their smartest dress uniforms, swords glinting in the evening sunlight, and they're marching out to say farewell to one man and his dog from this tiny unit – the 104.

We drag Ken out of the ambulance, and it's now that he has the last laugh on us. We go to lift the coffin and it feels like there are four of him in there. The coffin contains not just his body, but all of his kit, hence the extra weight. More fool us for removing some of the sandbags during rehearsals. I think to myself that Ken's got to be up there somewhere, laughing his rocks off as we stagger under the weight.

We reach the platform where the padre will read the service. We lower the coffin and pause, as he begins to say some words. I'm physically close to Ken, and I'm deaf to all that's around me. I find that I'm talking to him, muttering under my breath one last goodbye.

'Listen, lad, you were a cheeky little gobshite and I loved you to death, you know.' I glance at the coffin. 'Out here, you'd grown to be a great handler and a real comrade at arms. I'll try to always remember the good times, Ken, and I hope you and Sasha never suffered. I'm certain you didn't, lad, for both of you deserved only the best . . . Anyhow, soon be time to lift you up and into the whirlybird, and then you're away and we'll be saying our last goodbyes.'

We move towards the C130's open tail ramp. I've got my head next to Ken's and I'm talking to him the whole time. 'Ken, don't worry, lad, your family will be OK. We'll look after them, mate; we'll make sure they're all right.'

We march slowly into the aircraft's gaping hold and lay Ken's body on the cold steel floor. All of us have faces streaked with tears. Marianne, Sasha's previous handler, is with us. She's carrying Sasha's ashes in a brass shell case, one that the Engineers have engraved with her name, unit, dog number and a paw.

She places the shell by Ken's coffin, so Sasha can accompany her dad home.

CHAPTER TWENTY-TWO

As the C130 dwindles into a distant speck in the sky I go and have a quiet, teary moment with Treo. It's a funny thing; I came out here knowing that I was the combat veteran, and worrying about my dog, the combat virgin. I've ended up drawing my strength from him when I've been at my lowest ebb.

Out here in Afghanistan, Treo has given me something invaluable: blind loyalty and courage. He's never once faltered when I've asked him to step out to lead a patrol, even though we know the enemy is set on killing 'the black dog'. Treo's put steel in my soul. And now I've got to step up to my dog and be the old warrior every young handler needs me to be.

I need to dig deep to find the strength to carry on. It's not so much for myself or for Treo. We're the old dogs here. I can well remember the time I bagged up dozens of civilians massacred in Bosnia, when I served with the Cheshires. The Balkans War was a brutal conflict, one in which neighbour turned upon neighbour, and even infants and the very old weren't immune from the slaughter.

But this is different. This young lad was one of our own. And I need to give our young handlers the strength to walk back into the jaws of death, having just said the long goodbye to Ken and Sasha.

I gather the six of them together: Marianne, Ali, Cat, Debbie, Dan and Sean. I talk to them. I tell them we have to get back out there and do our work, and to do it for Ken and Sasha. I tell them there's nothing more we can do for the two of them now – they are going home to their families. We have to turn our grief into action, for we've got lives to save.

Before we depart from Camp Bastion, Martin gives a handwritten letter to each handler, including me. Mine reads:

Be strong: Ken would have wanted you to be. I can't thank you enough for what you've done looking after the boys and girls, when I know you wanted to grieve so much for Ken yourself. Thank you for being so brave and for being there for them . . .

Tommo's an officer, one who perhaps isn't supposed to show his feelings to those under his command. The way he's got around that is to write each of us a heartfelt letter. I'm so thankful that I go and tell him what a great thing it is that he's done. I don't know it yet, but I'll read that letter time and time again during some of the darkest moments that lie ahead of me in Sangin.

I say farewell to the other handlers on the Chinook flight out to our base. We've got one extra man-and-dog team with us. Steve Purdy is a gentle giant of a bloke. He's a real man mountain, and he makes even his big, long-haired German shepherd look diminutive by his side. Steve and his dog Reece will be the third K9 team that's joined Treo and me in Sangin. They're an

IP dog team, so they can get out on patrol and in amongst the enemy.

Reece looks like a total monster, he's so huge and so hairy. In fact, he's a great big teddy bear. In spite of his ferocious appearance, he's far less grumpy and irascible than Treo, and he's happy to let you hold and pet and cuddle him.

Steve and Reece demonstrate the same kind of man–dog bond that Treo and I share. In fact, at a distance you could just about mistake Steve and his dog for Treo and me. I hope the Taliban do just that. I hope they see another dark-coloured dog in the area, and it freaks them out big time. I hope they think Treo's managed to clone himself, and that the black dog just got to be even more of a problem.

Steve's heard about the number of IEDs there are in Sangin. Who hasn't? It's put the fear of God into him. But at the same time he knows that Treo's found every one that there was to find. He's been at the front of every patrol, and he's not missed a trick. My dog's been shot up, sniped at, bled all over and blown up, but he's brought every man on his patrol home alive.

We touch down at Sangin, exit the aircraft and almost immediately we're tasked to join a foot patrol heading down to PB Armagh. Steve and his dog will be coming with us, for Armagh is the ideal place to make use of an IP dog like Reece, one who can sense the enemy from a good distance away.

We exit the base and Treo seems back to his old self. I've shown him a flash of his ball and set him to seek. An instant later he's out front, head down, stump of a tail flicking to and fro as he hoovers up the hot, dusty Afghan air.

But at the same time he can sense another dog has joined his patrol, and it's kind of bugging him. I see him glance behind at Reece, and glare: *Hey, this is my gaff. What the hell's that big hairball doing with us?*

Major Shannon's received intel that the Taliban bomb teams are threading a string of IEDs around PB Armagh. That's going to be their stranglehold, and Treo and I are going to have our work cut out searching for them. But as luck would have it, it's going to be Steve and Reece who strike the first blow against the enemy that are laying siege.

That evening the Ranger lads decide to establish a hidden observation post (OP) in the bush to the front of the base. I explain to the Rangers what an IP dog can do: he's able to lie for hours in any position and sense the enemy. He's trained to remain silent, and indicate their location by pointing it out with his nose. Reece is a great asset for a mission like tonight's, and he and Steve join the team heading out to set up the OP.

Sure enough, in the depth of the night Reece detects enemy moving through the bush. The lads in the OP radio in a warning. We figure they're planning to try to hit us by surprise, at first light. But with Reece acting as our early warning system, we're going to be more than ready.

As the first rays of dawn are groping over the mountains to the east, the enemy hit us. A rocket-propelled grenade round tears apart the pre-dawn stillness. It hammers through the air above the OP, and explodes with a massive boom against the wall of the base. As the bush erupts with gunfire, the vegetation throws back the raw crunch and slam of battle in a deafening wave of sound.

I figure Steve and Reece must be getting one hell of a baptism of fire out in that OP. Man and dog, plus the Rangers positioned there, are forced to bug out under intense fire. They make it back to the base, which means we're free to unleash merry hell upon the enemy. A massive barrage of fire is slamming into the compound walls, rounds kicking up angry spurts of mud and dust all along the roofline.

The noise is deafening, and if there's one thing Treo hates it's loud bangs. He takes one look at all the chaos and bolts for his kennel: *I'm off; see you when all this madness is over.* The lads up on the roof start hammering away at the enemy. I throw on my body armour, grab my sawn-off SA80 and race up the stairs to join them.

I reach the roof to see it swathed in the blue-grey smoke of incoming RPG rounds, plus a curtain of burned cordite hanging thickly in the air. To our front, a hail of bullets is shredding leaves and branches as the enemy hit us with all they've got. Waves of screaming fighters come charging forwards, trying to rush the compound. It's like the Siege of the Alamo and Rorke's Drift rolled into one.

Within minutes I've belted off six mags from my Stumpy, and all the time I'm yelling: 'GET SOME FOR SASHA AND KEN!'

The barrel of my shortened weapon is smoking hot. I can't even touch it. There have been air strikes going in overhead, mortars slamming down, and the air's thick with the reek of battle.

There's a sudden lull in the firefight, and lads are running up and down the stairs, hauling fresh crates of ammo. I ask if anyone's got some spare rounds, so I can re-bomb my mags. All of a sudden we start laughing. We've just realised what we look like. We may appear to be battle-hardened warriors above the line of the wall, but below it we're still in our early morning shorts and flip-flops.

It's now that I remember Treo. In the heat of battle – and seeking bloody vengeance for Ken and Sasha – I've momentarily forgotten my dog. I race down the stone steps and crash through the door to our room. Treo's lying on my cot, his paws covering his ears and half obscuring his eyes.

I join him on the cot and gently take his paws away. 'OK, lad, all that noise you just heard, that was the bastard Taliban coming to have a right good go at us. So, you know, we gave them a right good going-over in return.'

He gazes up at me with two shining eyes. He's perked up at the sound of those words: *So, are you boys done with all of your bang-bang yet? Are you, Dad?*

'That's it, lad: all done for now.'

I take Treo out into his garden. We toss the ball around for a bit and play. He has a good roll in the grass, eats a few mouthfuls, and I give him a scratch on his tummy. The garden is bathed in early morning sunlight, and for a moment it strikes me as being quite lovely in this little, peaceful green oasis of ours.

The Rangers reckon the attack was a 'come on'. The enemy wanted to draw us out in hot pursuit, so they could steer us onto their hidden IEDs. Instead, we've stayed put and we've smashed them. Their fighters are busy gathering up the dead and wounded in the bush. We let them go about their grim business unmolested.

That evening Treo and I get recalled to the Sangin DC. We're to regroup with the Seven Platoon lads and prepare for a special mission together with Chavez's Marine Corps unit. Major

Shannon figures he's identified where the enemy have strung their IEDs around PB Armagh. I don't know where he's got the intel from – maybe he's recruited a hot informer – but he's got a map marked with twenty-three suspected points of IED-laying activity.

He's sending us out to those specific areas. We're either going to track down the bombs, or get torn to pieces looking for them. I head for our kennel, so I can explain to Treo exactly what's what. Steve and Reece are down at PB Armagh, so it's just the two of us again. I'm settling down to give Treo a briefing about the mission-from-hell, when we have a visitor. This one's very welcome, and I'm more than happy to stop what I'm doing and get the kettle on.

Caylie MacLean is the Seven Platoon medic. She's a fresh-faced brunette, and there's something very open and innocent about her features. I've seen her out on missions, and beneath her kindly exterior there's a core of hard steel. At first the Rangers kept asking this pretty young slip of a thing if she was all right whenever she was out on patrol. The only response she ever gave was: 'Course I am, lad, so shurrup asking.' That silenced those Ranger lads pretty damn fast.

Caylie hails from the Royal Army Medical Corps, so she's another bolt-on to the Rangers, just as Treo and I are. That's given us a special bond, one that's strengthened by her absolute love of my dog. Caylie's spent a good deal of time at the kennels, and being a lady's man Treo's warmed to her. I figure he senses that she's the one who's going to care for him, should anything truly horrible happen out there on patrol.

Handlers get given basic medical training, and I can treat many of the injuries Treo might suffer in the field. But I wouldn't want to have to deal with him suffering a life-threatening wound, especially not with my phobia of blood. In view of our coming nightmare mission, I ask Caylie the question that's at the forefront of my mind. If anything does happen to my dog, is she ready to put whatever she can into him, to try to save him?

'Dave, I'd do the same for Treo as I'd do for any other soldier,' she tells me. 'It goes without saying.'

'Sorry, love, I had to ask.'

We move out at first light. I give Treo the command and his nose starts going like a suction pump: *slurp, slurp, slurp*.

We've got Ranger Cupples acting as interpreter on this mission, because we're low on Afghan terps. One of ours has just turned out to be a closet Taliban, so we had to get rid of him pronto. It's proving difficult to recruit any replacements. Must be something to do with how the Taliban keep trying to murder them.

Over recent weeks I've noticed a change come over Ranger Cupples. We shared a room together for our last few days at PB Armagh, and Cupples just couldn't get enough of my dog. He was forever trying to feed him treats or cuddle him. Well, it takes Treo a good long while to let anyone but his dad give him his cuddles. Eventually, Treo would show he'd had enough. He'd turn on Cupples and let out his signature throaty growl. Cupples would jump back worriedly.

'Dave, your dog's growling at me,' he'd say.

'Well, don't bloody keep going near him then,' I'd tell him.

It became like a game, or a ritual between us: Cupples trying to pet Treo; Treo finally growling; Cupples jumping away from him. It always raised a laugh. But over time I noticed Cupples growing quieter and more withdrawn. I figured Afghanistan was getting to him.

Due to his role as interpreter, he spends more time than most conversing with the locals. I figure he's getting a real eyeful of the screwed-up nature of the war that we're fighting here. I figure maybe he's starting to see things from their perspective. Or maybe juggling his dual roles as radio operator and interpreter is proving all too much, and it's starting to fry his mind.

As Treo and I push ahead on the search, I give Cupples a friendly nod. 'You OK, lad?'

For a second his eyes meet mine, and there's a glazed and distant look in them. Then I see him pull himself back to the now.

'Yeah, Dave, I'm good . . . Oh, you know, you forgot to call me "sir".'

I fire back a few choice expletives – 'bloody Yank'; 'plastic Paddy' – and turn to focus on my dog. If Cupples is still working the wisecracks into me, I figure he's pretty much all right.

I check the map that Major Shannon's given me. He's marked up the foci of IED activity with a series of red dots. They cluster around PB Armagh on three sides: north, south and east. The western edge is believed to be pretty clear, because that's the way the Taliban use to move their IEDs. That route takes them north-wards towards Musa Qala – where Sean Cheetham is based with his black Labrador, Max – and on into Northern Helmand.

Treo and I turn a couple of corners and reach a narrow alleyway that threads between high mud-walls. I whistle him back to me and pause the patrol, so I can check the map again. We're west of Highway 611 and east of the River Helmand, in the narrow neck of territory that the Taliban claim as their own. The route ahead leads into an area that's marked up with five nasty red dots – IED blotches. This is Ground Zero for the bombing teams here in Sangin.

I study the alleyway that lies before us. It's a deserted length of sun-baked dirt with piles of leaves and rubble to either side. *Thu-thud; thu-thud; thu-thud.* My pulse thumps in my ears. The silence here is so deep and so residing, it's like the very air itself is holding its breath.

I feel a wet nose nuzzling my hand. It's Treo, and he's at my side, his stump wagging away and eager to sniff out the bombs. There's nothing obvious here that screams out violence and danger, but I've got a real bad feeling about this one. I've felt fear every day that we've led these patrols. It's been my constant mocking companion: *is this the day you're going to die?* But today feels different. Today the terror has me gripped in its vice-like grasp as never before.

I gaze down the alleyway that leads into IED Hell and I force the words out: 'Seek on, boy . . .' But they come out as a half-strangled whisper, from a throat that's bone-dry with fear.

Treo flashes me a momentary look: *Come on, Dad, we can do this. I can find them.*

Then he's off. He drops his muzzle low to the ground, and he's hoovering up the scent just inches off the dirt. His stumpy tail pokes out behind him, twitching away, and keeping time as his head sweeps this way and that: *Here I am, on the search, and I'm loving it.*

Treo's entire focus is on the air that he's channelling through his muzzle now. He's moving through a world defined by the molecules all around him. He lifts his head only now and then to check where he is, and that he's not about to blunder into something. He's happy that we're out on the search, which means a chance of earning his reward – playtime. But as for me, I'm shitting myself.

We're a third of the way down the alley, and we're moving along a narrow path with a mud wall to one side. Halfway down it I notice a break in the wall. It looks as if some stones have been removed to give access to the far side. I'm hyper-alert, and my threat radar is working overtime. I'm trying to figure out what lies beyond that gap, along with the countless other threats that I'm scanning the terrain for.

Treo's ahead of me, off-leash. Every time he places a paw on the baking-hot earth, I'm tensing for a blast. I see him pause before the gap in the wall. I see his nostrils widen, and suddenly he's sucking in great lungfuls of air. He turns his head to left and right, sampling the scent, until his nose is pressed up tight against the warm mud of the wall. On the other side is a telegraph pole, and Treo's got his black snout pointing directly at it.

'Careful, lad, careful. Easy does it now,' I'm muttering. I can feel my pulse hammering away like a machine gun. 'What d'you think it is you've got there?'

Treo glances back at me, then moves ahead a foot or so until he's level with the gap. His head snaps around until he's staring right through it. He pokes his snout and half his neck through, and his entire torso goes rigid. I can sense that he's staring at the base of that telegraph pole.

He flicks his head around and gives me a quick, intense, piercing look: *Bloody hell, Dad, best you get here and check this out.*

With that he leaps through the gap in the wall and he's gone. The smell of whatever it is he's found here has drawn him irresistibly towards it. In his eagerness and impatience he's charged ahead to show me – which means he's more than likely standing right on top of whatever it is that he's found.

I'm totally freaking out. I fly down the path screaming my head off at him: 'NOOOOOOOOO!'

I vault over the wall, lunge, grab his collar with the one hand and haul him back towards me. With the other I reach for the base of the telegraph pole. I've got to be certain. There's an old plastic sack lying there. I tug it aside. Beneath it, half buried in the dirt, is a blue plastic box with wires sticking out of it in all directions.

Time seems to slow to nothing. I feel my blood run cold.

Oh shit! Oh no, no, no, no! You bastards! You got us!

It's an RC device – a radio-controlled IED. Somewhere nearby there's a Taliban with a firing mechanism watching us. Right now he's thinking: *Yes! I've got them! I've got the black dog!*

I lift Treo with both hands, and together I throw the both of us back over the wall.

As we hit the deck I'm yelling: 'RC DEVICE! RC DEVICE! GET THE HELL OUT OF HERE!'

An instant later I'm on my feet pounding up the path, Treo tucked under my arm like a parcel. At any moment I'm expecting to get blown off my feet, and for the lights to go out once and for all. I swing Treo around until he's held in front of me, to shield him from the blast, which will rip up the alleyway like a tornado of fire and steel. I can feel the tension in my back knifing in between my shoulder blades as I tense myself for the devastating explosion.

But nothing comes.

I saw one big chunk of explosives lying at the base of that telegraph pole, and that alone was enough to blow Treo and me, plus any number of the Ranger lads, to kingdom come. But somehow we reach the forwardmost Rangers still very much alive. I don't know how the hell we've managed it. Maybe the device malfunctioned. Maybe the watcher had gone to take a pee. Maybe our ECM kit managed to jam the signal.

We pull everyone back. We go firm in a compound a safe distance away, and Speedy asks me what we found. I ask him for a few seconds to get my breath back and my pulse under control, for my heart's going like it's about to burst.

I draw a rough diagram. It's easier than trying to talk. I do the best I can with the scribble, my hands shaking as they are. As for Treo, he gets his nose right on the page, and he keeps kind of nodding: *Yep, you got it. That's exactly what I found.*

Our first priority is to close off the area, so the enemy can't come in and remove the bomb from under our noses. If they do, they can reset the IED somewhere else and have a second go. The Rangers throw a cordon around the bomb site, which means no one's allowed through. We've got Chavez and his bomb-disposal guys with us on this patrol, and right away they're readying themselves to move forward and defuse whatever it is we've found here.

Chavez takes a good long look at my scribbled diagram. He lets out a low whistle. 'Forget trying to dig this one out and decipher it. Screw that. Let's blow it.'

He grabs a pair of tinsnips, calls for his men to follow him, and they're off. The man's a true hero and a legend.

With Chavez and his EOD lot away doing their stuff, Treo finds a patch of soft grass to one side of the compound. It reminds me of the little oasis we declared 'Treo turf' down at PB Armagh. My dog loves munching on the fresh, sweet grass and I can afford to give him a good play with his ball.

I figure he deserves it. In fact, I don't know the half of it.

Right now, my dog deserves the biggest well done of his entire life.

CHAPTER TWENTY-THREE

Forty minutes later Chavez is back with us. He stares at Treo and me in silence for several seconds. 'Man, you're the luckiest dog team alive.'

'Why's that, Master-Sergeant?' I ask.

Chavez explains that what we'd found was a radio-controlled IED linked to five separate charges – more commonly known as a 'daisy-chain'. There are five individual bombs dug into the earth, linked together by detonation wire. The telegraph pole was the watcher's marker: once they saw us reach that point, they would have tried to set off the entire chain of explosives.

Two hundred metres to the east of us is a tower. It's either a mosque or a fortification set at the corner of a compound. Chavez figures that's the vantage point from where the watchers were waiting to trigger the daisy-chain. He can only think that our ECM kit managed to scramble the signal.

As for me, I reckon it's Treo's shamrock: I'm convinced that lady luck played a big part in keeping us alive today.

Chavez has found a path through the cornfield leading to the tower. That's the way the Taliban came in to plant the daisy-chain, and that's how they've been able to keep a check on it.

The buried charges are a mixture of 82 mm mortar rounds, plus some monster 105 mm howitzer shells, any number of which they've more than likely scavenged off British forces. How many men would have been taken out if that lot had blown, God only knows, not to mention one man and his shaggy black dog.

Chavez tells me that when I went through the gap in the wall to rescue Treo, I actually trod with my big British army boot on top of one of the charges. I was standing on it whilst I reached down and pulled the sack aside. If the enemy had triggered it then, all that would have been left of Treo and me would be a fine pink mist drifting on the air.

Chavez and his team have dug out the earth beneath the charges, and laid detonators below each. He's ready to blow the entire lot sky high. We're sitting there in the garden of that compound when he announces in his deep-chested American accent: 'Fire in the hole, guys!'

It's like we're on a film set, and it's one of the funniest of moments. It breaks the tension completely. We count five big explosions: *Boom! Boom! Boom! Boom! Boom!*

Chavez returns to the scene, just to ensure he got them all. I'm left sitting in the garden with my eyes on Treo, sharing this unique moment between us. My dog and I are experiencing the incredible high of having stood on top of a daisy-chain IED, yet somehow having cheated death yet again.

I can't explain how, but I know instinctively that Treo gets it. Whilst he knows this is a game, at the same time he knows how horribly, deadly serious it can get. This is life and death that we're toying with here, and Treo knows it just as well as if he's understood every word that Chavez has told us.

Word spreads as to the nature of the find. The Rangers gather. They are ecstatic, and the problem now is keeping Treo's feet on the ground. He knows he's the big I Am. He's strutting around on the grass: *Look at me. I'm the one who found it.* Usually, he's pretty much aloof from everyone. Now he's rolling on his back and letting them stroke, scratch and rub him: *Yeah, come on, love my belly! I'm the unbeatable bomb-sniffing dog!*

Once Chavez is done, Speedy gets us to move out. I pull out the ball from my pocket and show it to Treo. I make as if to throw it down the path ahead of us: 'Seek on, boy, seek on.'

Instantly, he's forgotten his audience and he's off on the search. We press onwards, passing the point where the IED was planted. I say a quick prayer: *Thank you for delivering me and my dog, plus the Rangers, from this evil.*

The message 'DOG FIND' has been cabled back to the Sangin HQ. By the time we're back at base everyone knows what Treo's found. During the debrief that evening, Major Shannon gives Treo and me a big 'well done'. I have to admit I lap it up. I'm ecstatic. I feel as if one man and his dog were put together five years ago for a very specific reason. We are the team. This is our *raison d'être*. Here in Sangin, we're living it.

That evening the Ranger lads rustle up the biggest bone that I've ever seen from the cookhouse. It's a bone fit for a hero, jokes Ranger Cupples. He holds it out gingerly, and Treo grabs it in his jaws and drags it into his kennel. I just know he's going to keep me awake half the night gnawing on it. Still, I figure he's earned it. I have never felt quite so proud of my boy, my dog.

Major Shannon has built up detailed intel on some ninety IEDs and mines that have been strung around the base in the past weeks, to encircle and entrap it. Treo and I have unearthed a good number of them, but scores more have been detonated by hapless Afghan civilians. Yet at least we've not lost a single British soldier on our watch.

The major declares a two-day period of rest and recuperation. It's much-needed time to unwind. It's a chance for Treo to do exactly as he wants, him being off the relentless treadmill of the search. He can give his nose some down time and rest his senses. It's time for him just to be a dog.

As for me, I lounge around the kennel in shorts and flip-flops and catch up on writing some letters home. I chew the fat with the Ranger lads, take a few souvenir photos, and generally try to feel a little more human. But more than anything else, I'm just savouring the pure joy of being alive.

I reflect upon the last twenty-four hours and what we've learned. I reckon Treo and I are going to hunt for the IEDs with an added hunger now. What's driving that hunger is coming face-to-face with the lethal power of that daisy-chain IED. You can think you know something. You can think you understand it. But there's nothing like coming face-to-face with the murderous evil of such a device to really sharpen your hunger to beat the bomb makers.

It's now that we get paid an unexpected visit down at the kennels. This rufty-tufty group of Special Forces types comes in from a desert operation. There's an American and an Aussie dog handler embedded within their unit, and they naturally gravitate to Treo and me.

Brad, the American handler, has a solid-looking German shepherd, but it's the Aussie handler, Jim, whose dog really grabs my attention. He's a beautiful brindled (mixed black and brown) Belgian Malinois – what we handlers call a 'Mal' for short. The Malinois looks like a slightly smaller, but more solid and powerful version of a German shepherd.

We take the dogs to give them a good swim in the river. Treo teaches the shepherd and the Mal the belly-flop-from-the-bridge trick, and soon they're best of friends. That done, I ask the guys if they'd like to do some joint training. I've got a number of hides set up around the base – piles of scrap metal or discarded building materials, within which I've hidden tiny amounts of explosives. If Treo and I come in off patrol and he's not found anything, I send him to search a few of those, so he gets a find and his reward.

We head out as three man-and-dog teams – a Brit, an Aussie and a Yank – and there's a healthy spirit of competition. I watch the guys do their searches, but right from the start they're doing everything on-leash. I ask them why they don't let their dogs run free, so as to give them their head. I figure keeping them leashed the whole time inhibits the dogs, which lessens their ability to search.

To better demonstrate what I mean I show them Treo at work. He wanders off on his own and plonks his butt down at find number one. Brad and Jim are transfixed as they watch my dog move from point to point – tracking the scent, and pinning it to source. I've put some really challenging hides out, to truly test him, but it's almost as if he doesn't need his handler, he's that good at what he does.

'Do me a favour, guys,' I tell them. 'Let's run through this again, but this time do it with your dogs off-leash.'

'Well, you know, we'd love to,' Brad remarks. 'But we're not allowed to unclip our dogs.'

He goes on to explain what I already suspect – that their animals are joint Search- and Patrol-trained. That means they're trained to find arms and explosives, but also to chase, bring down and hold a suspect. On one level that's good. It means you can go out on patrol and use your dog both to find the bombs and to apprehend a fleeing enemy. But it also means your dog's not free to follow his nose and his intuition when on the search.

'Listen, guys, you're in a safe area,' I tell them. 'This is off-limits, 'cause it's known as Treo's turf. You risk nothing by letting them off-leash here.'

With that the guys seem convinced. First Brad's shepherd and then Jim's Mal are sent around the search course. Initially, both dogs seem a little unsure of themselves, without the feel of their handler on their shoulder and at the end of the leash. But it doesn't take long for each dog to find his confidence, and to sniff out the hidden devices completely independently.

The exercise done, Brad and Jim have to set off on another mission. Before leaving, they thank me for the training. Doing search work off-leash is a whole new experience, and they're amazed that their dogs did so well. They could see how they ranged more freely and searched more rapidly, which would speed up the progress of a patrol, so making it less of a target. They figure they've learned some useful lessons, ones that they'll take back to their home K9 units.

In the British K9 world we don't dual-train our dogs. A search dog like Treo will only ever be a search dog. That way, it leaves him free to achieve his best. Here in Sangin, the results speak for themselves. I think we've got it right, and I wouldn't want it any other way.

Our two days' down time fly by, after which Treo and I are constantly out on patrols. We try to avoid obvious chokepoints and target areas. We go over walls and along rooftops. We carry the scaling ladders everywhere, and I'm forever humping Treo onto my shoulders, or carrying him one-handed over obstacles.

At times I'm going 'Bup! Bup! Bup!' when I need him to jump something. He's looking at me as if he's saying: *What? What you talking about, Dad, I can't make that.*

'Course you can,' I tell him. 'Good boy. Get over, you're all right.'

When he's jumped and made it, his whole backside wiggles happily in time to the wagging of his stumpy tail.

By now my dog and I are dictating the pace, the route and the progress of just about every patrol. The myth of Treo's abilities has spread far and wide. I can see this incredible trust and confidence written large on the faces of the Rangers: *As long as the dog's in front of us, we're OK. Go on, Treo, sniff it out.*

We range further afield in the hunt for IEDs. We search around the two, outlier bases to Sangin – PB Suffolk to the south, and PB Tangiers to the north. The days pass and this is what we're here for. It's the meaning of our lives. But with each search the fear escalates.

In an effort to vary our route and fox the IED-laying teams, we start using these rickety crossing points that snake across the Helmand River. The more my fear worsens, the more Treo's confidence seems to grow. He starts running over those makeshift bridges and diving into the Helmand River, just for the sheer wild doggy craziness of it all.

I'm screaming at him: 'GET HERE! GET HERE! NOW!'

He's swept hundreds of metres downstream, and I'm about to dive in and grab him when he clambers out and comes bounding back to me, a huge grin on his bedraggled features. He skids to a halt right at my feet and I just know what's coming. Sure enough, he does the biggest doggy shake you've ever seen, and in an instant I'm engulfed in a Treo-shower.

In Afghanistan, my dog has developed this uncanny ability to keep getting me wet. If he's not pulling me into a river, or forcing me to go in and pull him out, he's jumping off a bridge and coming to shake his wet coat all over his dad. It's a good thing it's so unbearably hot here, and that I can always do with a good dousing down.

I know I've got to let my dog be a dog. I know he just wants the chance to cool off and to play. But every second he's out of my sight being swept down a river I've got this terror gripping me that the Taliban will grab my dog and mess him up badly.

I don't want to rein Treo in too much, or he'll lose his eagerness to work. But at the same time I've got to get him to work at a pace that we can use, and a safe one. I clip him onto his long paracord lead, and decide to keep him like that for a while.

He gives me a knowing look, one tinged with a smattering of remorse: *It's OK, you're the man and I'm the dog. I know that. I'll wind my neck in* . . . I do need Treo to wind himself in. I need him to let me lead, and to work with me to the max, for we've only got a few weeks left before we'll be out of here, and we have to make sure we bring all the lads home alive.

My dog and I develop a new trigger technique – the trigger that signifies to Treo that he's on the search. Before now the trigger has always been when he sees me pull out his harness. I'd remove his collar, strap the harness onto him, and then he'd know for sure: *I'm on the search.*

But as we up the tempo of operations, I don't have time for that any more. By the time I've done the stop-collar-off-harness-on thing, the enemy may have pinged us and opened fire, or snuck in behind us and planted a bomb. Instead, I start him off in his harness from base. But I can't have him always thinking he's searching, or he'll exhaust himself – so the new trigger is when I remove his collar.

Prior to that he's on standby. Collar removed: he's working.

It isn't so much a process of teaching Treo, as learning on the job. He notices me releasing his collar, and at the same time giving him the seek on command. It doesn't take long for him to realise: *Aha! That's the trigger. It's when you take the collar off, not the harness going on, isn't it, Dad?*

There's another, crucial reason why I want him in-harness from the start of patrols. I've realised how reassuring it is for the Ranger lads. They've become so tuned in to how my dog and I work, that they've figured out that in-harness means search mode. Conversely, out of harness means the opposite, and if they see Treo like that it ups their anxiety levels.

With this new trigger system, I can keep the guys fully reassured, whilst still not having Treo constantly on the search, which would finish him. And as luck would have it, having my dog in-harness the whole time is going to prove the saving of him – although I don't know that yet.

Reports come in to base that one of the Afghan National Army soldiers has been assassinated. For some unknowable reason he

Searching inside the dark confines of a building was always a nerve-wracking experience, for both me and my dog.

Fellow handler Marianne Hay and her dog, Leanna, out on patrol with me and Treo.

A well-earned rest. After months spent searching for the bombs you get the 'thousand-yard stare' in your eyes.

The local kids loved my dog. As 80 per cent of IEDs killed innocent Afghan villagers, we were there protecting them as much as we were our fellow soldiers.

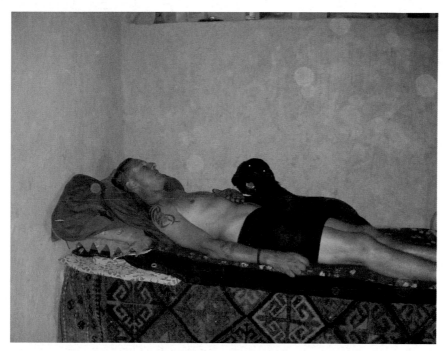

Treo kept a watch over me as I slept. More often than not we'd bed down together, especially when overnighting on operations.

Sometimes I could tell he needed his dad as much as I needed him. A good cuddle and a chat, and he'd be raring to go again.

7 Platoon, Ranger Company. I was proud to serve with these lads. I'm standing in the second row, second from right. Kneeling third from left is EBEX operator Davy Miller. Standing first on left is the platoon Sergeant Trevor 'Speedy' Coult, and third from left (with antennae) is Ranger Justin Cupples.

Treo caught red-handed. He's with two of our medics, but they don't seem too bothered that some poor sod is walking about the base with only one shoe.

Treo and me with some of the Rangers. As per usual, Treo looks very chilled out.

Dogs of war. Treo shooting a jealous look at the ball the beautiful Malinois, who arrived with Aussie handler Jim, is holding in his gob. Looking on is American dog handler, Brad.

The heat in Afghanistan could really take its toll on both man and dog. There was nothing Treo liked more than sploshing around in water whenever he got the chance. Trouble was, whenever we went static like this the enemy tended to drop mortars on us or shoot at us, for they knew 'the black dog' was defeating their bombing teams.

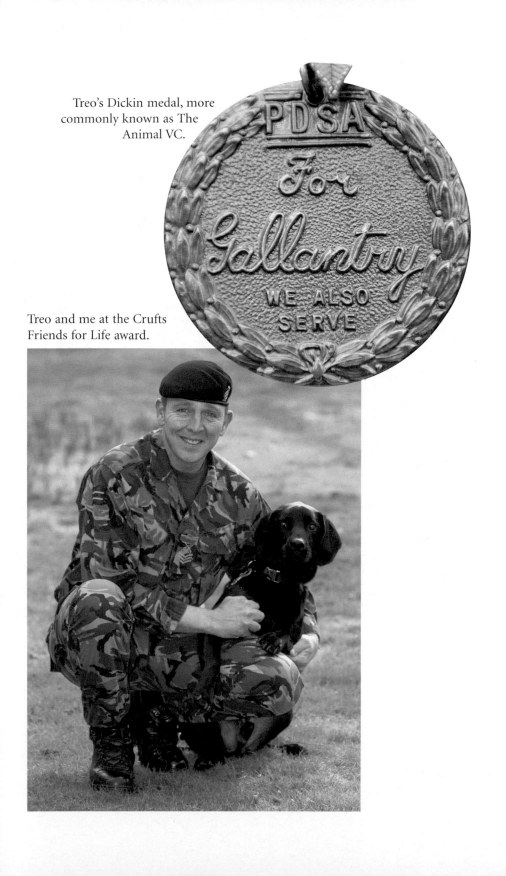

Treo's Dickin medal, more commonly known as The Animal VC.

Treo and me at the Crufts Friends for Life award.

Back home, today. Treo and me retired out of the Army together, so we were never parted.

thought it was a good idea to wander through the marketplace in full uniform. He didn't get very far. Almost immediately afterwards, a second ANA soldier is killed. He was manning one of their observation towers overlooking the town. Unbeknown to him the Taliban had managed to plant an IED in there.

Boom.

As a result, the ANA refuse to go out on ops around town, and they won't man their observation posts any more. Major Shannon calls me in and asks if I'll go and search their watchtowers, so he can declare them safe. I tell him that I'll do just the one, as a demonstration that they've not all been rigged with IEDs. The major seems to think that's good enough, so I ready Treo to do just the one search.

We head out in our new search mode, with Treo in his harness from the very start; I'll only remove his collar when we're up in the tower. We make our way down to the ANA position with an escort of redoubtable Rangers in support. We reach the location of the watchtower and stop before it, assessing how best to do this.

The watchtower is built from wooden struts and sandbags, and it sits on the roof of an existing building. There are two possible routes up to it. One involves going up a long and rickety-looking ladder. It's a no-no for Treo. The other involves climbing along the apex of a wall for a good twenty metres or so. That's much more my dog's thing. It's been raining, so it's a little slippery, but it should present no real problem for four paws and claws.

I lift Treo onto my shoulder, but I'm still not able to get him up onto the wall. I take a couple of steps up the ladder, which is juddering under our combined weight, reach across and plonk Treo onto the wall. He scrabbles with his paws, and then he's up there looking confident and standing tall. The wall goes up at approaching a forty-five-degree angle, but Treo's always been good with heights. I figure he'll do just fine.

I continue up the ladder as my dog scrabbles his way up the wall beside me. I glance down, and we've got a thin line of Rangers spread out all around us. I hope no one's getting through that to have a go at my dog. I turn back to the task in hand but just as I do so I hear a faint yelp and Treo's gone. He's fallen off the wall and disappeared down the far side.

This is the nightmare scenario. Whilst the fall won't have been enough to kill him, it sure as hell may have injured him. He could have broken a limb if he's landed badly, and that'll be the end of Treo and Afghanistan. But worst of all, if there are any Taliban watching – and they're sure as hell to be out there, eyes on the black dog – now is the moment to move in and seize him.

I pound my way upwards, the ladder bucking and bouncing horribly, and I grab hold of the top of the wall. As I haul myself onto the apex I'm dreading what I'm going to find on the far side. But as I peer over, just a few feet below me I see Treo, somehow suspended in mid-air. For a moment I can't believe it. I stare at him in utter astonishment.

He's dangling from his leash where it's caught on a nail in the wall.

He stares back at me, irritably: *Get me the hell out of here, won't you!*

I lean down and grab the leash. My dog is swaying gently backwards and forwards, and for a split second I leave him to swing like a pendulum. Treo glares up at me. He knows exactly what I'm doing. He knows I'm taking the mickey out of him, and he can see the laughter in my eyes.

The longer I tease him, the more annoyed he gets. *Bloody get me out of here! Pull me up, Dad! I am not some conker on the end of a string.*

I swing him back and forth a little, and I'm laughing at him openly. My dog is not impressed. He's just suffered a serious loss of cool, and I'm making it worse. He scowls: *You just wait until I get up there!*

As I start to haul him in a thought hits me. If Treo hadn't been in his harness he'd have taken the fall wearing only his collar, and that would have strangled him. I'm aware that the harness may have just saved my dog's life.

I get him onto the wall and check him over. He seems just fine. 'OK, big fella, you're good to go. Let's leave all of that alone now, and do what we've come here to do . . .'

But my dog's still in a temper with me. There's no bigger sin in Treo's book than laughing at him, especially when he's just suffered a major loss of face. I do my best to apologise, but he can tell that I don't really mean it. I can't help sniggering. As we move ahead towards the watchtower, he has a nip at my ankles. It's his way of getting some payback on his dad.

We check the watchtower for devices and it's perfectly clear. We radio in the result and the message comes back that the ANA commander on base is 'very pleased' with Treo. Whilst the ANA lot resent Treo's very presence here – it's something to do with dogs being 'dirty' in their eyes – they love him to death when he's out safeguarding their lives.

Major Shannon tells me the ANA commander wants Treo and me to check every watchtower. I tell the major that we are most definitely done with it. Had the ANA shown just the slightest respect for my dog, we might have done the searches for them. I don't expect everyone to love my dog. Not everyone has to be a dog lover. But if you expect him to put his life on the line for you, show a little decency and thanks.

We get back to base and head for the kennel. I remove Treo's harness and for a moment I pause. I caress the tough, coarse material of the thing. It's an unremarkable black canvas frame, one that straps under his neck, chest, and around his back in a wrap-around rig.

And it's that mundane piece of kit that has saved my dog today.

CHAPTER TWENTY-FOUR

We're five months into Sangin with just a few weeks before we leave. Treo and I up the workload still further, for we're desperate to keep one step ahead of the bomb makers. If we're not eating or sleeping, or grabbing some rare Treo playtime, we're out pounding the streets and alleys and pathways.

We get called out to search the Rat Run, a maze of narrow paths and compounds just to the south-east of PB Suffolk. British forces rarely go into the Rat Run, for it's a horrendous tangle of chokepoints, blind corners and shadowy dead ends.

We head in there and start clearing compounds, and Treo sniffs out some weaponry almost immediately. Arms finds are so commonplace these days they hardly merit a mention. But there's this one piece that grabs my attention. It looks like some kind of mean Taliban sniper rifle. It strikes me as being the ideal gun with which to shoot and kill a black search dog from several hundred metres away. I'm happy to see it go into the bag with all the rest of the weaponry.

We're out of that compound and clearing a road when we see a white sedan crawling towards us down a narrow road. The driver's acting suspiciously so we decide to stop and search it.

The occupants refuse to get out – that's until I put Treo through the vehicle. My dog goes in one door, and the driver and passengers bail out the others.

We find nothing of interest, but we figure they've been briefed to slow us down so the enemy can hit us. We're on tenterhooks. There's a motorbike chugging along behind the car. We make the guy stop a long way ahead of us. We order him to lift his robes so we can check for explosive belts. There's nothing visible, but I decide to get Treo to give him and his bike the once-over.

My dog starts going crazy around the saddle area. He's sniffing and pawing all over it, and he's got this mad excitement burning in his eyes. My mind flips back to the suicide bomber, the one who blew up my dog but forgot to pack his shrapnel. The next moment I'm convinced that's what Treo's onto here.

I reckon the biker hasn't got a suicide belt visible, because the charge is packed under his saddle and poised to blow his nuts off. If it does, it'll take my black dog with them, and probably the rest of us as well.

I start yelling for Treo to get away. 'GET BACK HERE! NOW! NOOOOOOW!'

My dog turns, glances calmly over his shoulder and shakes his head at me. He's got this look of absolute certainty in his eyes, one that silences me right away. *It's not that, Dad. It's not explosives. No one's about to blow up your dog. But come and see – there's something really weird in here.*

I move forward, my Stubby in the aim. I order the biker off his motorcycle. I see him flip out the stand reluctantly and step a pace away from his machine. I wave the muzzle of my SA80 at him, making it clear I want him further back. Under the threat of being shot he takes a few sullen paces to one side.

I reach out and flip open the motorbike's saddle. The space underneath is crammed full of small brown blocks, each of which is wrapped in cellophane. I know it can't be a bomb, because there are no wires visible, and the thing's not packed full of shrapnel. I know the bike itself if blown up would turn into lots of nasty metal projectiles, but an explosion at saddle level would force the shrapnel into the ground, and so it wouldn't be much use as a bomb.

I take one of the brown blocks and raise it to my nose. No wonder Treo was going wild. The scent is pungent and heady and intoxicating, and like nothing I've ever smelled before. I'm sure Treo hasn't either. I know instinctively what it is: opium. The biker must be one of the Taliban's drugs runners, and I figure the car out front was to decoy us away from the opium package.

Treo's not trained to find narcotics, but the smell was just so exotic and overpowering that he had to tell me about it. We take the biker prisoner, and confiscate his haul of dope. Back at PB Suffolk we deliver a pile of confiscated weaponry – including the sniper rifle – plus the opium stash into the base commander's hands. He seems amazed at what Treo's managed to winkle out from just a couple of hours within the Rat Run.

'Hey, if we need you up here again, will you come?' he asks me.

'Sir, that's what we're here for.'

We're in late from searching the Rat Run, and I'm warned off that we're needed for a mission at first light the following morning. At least we'll get a few hours' uninterrupted sleep, or so I hope.

But that night I have a horrendous dream. I wake bolt upright and drenched in sweat. I'm physically shaking and I know I've been screaming out in the depths of my slumber. I can hear Treo whimpering and whining from his kennel, for he's heard his dad thrashing about madly and yelling. He's beside himself with worry. He knows it's the middle of the night and that something bad is happening, and that he can't get out to protect me.

I pad over to his door and I go to unlatch his cage. As I do so, the images from my dream come crowding in, like freeze-frames from a movie beaming across my subconscious at warp speed. I see a device; then a whole string of them; I see they're strung together with electrical wire, and that it's wrapped around someone's neck. The image zooms out and I see that the neck belongs to a body, and the body is that of Dave Heyhoe.

The images are dark and frightening, and they freak me out completely. I grab Treo and pull him in towards me. He jumps up into my arms and I can tell that he's overjoyed to see that I'm OK. But am I OK? Or am I starting to lose it? In truth, I really don't know. That dream keeps taunting me. The images just won't go away. I feel fear. Fear of sleep. Fear of returning to the nightmare.

I wonder what it means.

Is it a premonition? Have I seen the future? One thing I know for sure: that necklace-string of charges is like nothing I've ever seen out here before.

We set out at first light. We're joining Lieutenant Wilcock's Eight Platoon, the guy who took a while to get to really dig my dog. Now, he's a total Treo convert. He just can't get enough of my boy. We're heading to an area about a kilometre to the west of us. Major Shannon's pinged it as a focus of intense activity and we're going to investigate just what has been going on out there.

We leave early-doors by Gate Three, a little-used exit that takes us due west. We've picked a route that weaves through high reed-beds, in an effort to hide our approach from any would-be watchers. The reeds are so tall that they'll prevent me from being able to see my dog, so I've got him on his paracord leash, like an umbilical cord. That way, I shouldn't lose him.

Trouble is, my dog goes one way and I go the other, and suddenly we're wrapped around this big plug of reeds. I can't set him free, for I just know that I'll lose him. I have no choice but to reconcile myself to making painfully slow progress, and to tying the patrol in knots half the time.

We push ahead at a dead slow for hours on end. Occasionally, we come across a farmer. Or maybe he's a Taliban. There's no telling. We stop and ask each in turn if he's seen anything suspicious? Any strangers around recently? Any foreigners? By 'foreigners' we mean Pakistanis, Iranians or Arabs – the non-Afghan jihadis who've come to join the fighting here in an effort to kill a Brit or an American.

We ask if they've seen anyone digging holes in paths or burying anything suspicious. The answers we get are monosyllabic and evasive. That's obvious, even for those like me who can't speak the language. For Ranger Cupples, who's tasked with doing the translations today, it's another face-to-face lesson in how much they seem to hate us, or at least to not want us here.

It's mid-afternoon and we're heading down a path that loops back towards the base. There's a tributary of the Helmand River on one side, and thick verdant reed beds on the other. The terrain is a maze of pathways but they all seem to converge on this one place, where there's a rickety crossing over the river.

Acting on a whim, I send Treo ahead of me to check out that river crossing. You never know, we may want to use it in the near future, so no harm checking that it's clear. He's approaching the crossing where there's a high wall on his right-hand side. As he nears the wall, he starts to air up big time. I've rarely seen such a massive change of behaviour in my dog.

I've got my eyes glued to him as I hurry forward to get a better view of things. Treo checks step, doing a little foot-dance as he turns around himself, his whole body being led by his nose, and then he's edging steadily forwards, nostrils flaring noisily. All of a sudden he stops, then starts pawing madly at the earth.

I whistle him back to me, but I see a real reluctance in my dog as he turns to leave whatever it is that he's found. I call the patrol to a halt. Davey goes forward with his EBEX machine. There's a faint muffled bleep, but Davey's not so sure that it means anything. It's not a strong respond, so it may in fact be a false one.

I send Treo forward again, and again he's absolutely certain. But this time when I try to whistle him back to me he flatly refuses to come. Instead, he starts to dig. There's dirt and shit flying from his front paws. He's like a dog possessed.

I lose it. I'm yelling at him: 'OY! TREO! NO! Leave it! Leave it! LEAVE IT!'

But my dog just can't seem to pull away.

As I scream for him to come to me, I've got this dark image crashing through my head like some unwelcome nightmare.

Then I realise what it is: *it* is *the nightmare*. It's the dream that I had the night before that so freaked me out. It's come back to haunt my waking hours. It's that string of bombs, wrapped around my throat like some necklace from hell.

Treo can't help himself. He knows what it is that he's found here. The draw of that killer device is so strong, he just can't leave it alone. *Can't stop digging. Got to find it. Got to stop it from killing my dad.*

I charge forwards, grab him by his harness and haul him up into the air, turn on my heel and I'm gone. I'm sprinting back up the path and away from death like I've got the Grim Reaper himself right on my tail. I barrel past the Rangers, screaming for them to get out of there before it blows.

When finally I stop and let Treo down, I'm hyperventilating. The breaths just won't seem to come. My throat's rasping as I try to find some words for my dog. I don't want to admonish him. I don't want to punish him. I want to give him all the praise that I have, for I know in my heart that he's just saved my life – our lives – all over.

The call goes out for Master Sergeant Chavez and his team to join us. It's then that all hell breaks loose.

There's a violent burst of orange-yellow from out of the woodland to the east of us. It's like a mortar flash, only horizontal, and it's aimed right at our position. It's followed instantly by another, the flame of the second weapon lighting up the billowing cloud of exhaust smoke hanging beneath the trees.

Two black arrows, each the size and shape of a Coke bottle on its side, power their way towards us, trailing flame in their wake. One seems aimed at Treo's head, the other at mine. My dog and I dive for cover at the same moment. As we hit the dirt, the two warheads scream through the air where we've just been standing and detonate against a compound wall, showering us in blasted chunks of mud and dirt.

The exhaust from the RPG's sustainer motors envelops us in a choking grey-brown fog. Those RPGs are the signal for the main attack. The bush all around us erupts in a volcano of tracer fire. It ripples towards our position until the air itself seems awash with flame.

Just to the front of where we've taken cover I see rounds sparking and ricocheting off the path that Treo and I walked. The enemy gunners have their weapons zeroed in there, and they're hosing it down with a murderous rate of fire. I've no idea where they've all appeared from, because this place was pretty near deserted when first we came through. This is a well-coordinated, concerted attack, and it would be terrifying if we weren't so used to this kind of thing by now.

We've been whacked so many times that somehow the rounds and the rockets smashing into the walls all around us almost don't seem real any more. I see Rangers getting up and strolling over to take up a better firing position, as if they are bulletproof or something. This has kind of become the new normal for us by now.

With calm, almost surreal, professionalism and aggression we beat off the attack. The enemy melts back into the surrounding bush. I'm convinced I know why they hit us, and with such sustained ferocity. They've been watching, and they realised what my dog's onto. They were trying to drive us away from his find, so as to prevent us from lifting whatever it is that's buried there.

I'm certain this is the case – as certain as I've ever been about anything.

The bulky figure of Chavez arrives with his marines in tow. He asks me what we've got. I describe to him the route we walked in on, which should be clear, for Treo's just been across it.

'You follow that route, it'll take you to this half-dug hole. That's where whatever it is is.'

Chavez raises one eyebrow. 'You guys tried to dig it out?'

I shake my head. 'Not me. Treo. I've never seen my dog like it before. Whatever it is, he was going crazy down there. I've got a bad feeling about this one, Master Sergeant. Be bloody careful.'

Chavez grins. 'Man, Careful is my middle name. Soon be time for fire in the hole!'

I smile. I love those words. Each time Chavez says them, it marks another victory for us over the Taliban's bomb makers.

Chavez is gone for a good long time, longer than I've ever known it. Half an hour becomes an hour, and still he's not back. I'm tempted to creep forward to have a peek. Instead, I spend my time talking to and playing with my dog.

It's a good ninety minutes before the Master Sergeant clambers his way up the track. He's looking totally exhausted, finished. He plonks his butt next to mine in a cloud of dust, his back to the wall that my dog and I are leaning against. He swivels his head around and his eyes meet my gaze. They're red-raw from staring into whatever evil it is that he's unearthed.

'Man . . .' Chavez shakes his head. 'You ain't gonna believe this, 'cause neither the hell do I.'

'What? What is it, mate?'

I'm trying to stop the images from the nightmare crashing

through my head. I know what it is that Chavez has found here, but it's just so freaking spooky I don't want to go there.

'Never seen nothing like it,' Chavez murmurs. 'I dug where Treo the super-hound dug, and sure enough I found the first charge. I felt around and found some wires heading off to either side. I traced those to another couple of charges. So I thought to myself: daisy-chain.'

'How many charges?'

'I traced six. Laid in a ring, connected with electrical wire in a circuit. Daisy-chain, right?'

'Sounds like a daisy-chain to me.'

'Right. I'm just about to snip the wire when something makes me pause. I think: *Hold on, where's the trigger device and the RC unit?* I've found the two six-volt batteries that give power to the thing, but I can't seem to find the trigger set-up. I check again, all around the freaking chain, but there isn't one.'

Chavez pauses, wiping a grimy hand across his forehead. 'You know, I put my tinsnips down and I thought to myself, *What the hell is this?* I checked for a command wire, in case I'd missed it. I figured maybe there was a wire buried deep, one that snaked off into the bush so some fucker hiding there could detonate it manually. But nothing.

'I took stock for a few seconds,' Chavez continues. 'Then I thought: *The dog went crazy over this thing. Half dug it up. What did the dog know that I don't? And the dog handler: he gave me that extra warning.* I thought about how the Taliban had tried to force you guys to abandon it by hitting you so hard. I thought: *There's gotta be something different about this thing, an extra layer of evil. Something so bad that it drove your dog wild.*'

Chavez fixes me with this wide-eyed stare. 'Then it came to me: *Collapsing circuit. It's a freakin' collapsing circuit.* And you know what? You only ever build a collapsing circuit when you want to kill the guy who snips the wire. You know who they set this one for: they set it for you and your dog, or me and my team. No one else is going to be cutting those wires. And you know what? Man, they near as hell got us.'

Chavez goes on to explain that the last time they used collapsing-circuit IEDs was back in the eighties, when the Afghans were fighting the Soviets. He explains how the collapsing-circuit is a self-activating device. It needs no external trigger. If someone cuts a wire, that triggers the entire thing to blow. And it would have been some kind of blast. There were 81 mm mortar rounds, empty illume rounds packed with ANAL, plus three RPG rounds taped together as one charge. It would have been the mother of all explosions.

'No wonder they didn't want us to find it,' I tell him. 'This was the big one.'

'Yeah, the mother of all IEDs. And you know what? The only thing the Taliban hadn't considered in all this was a black dog's nose coming in and sniffing it out.'

'Plus Master Sergeant Chavez realising it was a collapsing circuit, and not snipping the wire. You know, my dog can't take all the credit all the time.'

Chavez gets to his feet and glances down at me. 'Far as I see it, that dog of yours is worth his weight in gold.' I see him square his shoulders. 'It's time, guys. Fire in the hole time.'

Chavez proceeds to blow all of the charges in a series of massive blasts. As for me, I'm still kind of spooked. I'd seen this device – or something very like it – the night before, in my dreams. No doubt about it, this is freaky. Once he's checked that all the charges are blown, Chavez says he needs to get back to base. He's low on water, and his men are done in.

We make the walk together as one patrol, Seven Platoon plus Chavez's Marine Corps team. It's a kilometre or less along the river, and we're back through the gates in short shift. We de-bomb our mags, and I'm turning for the kennel when Chavez grabs me by the arm.

'Say, mind if I have a word with you alone?'

We find a corner that's pretty much deserted. Chavez turns to face me. He's got a look bordering on tears in his eyes.

'I just want you to know if it wasn't for you and your dog today, me and my team would now be dead.' He's all choked up with emotion. 'It's that plain goddamn simple.'

I do my best to play it down. 'That's what we're here for, mate. It's what we're paid to do. Treo and I were just doing our job.' But the goose bumps I'm feeling are like nothing I've ever experienced before.

Treo gets an extra bowl of food that evening. After that, we sit up and have a good long cuddle. I'd sent my dog in there in the first place because that unknowable sixth-sense was telling me that something wasn't right. I feel like this is what my dog and I were put on this earth to do. I feel on top of the world.

I go to bed that night a very happy man, and my sleep is blissfully free of nightmares.

CHAPTER TWENTY-FIVE

Early the following morning Chavez pays us a visit at the kennel. He's written my dog and me a testimonial. It's all a bit American, but still I love him for it.

'Treo located a string of IEDs that saved a number of soldiers from death or injury. The skill of this working dog is unsurpassed by anything I have ever seen or had the pleasure of working with before. I believe Treo has saved scores of lives . . .'

It's signed 'Tanos Chavez, Master Sergeant, United States Marine Corps'. I'll treasure that for the rest of my days.

By now, I've lost count of the number of devices that Treo's sniffed out. It's reached the stage where I see Treo's nose as somehow infallible, and Treo as all but indestructible. The Ranger lads pretty much view him like that too, not to mention Chavez and his crew. We've all got ultimate faith and pride in our dog soldier, and I guess they say that pride comes before a fall.

September comes around, and it's only days now before Treo and I will be getting out of here. I keep telling myself that my dog and I just have to last the final lap. The one thing that we can't afford to do is to relax or get sloppy just when we're about to go home.

We're scheduled to head out on a night patrol with our favourite boys, Seven Platoon. We've been out with those guys so often now, it's become like second nature working with them. It's eleven o'clock by the time we leave the Sangin base. We exit through a side entrance, one that we've nicknamed Pizza Hut Gate, because the building right opposite looks like a run-down pizza joint.

A couple of hundred metres later we swing right, into a host of narrow alleyways that lead into the depths of Sangin town. It's typical search territory – narrow, twisting, dark as hell and with a blind spot at every corner. It's where my dog and I have learned to thrive. I'm aware that we were last here several weeks back, so there's a good chance a crop of new devices will have been planted.

We push onwards, and Treo's got his nose right in the search. He never seems to tire of this, does my boy. There are high walls to either side, and my dog's out front twenty metres ahead of me sniffing for all he's worth. We head up an alleyway, swing immediately left and right, and emerge on a dark and deserted T-junction.

Right in the middle of that T-junction I see Treo pause. He starts doing the weirdest of things: he begins to turn around and around in the open, as if he's chasing his stubby little tail. I whisper at him that this is no time for games, and I push him on towards the next alleyway. But we've gone no more than five paces when my dog turns around and heads back into the open again.

Once more he starts doing that turn-around-in-circles routine. But it's now that I realise that he isn't chasing his tail: he's sniffing and snuffling around in a ring. He's got a puzzled look in his eyes as he goes, like he's thinking: *What the hell?*

I see his head go down and he's sucking up the dust in great slurps. In the still night air I can hear his nose going like a hoover, even from where I'm standing. Finally, he stares at one patch of ground, and he goes down on his tummy, his eyes glued to that slice of earth.

It's an odd way to indicate. It's like he's still not certain, but if there is anything here he figures that's where it's at. I call Treo back and send Davey forward with his EBEX. He passes it over the area and gets a barely audible bleep.

'I've got a faint reading on the EBEX,' he whispers.

I send Treo forward again. By now this is standard procedure. We double-confirm before we bother to call Chavez. Treo's half sure there's something there. It's kind of a stalemate.

Ronnie offers to go forward and triple check. I watch him snake across towards the spot on his belly, and pull out his knife. Gently, ever so softly for a man of his size, he picks away at the hard-packed dirt. There's a faint click of a knife blade making contact with something metallic.

Ronnie rolls away and gives the signal: there's something there all right. We call Ranger Cupples forward, and Cupples does what's needed. He puts out the call to Chavez via the patrol radio: 'Dog Find.' He gives our position, and Chavez confirms that he's on his way.

As we can't go back across the T-junction, for fear of triggering whatever's buried there, we need to seal off as many routes as we can that lead onto it. We do just that, move back a good distance, and sit ourselves down at the base of a compound wall.

I start giving Treo the praise that he deserves. I give him a few good pats and tell him what a fine job he's done.

I've noticed that my dog is no longer acting like the big 'I Am' whenever he finds something. As the weeks pass, he's growing humbler and more mature. All the look on his face says to me now is: *Got another one, didn't we, Dad?*

I warn Cupples to make sure that Chavez comes in via the same path that we used. Otherwise, he could take a route that brings him over the location of the device. Cupples sends a short message to base to that effect. I'm struck by how quiet Cupples – the thinking-man's soldier – has become during the time we've spent at war here. I figure that he – like me – is more than ready to get home.

It takes two long hours for Chavez to make it out to us. When finally I see his burly figure come jogging in our direction, I practically have a heart attack. He's come in using a route that's taken him directly over whatever's buried at that T-junction. Chavez is pissed as hell when he learns what's happened. Somehow, Ranger Cupples' radio warning hadn't made it through to him.

Chavez doesn't let it bug him for too long. I hear this hushed cry: 'Where's my doggy friend?' He breaks into the widest of smiles when he espies Treo and me. 'Great job, guys. So, where is it?'

I send Treo forward to indicate where he's made the find. Treo goes down on his belly again, right at the very spot.

'Pull your dog back,' says Chavez, ''cause we're going in.'

He gets his kit ready, then deploys his team to safeguard him whilst he's dealing with whatever we've got. I plonk myself down next to Ronnie, in a position where we can peer around the corner and watch Chavez work. He shuffles forward and goes down on his belly. I see him start scraping at the dirt with his knife.

As Chavez picks away at the earth, I keep thinking to myself: *There's got to be more than the one charge . . . There's just got to be more . . .*

I say to Ronnie. 'Hold Treo, will you, mate.'

I creep forward until I've got a good view of the T-junction. I start trying to think like a bastard Taliban bomb maker. Where would I have positioned the charges? I figure there has to be one to the right, one to the left and one to the front of Chavez, so as to blow the entire junction.

I'm within spitting distance of him. 'Master Sergeant,' I hiss. 'Master Sergeant.'

'Send it!' he says. *Say what you need to say.* He's as tense as hell.

'I don't believe there's only the one. I believe there'll be a triangle of charges . . .'

'Don't I know it! Now back off. No point getting us all killed . . .'

I slink off with my tail between my legs, and return to Ronnie and Treo.

I can hear the chat going back and forth between Chavez and his team. He's giving a kind of a running commentary as he digs. Where Treo went belly-down, he uncovers a six-volt battery wired to an illume round packed with high explosives. There's a cellphone trigger wired to the battery, and the entire lot is wrapped in protective plastic. The ground is hard as iron, and

Chavez figures the Taliban have smoothed it over with water and left it to bake hard in the sun.

From there he traces wires leading out to two more charges, both of which are 81 mm mortar rounds. From that triangle of charges, a further wire snakes underground away from the T-junction, through a compound wall and off into the midst of an orchard. It seems this was a belt and braces operation. If the cellphone failed to set off the chain of charges, a watcher on the end of the command wire could have triggered it manually.

Presumably, it's our ECM kit that has jammed the cellphone signal. As to the watcher on the end of that command wire, maybe the guy had fallen asleep at his post, ours being a night patrol.

The configuration of the device explains Treo's odd behaviour. He was turning round and around himself, because he could sense all three charges, and he couldn't work out exactly where to sit at source. He'd detected each of their scents, and he'd opted to go for the strongest smell, the main charge and the trigger.

Chavez gets everyone to move back into good cover before he utters the magic words: 'Fire in the hole!' He touches two bare wires together and a series of three powerful explosions tear the night apart. That's it: device terminated.

We decide to stay firm for a good hour, waiting and watching in absolute silence. We want to see if any of the bomb makers return to the scene of the crime, to check if they got anyone. If they do, we'll kill or capture the bastards.

But no one shows.

We push onwards, skirting by the craters created by Chavez's demolition work. We make directly for a deserted compound where we've camped out overnight on previous ops.

We post sentries around the walls, and then it's time to get some sleep, at least for the remaining hours of darkness. Treo and I bed down on the bare dirt of the compound. My dog falls asleep using my helmet as his pillow, he's that tired. I snuggle up to his warm body, curl around him, and Treo's now my comfort blanket. I get my head next to his, tune into his gentle snoring, and I'm soon gone.

We're up at first light, feeling reasonably well rested. But I'm stiff from the cold, and so I figure is my dog. Best thing to do is to get moving. We head out, me giving Treo a flash of his ball as we go. We start patrolling, edging into a labyrinth of alleyways that take us ever deeper into the heart of Sangin town. The harsh light throws knife-cut shadows across our path as Treo and I edge forwards into the unknown.

We're two hours out and we call a halt in a small square, one that lies between a scatter of compounds. Speedy figures we'll set up a flash checkpoint here, so we can stop and search anyone coming through. You never know what unsuspecting souls may be on the move at this time of the morning, and this deep into bandit country.

It gives me the chance for a good play with Treo. I offer him his ball. Trouble is, he's not interested. Instead, my dog's got chicken mayhem in mind. There are a dozen chooks scratching around in the dust of the square and they seem oblivious to the fact that Treo is eyeing them hungrily.

I let out this deep, indulgent sigh. 'OK, big fella, best you go for it.'

I unclip his lead, and he checks me out: *Oh, can I? Can I? Will you really let me?*

I nod in the direction of the nearest chook. 'Like I said, big fella, go for it.'

An instant later Treo's pounced on the chicken and he's got it pinned in his jaws. He growls menacingly, then does the oddest of things: he lets it go. The chook gets on its feet and stumbles forwards unsteadily, seemingly unable to believe that it's still alive. Then Treo's pounced on it again, and he's got it pinned down once more.

Aha, I think, *I get it now. This is the chicken-chasing game.*

He lets it go for a second time, but by now the chicken's had enough. Treo tries to set it off on the run but the bird's not budging. I see my dog go up to it and give it an encouraging pat on the bum. *Come on then, move!* Eventually, the chicken gets the message and scuttles off a few paces. Instantly, Treo's on it again.

This goes on for a good twenty minutes. Treo's antics are having a serious impact on the Rangers' ability to do their stop-and-search properly. They can't keep their eyes off my dog, and each time he pats the chook on the bum – *come on, move along* – they're in stitches.

A figure sits down beside me. It's Ranger Cupples.

I nod in Treo's direction. 'It's like watching a kid play tag.'

Cupples smiles. 'He sure is one funny dog. You know, it's like we're back at home having a bit of fun with the animals in the park.'

That's the thing about my dog. He brings so much humour to any situation, even in the dark heart of war. He takes us away from the harsh reality that we're facing here, and into a place that's warm and homely and secure. Just for one short Treo-moment the Rangers aren't in Sangin any more. They're at home and they're watching their dogs play chase-the-pigeon in the park.

But there's only so much time we can afford to play for. This is a big, open space, and I figure that any watcher could get a cross-hair on my dog pretty easily, especially when he's repeatedly patting that chook on the butt to make it move.

'You've got two minutes!' I shout over at him. 'Two minutes and we're on the move.'

I feel like I'm calling a child in for his tea. I start to get my gear on, and Treo knows we're moving out. He gives the chicken a last pat on the bum, but it's more than had enough. It takes a couple of steps forward, then plonks itself down with a real finality. Treo pounces and practically squashes the poor thing flat, before he's bounding back to be at my side. Game over.

I reach down and clip his collar on. He knows he's not in search mode any more. The route back is the same way that we came through this morning, and I figure it's clear. We set off, Treo and me leading, but with my dog scurrying backwards and forwards all around me in semi-play. He's had a good bit of fun with his chicken, and he's not on the search, so there's a relaxed feel about us right now.

We turn a corner of an alleyway and I place a boot on the hard, sandy surface. *KABOOOOOM!*

I feel myself lifted off the ground as if by a giant fist, and the next moment I'm floating through the air in agonising slow motion. I land with a sickening crunch, and an instant later I've lost consciousness.

I come to with an unbearable ringing drilling into my skull. My vision's swimming in sparks of fire and deep black, and I don't seem able to stand. As my sight starts to clear I see a thick curtain of darkness all around me, and the distinctive smell of explosives hangs heavy in the air.

I know that I've been blown up, but my first conscious thoughts are for my dog: *Where's Treo? Where's Treo? Where's my boy, my son, my dog?*

I search with my eyes, frantically scanning the opaque wall of drifting shadows. *I can't see him anywhere.* For a moment I imagine Treo lying nearby, desperate for his dad to comfort him as he bleeds out his last. I feel consumed by this crushing wave of guilt that I have somehow survived, yet I've failed to safeguard my dog.

And then I see him. This tiny black figure comes staggering through the blasted smoke and dust.

CHAPTER TWENTY-SIX

My dog's barely able to walk. He keeps staggering into the alley walls and half falling over. I've got not the slightest idea how badly he's been wounded. But thank God he's still alive.

I know in my heart that he's searching for me. However badly hurt he is, he only has thoughts for his dad, just as I only have thoughts for my dog.

'TREO LAD! TREO LAD! OVER HERE! OVER HERE!'

I see his head swivel in my direction, and a pair of eyes light up with the pure joy of recognition. *Oh thank God, Dad, thank God. Thank God you're still alive.*

As he stumbles across to me, I raise myself on one elbow and hold out an arm to embrace him. I realise then that I'm lying in some kind of crater. I guess this is what remains of whatever device has gone up under us, and I can't for the life of me imagine how my dog and I can still be alive.

Treo reaches me, flops down beside me, and starts to madly lick at my face. My dog is plastered from head to toe in blasted mud and dirt and God only knows what else. As I go to check him over, I feel hands lifting me up and dragging me out of the blast area, whilst another set of arms reaches protectively for my dog.

It's Ronnie and Speedy and Ranger Cupples, and they're yelling over and over and over: 'Dave! Are you OK? Are you OK? Are you OK?'

I can see them mouthing the words at me but I can barely hear a thing that they're saying, I'm so deafened.

The Rangers haul my dog and me back to safety. I'm confused and I guess I'm badly in shock. My mind drifts into rainbow shades of grey, and for a moment I wonder if this is for real. *Am I really alive? Did we really survive all of that? Or am I imagining all this, and in reality my dog and I have just been killed?*

Caylie, the patrol medic, appears at my side. She kneels and starts checking me over. I try telling her to go and see my dog first, but the words just won't come. Gradually, I see her expression change. It goes from one of total fear and worry to one of absolute joy and amazement. She turns to Ronnie and the other lads and mouths.

'Bugger me, it looks as if he's perfectly all right!'

She hurries over to check on Treo. She runs her hands up and down his body and his limbs a few good times, then she cracks the biggest ever smile.

'It's a bloody miracle! Treo seems fine 'n' all!'

All around me there are Rangers breaking out into smiles and laughing with sheer relief.

'Sure, the dog's OK.'

'He's feckin' bulletproof.'

'Sure, if they'd have hurt the dog . . .'

'It's a miracle, end of story . . .'

Chavez goes down into the crater and he starts doing his stuff.

He comes back holding a few shattered fragments of whatever it is that he's found.

He crouches down beside me. 'That, my doggy friend, was a command wire device.' He's having to speak in my earhole to make himself heard. 'Looks like a single charge. But you know what – they put the charge in upside down. It blew the shrapnel downwards into the earth, not up into you guys. All you took was the backblast.'

Finally, the enemy has managed to get us – to blow up the handler and his black dog. But what were the chances of them putting the charges in the wrong way round? What were the chances? It feels like an action-replay of the moment the suicide bomber got us. He'd forgotten to bring his shrapnel with him: they've forgotten to place the charge this-side-up. What are the chances?

We move as quickly as we can now to get my dog and me back to the relative safety of the compound in which we spent the night. Once there, we go firm in all around defence. I sit with Treo, and the two of us hold each other tight. I've noticed during that short walk that Treo's trying to keep his weight off the one leg. I run my hands up and down it, trying to feel for broken skin, or the crunch of fractured bone.

I can't feel any breaks in his skin. I check my hands for any blood. There is none. It doesn't look as if he's been fragged with any shrapnel. He was hit by the blast wave, just as I was, but that appears to be about all. My dog's quieter and more withdrawn than I've seen him in an age. He's not the chicken-chasing super-dog of this morning. He's withdrawn into himself, and all he wants is to be with his dad.

I get him to take a few shaky, unsteady steps. He's definitely limping. I figure that as the blast went off under him it must have driven some nasty pieces of gravel into his front paw. All the shrapnel may have been blown downwards, but not the grit and dirt. It must have damaged his pads, which are one of the most delicate parts of a dog's body.

Or maybe when he was blown into the air he came down hard and landed badly. Maybe he's strained something at the point of impact. Either way, there's not a lot I can do about it now. I need to get him home and into his kennel. Then I can soak and sponge his paws, check him over properly, and get him well again.

I look over at Speedy: 'The dog's lame. He can't search any more.'

Speedy nods. 'We're chancing our arm staying any longer anyways, Dave. We found a device on the way out. A device has gone up underneath the two of youse. We need to get back to base and re-evaluate what we're doing.'

Ranger Cupples sends a radio message to the Sangin HQ. 'Device triggered. No casualties. We're coming in.'

We decide to take the route back that we came in on. Treo won't be able to search, and we figure it's the safest way out.

Last thing I do before leaving the compound is to check my camera. It's the new one that my sister posted out to me. I pull the Olympus out of my breast pocket, and miraculously there doesn't seem to be a scratch on it. I flick on the power switch and frame Treo for a photo. He's covered in dust and dirt from the blast, but otherwise he looks pretty much OK.

'Smile for the camera, big lad,' I tell him, ''cause it could have been a whole lot worse for us.'

Treo obliges with a half smile, white canines creeping over drooly black gums. It's like he's saying: *I'm real sorry I didn't find that one, Dad.*

'Listen, lad, I didn't have you searching, so if anyone's at fault here . . .' I click the button and the shutter whirs, 'then it's me.'

I check the image in the playback screen. Bugger me, the camera seems to be working perfectly. So far, it's survived being dived on, half pulled into the Helmand River, and now it's been blown up. My sister's done me right with this one.

As we pass through the compound's shattered doorway, I can't help but have this rush of conflicting thoughts. *We missed one. They got us. So am I getting sloppy? Or did they just get lucky? Or were they just unlucky, 'cause it was planted upside down. Who knows?*

Treo's hurt and he's off the search, so there's no point us taking the lead. Davey goes first, doing a rapid sweep with the EBEX, Ronnie follows, and next comes me and my dog. We thread our way back through the maze of alleyways, passing by the T-junction where Chavez blew the device the night before.

We're a few hundred metres from the camp gates when we turn a corner and walk up the side of a compound, the narrow path threading between that and a wall of vegetation on the opposite side. Davey pushes on past the compound and out into some open fields of corn.

As he does so, I notice an Afghan male standing to one side. He's bent double, as if he's tending the crops in his field. As I pass him by I hear him yell out something in the local language. I'm a couple of steps behind Ronnie as we emerge into the open, and for just an instant I wonder what the Afghan farmer was saying.

The next moment: *BOOM!*

Ronnie and I are thrown forwards by this massive blast. It punches into my back and hurls me into the earth face first. I come up spitting mud, and as I turn my head to search for my dog I see the Afghan 'farmer' taking to his heels. I know instantly what has happened: he was the trigger man, and behind us a device has gone up under the patrol.

I grab Treo, and Ronnie and I help each other to our feet. We're yelling at each other: 'NO! NO! NO! NO! NO!'

With my dog on one side of me and Ronnie on the other, I run back into the smoke and dust. I see a figure lying to one side of the path. I know at once who it is, for the radio antennae on his back are so distinctive.

It's Ranger Cupples.

The poor lad's been blasted off his feet into the Afghan dust.

Ronnie starts screaming: 'MEDIC! MEDIC! MEDIC! MAN DOWN! MAN DOWN! MAN DOWN!'

For the second time that morning, Caylie comes sprinting forwards. She doesn't panic. She doesn't fluster. In an instant she's down in the dirt trying her best to save him. She's trying to tourniquet his wounds to stop all the bleeding. I tear my eyes away from her, as she battles against all odds to save that young soldier's life.

Ronnie and I move back towards the open field. We've got our weapons in the aim, and we're screaming at anyone who comes nearer to back the hell right off. We're hyper-aware of the risk of snipers or a follow-up attack, and all we want is for Caylie to be left alone to do her stuff and to save him.

I've got Treo gripped hard between my knees. My boy's not

going anywhere. But inside my head this voice keeps screaming over and over and over: *You should have been searching. You should have been searching. You should have been on the search . . .*

I've no idea how long we've been standing there, screaming at the locals to make themselves very scarce, when word comes through to Ronnie and me. It's what we've been dreading. In spite of all she's done, Caylie hasn't been able to save him. Ranger Cupples has bled out into the Afghan dust, and he's left us. He's gone.

I wander over to the cover of the nearest wall. I sink down, with Treo between my knees. I can't get the horrific image out of my head. I feel totally drained of all energy and the will to live. I slump over my rifle and my dog, and I'm just gone.

It's a while before I hear a voice beside me, yelling: 'Dave! *Dave!* Get your finger out of your bloody backside!'

I turn to see Ronnie, gesticulating wildly at the field beyond. 'Listen, we can't do nothing about it here, but we can try and find the bastards who did this!'

We push outwards into the cornfield, but all my strength of mind and my spirit has died. I'm gone. Just gone.

Within minutes, Frankie O'Connor arrives with reinforcements. He can see that we're in shock and he takes immediate command. The priority now is to get Ranger Cupples' body back to base as directly as possible, and the rest of us into the safety of its walls.

We've got one injured, as well as our man killed in action. Sly, my favourite terp, has been blown up and taken some shrapnel to the face and other injuries. He's going to be OK but we need to get him evacuated to Camp Bastion as soon as. We need to get us out of here. That's the overriding priority right now.

Before we can leave, Frankie calls me over. He places one hand on my shoulder, yet the guilt's so bad I can't look him in the eye.

'Listen, Dave, I'm not going anywhere until I'm sure we've got all of him. I want you to go check.'

I nod dumbly, call Treo and we set off into the bloodied reed beds to the side of the path. I'm in there, searching, and in no time at all I know that I just can't go on. I feel sick, dizzy, nauseous, and just gone. I call Treo back to me and we drag ourselves out.

I turn to Frankie. 'Look, sir, I just can't do it . . . I just can't do it and neither can my dog . . .'

I don't know if I'm crying. I probably am. I'm cracking up and breaking down.

'Davey-boy, don't worry about it,' Frankie tells me. 'It's OK. You've done all right. Let's take him home.'

We start the walk back towards the base. I pass by the stretcher. I think of Ranger Cupples, and the months we spent together getting to know each other and how he loved my dog. And now, today, just days before he was going home, we've lost him, and all because I'd taken Treo off the search.

Those last two hundred and fifty metres feel like fifty kilometres to me. All I can see in my mind's eye is that stretcher, with that bloodied form lying upon it. We file through the gates like a patrol of zombies. We unload our weapons and I head off to the kennel area with my dog.

I don't even bother to take off my kit. Covered in mud and blood as we are, Treo and I climb onto my camp bed. I begin to cry. I feel devastated. A broken man. It wasn't my dog's fault out there today. It's not his fault a device blew up under us when he wasn't on the search. It's me who'd told him to stop searching.

I'd just presumed the Taliban never had the chance to put another device in, not in the few short hours since we'd cleared that path. And as they say, presumption is the mother of all fuck-ups. How wrong, how fatally wrong I've been proven today.

I sit in the kennel for hours, letting my tears flow. I stroke Treo, and try to comfort him and to check that he's OK. He's been blown away from his dad twice in one morning, and I've no idea what psychological harm that may have done to him. But I don't have much left now. All I can see in my mind's eye is Ranger Cupples, bleeding out his last. It's haunting me. It's killing me.

I keep hearing an odd, uncertain knocking on the door. A head pops round. 'Dave, it wasn't your fault.'

But I'm not hearing those words, and I'm not registering who it is any more.

It's not until that evening when Chavez comes to see me that I finally crawl out from whatever dark place it is that's consumed me. Chavez has come to have a fatherly kind of chat. He knows I think I'm to blame, and he figures he can explain to me enough about how that device was planted to convince me otherwise.

He explains that they'd dug in two charges. The main device was buried in the path, but the other was hidden in a wall, and set back the same kind of distance that I would move from a suspect device once my dog had found it. Chavez is convinced they set the devices so as to kill me and my dog. It was a command-wire-triggered IED, so no way would we have been able to jam the trigger signal.

Had Treo been on the search he'd have found the first device, no question. We'd have moved back a safe distance and plonked ourselves down on the wall to await Chavez. We'd then have been sitting right next to the secondary charge, with it positioned at our head height. The Afghan 'farmer' would then have yelled out a warning to the trigger man, sitting at the end of the command wire. And that would have been the end of me and my dog.

Chavez tells me all of this in an effort to raise my spirits, and to make me feel less guilty. But in a sense it makes it worse. I'm thirty-eight years old, and the only child I have is my boy, my dog. I've have a life. Sure, I love my dog. But Cupples deserved to live, and to be the father of the kids that need him home. What Chavez has told me – with the best of intentions – has ripped another part out of me.

There's only one being with the power to pull me out of the black hole that I'm in. It's Treo. He is so loving, and so very good at understanding his dad. With Chavez gone, he comes and leans his whole body against me, and he gives me a big lick up the side of my face.

He raises a paw to touch my cheek where it's slick with tears: *It's OK, Dad, really, it's OK. You're not to blame. It's me. I'm the one who went lame.*

That sets me off again. I realise how close I've come to losing my best friend twice in one day.

CHAPTER TWENTY-SEVEN

I lie awake that night in the darkness. I think of Cupples' family getting the knock on the door. I imagine that being me, and the crushing blow to my mother of hearing the news. I imagine her having to tell my sister. I imagine Bob having to make all the arrangements for the funeral.

I carry a letter with me on patrol. It describes exactly how I'd like my folks to arrange my funeral. It's my in-case-of-death letter. I wonder if Cupples carried one with him. I wonder if it survived that devastating blast.

I wander aimlessly around the night-dark camp, thinking about what I could have done to save him. I've lost someone at the eleventh hour, a good man and a father who had become a friend. I've done so by stopping Treo searching. My confidence is shattered. I vow that it's over. I won't go out again. My time searching is done.

The following morning I go to see the doctor. He takes one look at me and exclaims: 'My God, Dave, you look like you haven't slept for days.'

I tell him that's exactly how I feel. I need something to help me with the nights. But most of all I need out of here. I need to get myself gone. He prescribes some sleeping tablets, and warns me to take it easy. He doesn't say as much, but we both know I'm close to cracking up.

I keep getting word from Major Shannon that he's going to need my dog and me out on patrols sometime soon. I send word back that Treo's lame, and we're not going anywhere. In truth, it's just an excuse. I've checked Treo over. I've cleaned out any blasted grit from his paws. He's walking just fine now.

There's no physical injury to either of us. There's nothing physically wrong. It's just my mind that's been damaged so badly. I know lives are in danger if we don't go out on patrol, but I can't face losing another person. And if my dog and I aren't working at 100 per cent, we will lose someone, of that I'm certain.

I can't face that. I can't face any more blood on my hands. Who will it be next? Speedy? Davey? Lieutenant Wilcock? Ronnie even?

I lock myself away with Treo, and hour after hour I go over everything that happened. And somehow, my dog has this gift of making it good again. It's like when you're a kid and you fall off your bike. You get your mother's arms around you and somehow it makes the hurt go away. I feel the same thing from Treo. I've asked so much of him already, and yet still he's able to pour his love into me, and to raise me up again.

It's three days after losing Ranger Cupples when Seven Platoon head out on their next patrol. I've been told I'm to get my dog and me on it, but still I'm refusing to go. I'm adamant. I am not going out. Speedy and Ronnie wander down to the kennel. They sit in the brew area with all their kit on, and they call me out of the darkness.

I emerge from the kennel with Treo, and my dog takes one look at the lads in all their patrol gear and he starts going up the walls. *Ooo! Ooo! Can we, Dad, can we? Can we get out on patrol? I'm bored of you crying. Let's get out and search!*

I ask them what's up.

In response, Ronnie gives me a much-needed reality check. In his down-to-earth way he tells me that he understands how I feel, but that they've all lost Ranger Cupples. The show has to go on.

'We're not going out on patrol without you, Dave, it's as simple as that,' he says. 'So get your shit together, get your dog harnessed, and get ready.'

I know that I can't let them take the risk of going out without us. I ready Treo, and he's raring to go. I can sense his eagerness and his energy to get back on the search. But for me, it's all changed. I'm not going out with passion any more. I'm going out driven by a cold, icy rage and with a dark hatred in my heart. And it's dangerous.

Because I can't face missing another bomb or losing anyone, I start driving myself and Treo as never before. I can't bring Ranger Cupples back, but I tell myself I can make damn sure that I don't lose another man amongst us, or a dog. I push and push Treo, but he just keeps delivering. I think he knows if we fail to find a device it's going to completely fry my mind. I'm on terminal burnout.

War can bring out the very best and the worst in people. It's only ever brought out the best in my dog. But I know I'm long overdue to go home. I'm on the edge. I've lost a big part of myself here in Sangin, and in this death that's consumed me. I'm worried that I'm pushing too hard, too aggressively, and that I'm putting Treo's life at risk. I'm better off out of here.

Chavez does a detailed analysis of the device that killed Cupples. He shares his findings with me. He found a command wire running from one of the craters to a small break in a compound wall. A crack in the wall provided the watchers with a good view of the patrol as we passed. When we were in the 'kill zone' the watcher triggered the IED.

The firing point offered the trigger team a good escape route westwards into the Green Zone. That's how they got away. They're beyond the reach of our justice or our retribution. No amount of searching or kicking down doors will ever lead us to them. Ranger Cupples is gone, and we'll never get his killers, and just knowing that tortures me.

The twenty-first of September is our last day in Sangin. It comes around not a moment too soon. A Chinook is due in that afternoon to collect me and my dog, but Major Shannon's got one mission for us to do before then. We're to head out with Seven Platoon on one last search patrol.

I see the major at the base gates, and he and I exchange a glance. 'Sir, I'm going back in a matter of hours on the helo,' I tell him. 'D'you not think I'm pushing the boundaries here in terms of this could be the last one?'

He gives a wry smile. 'You and your black dog – unbeatable. Just one last time, Davey, and you're out of here.'

We exit the gates and I show Treo his tennis ball. As I give him the seek on command, I'm aware that this is the closing chapter for us here in Afghanistan. My dog bounds off ahead, as if he wants to get as much searching as he can under his belt before we're finally done.

One of the Rangers on my shoulder makes a comment. 'Not long, now, Dave, and you're out of here. I can't believe you'll be leaving us.'

I glance back at him. 'I think we've done our time here, lad, I think we've done our time . . .'

We push a few kilometres north-east, for no other reason than we haven't been around this area for a good long time. We've been out a couple of hours when we stumble upon this bizarre-looking compound. It's bigger and smarter than normal, and that's just from the outside. Once we're in, we realise what a palace the place is compared to your normal Sangin dive.

It's set on a massive, well-tended plot, which is absent the usual chickens and rats, plus fighting hound tethered by the gate. In the main living room there's the strangest thing of all – a white and very grand-looking piano. We're well aware that only two types of people own places like this here in Helmand: drugs-lords and warlords. The owner of the gaff is this stiff old boy, and I wonder which of the two he is.

I put Treo through the house and he's plodding about as if he's more than a little bored. *Done it. Seen it. Time to get home.* He doesn't show the slightest interest in anything, until he gets to the piano. At first he walks past it, but then he turns around and comes beetling back. He plonks his behind on the carpet, and he stares at a rolled-up rug lying atop the piano. The next instant he's got his front paws on the piano keys – *plonk, pling, plang* – and he's sniffing all along the rug.

I call him back, go forward myself and peer inside. There's

some kind of weapon in there. I call the owner of the house and get him to roll out the rug. Inside, there's a brand-spanking new AK-47, complete with a magazine fully loaded with 7.62 mm rounds. The gun goes into the bag, along with one or two other weapons that we find hidden around his gaff, and we're done.

We exit the compound and head back to base. Treo's made his last find, he's had his play with his ball and he's happy. It's hardly a daisy-chain IED that he's got here, but it's his last day and his last patrol and still he's made a difference. He's done his stint in hell and it's high time we got ourselves out of here.

On the walk back I'm looking at every building and alleyway, knowing that we've searched them all. Nine times out of ten we've found whatever there was to be found. I can feel the guilt of Ranger Cupples weighing heavily on my shoulders, but at the same time I know that we've lost only the one soldier in six long months. Maybe my dog and I have done OK after all.

We come in through the gates and I unload my weapon for the last time. The Rangers still have a few more days on the ground here. I do not want to leave these young men who have become like my brothers. The last thing on earth I want to do is go. But at the same time I know I'm sipping on fumes here, and I'm about to crash and burn. It's my time.

An hour before the Chinook is due I get summoned to the briefing room. I find myself sitting there as Major Shannon gives his orders, wondering what the hell I've been asked here for. I have this horrid feeling that the major's going to turn to me and say: 'By the way, Dave, we need you out on this one last mission . . .'

Sure enough, at the end of the orders he turns my way. I'm

bracing myself for having to say the biggest, strongest 'no way' of my entire career.

'Lastly, I need to have words with Dave Dog,' the major announces. He's stern-faced as he pulls out a piece of paper from his pocket and begins to read. 'Corporal Dave Heyhoe and his Arms Explosive Search dog Treo have been embedded with C Company, Royal Irish Regiment, for the last five months. During that time they unearthed scores of IEDs, arms caches . . .'

By this time I've pretty much gone deaf to his words. It sounds as if the major is reading out some kind of a medal citation, and as he describes the key missions my dog and I have been on I'm suddenly back on those searches, my dog's nose huffing away and the adrenalin pumping through my veins.

I only come back to the reality of the moment as the major's winding up. He tells me that we've saved the lives of so many of his men, and he lets me know that no dog team can ever replace Treo and me. That means one hell of a lot, especially coming from a man of the major's calibre.

The major rounds off with this. 'Dave, from all of us here, I'd like to give you my deepest thanks for all that you and Treo have achieved.'

There's a deafening round of applause. Familiar, and less familiar faces start grabbing my hand and wishing me luck for the journey home.

From there, the major and the lads of Seven Platoon escort Treo and me to the helipad. The whocka-whocka comes in low and fast down the Sangin Valley. Treo and I run up the open ramp, the powerful downwash of the rotors buffeting our heads, and the cries of the Rangers ringing in our ears.

We sit on the open tail ramp and wave our goodbyes. As the helo claws into the sky I've got my dog between my knees gripped hard. The Chinook banks around and Sangin fades. Treo turns to look at me. There's this deep sadness on his face, like he's leaving behind a place and a bunch of people that he's truly grown to love.

His eyes say it all: *Bugger it, Dad, nothing is for ever. I guess it couldn't last.*

EPILOGUE

I suppose it's hardly surprising, but it's taken several years for me to feel able to tell our story. Before leaving Afghanistan, we were delayed several days at Camp Bastion. On one level it was a blessing. It meant that Treo and I could meet the Rangers when they were flown out of Sangin, and count them all in.

Shortly after arriving back in the UK, I started to suffer from all the classic symptoms of Post Traumatic Stress Disorder (PTSD). I didn't realise it at the time. I didn't for a long while. I just thought I'd been hit bad by Ranger Cupples' and Ken and Sasha's deaths, and in time I would get over it.

I don't know if Treo suffered as much as I did, or even in similar ways. All I do know is that when, a few months after I returned, I decided I'd have to leave the Army, no one could force the two of us apart. The RAVC tried. They argued they wanted to assign Treo to another handler. By then he'd won the *Sun*'s 'Millies' award, and he was something of a superstar.

But Treo was having none of it. I'd warned them. 'Just you try taking my boy away from me,' I'd said. He'd get sent out to train with a new handler, but just a whiff of his dad, or the slightest squeak from me, and he'd turn his back on whatever he was doing and come running. In truth, I couldn't bear to see him with another. And in truth, he couldn't bear to be parted from his dad.

Eventually, the RAVC relented. When I retired from the Army, Treo came with me. We moved into a house in the Lincolnshire Fens. I was thirty-eight years old when I deployed to Afghanistan, and I'd come back to the UK two days short of my thirty-ninth birthday. But I'd also come home seriously messed up, although it took me a long while to face up to that reality.

Every day Treo and I walked the Fens. And as we walked and walked, Sangin was never far from our minds. I kept thinking – and I'm sure Treo did too – where is the dust, the fifty degree heat, the bullets, the blood, the IEDs?

Ronnie from Seven Platoon had been interviewed for the Millies, and his words had played on the screen at the awards ceremony: 'If this dog was not with my company on that particular tour the casualty rate would have been tenfold.'

There were other, similar tributes from across the board. Major Shannon had put my dog and me forward for a gallantry award. So had the Parachute Regiment, and Master Sergeant Chavez had even tried to put us up for a medal in the USA. But as far as I was concerned, I felt far from being a hero. I was wallowing in the darkness. I couldn't get the nightmarish images out of my mind.

Mostly, they were of Ken and Sasha, or of Ranger Cupples. I had nights when I didn't sleep at all; nights when I really needed to be close to my Treo. I'd met Ken's family when we'd held a proper military service, shortly after our return to the UK. I'd talked to them individually, and they were lit up to hear that their son's life had touched so many people.

I realised I was missing the adrenalin rush of the search, so I joined a local go-karting club. I asked Ken's family if I might paint a mural of him on my kart. Karting was something that Ken used to talk about all the time. Outside of his family and the Army, that was his passion. Ken's folks said they'd be honoured to have his likeness on my kart. I painted a picture of him and Sasha in the Afghan heat and dust, out front leading a patrol. His folks asked me to go out and win some races in the name of their son and his dog.

Wherever I took Treo in our new life as civvies, I noticed that he couldn't seem to stop searching. I'd take him down to the local park, and he was forever checking out the bins and the hedges and even the kids' play area. I kept telling him that he could have his tennis ball any time he wanted it now, but whenever I showed it to him I could see that look in his eyes: *Right, Dad, I'm on it. Where are we starting the search?*

I'd bend down and gaze into his eyes: 'It's OK, big fella, we don't need to search any more. There are no more IEDs. We're home.'

Partly because my dog just didn't want to let go, I got us a job as a man-and-dog security team at the Olympic site. The money was good, but all we ever got to do was stand gate duty, or search endless lines of vehicles. One day we were doing yet another vehicle search, and Treo turned around to me and said: *Dad, I'm so bored. Why're we doing this to ourselves? Why're we here?*

That very day I handed in my resignation, and we never worked there again. Treo was telling me that he'd had enough. It was his time. He was ready to let go.

Amongst the many accolades that Treo won was the Dickin

Medal, more commonly known as 'The Animal Victoria Cross'. The medal was established by the People's Dispensary for Sick Animals (PDSA), a British veterinary charity, and each one is inscribed with the words 'We Also Serve'. The last Dickin Medal was given out in 2007, to another war dog, and Treo remains the most recent recipient. Fittingly, Treo and I also went on to be finalists in the Crufts Friends for Life Award, and we put in a special appearance at our football club, Manchester City, in front of tens of thousands of spectators.

We travelled down to the Imperial War Museum for the Dickin Award ceremony. There I met Treo's original family, the Abbotts. It was nice to see them – the family without whom I'd never have met my boy. Unusually for my dog, he ran over to them right away and started rubbing up against their legs. He remembered them. He knew their smell. It was eight years since he'd last been with them, but a dog never forgets.

I thanked the Abbott family for letting Treo realise his true potential – for helping him grow from that little puppy into a hero of a dog. They say time is the greatest healer. Over time, and thanks to the companionship of my hero dog, I did begin to heal. But there was another factor that came into play here, one that would change my life for ever.

During the six months that we were in Afghanistan, Treo and I secured forty-five separate, verified finds – arms, explosive caches and IEDs. Yet somehow we both made it home uninjured and alive. Looking back on our time, I'm sure now there was someone up there watching over us. There has to have been. Nothing else makes any sense. Nothing else can explain how my dog and I made it out of there alive.

Thanks to that protector, I was given a second chance at life in the UK. I made contact with an old girlfriend, a lovely lady called Rachel. We met up, talked and laughed like old times, and one thing led to another. Rachel didn't seem to mind that I was a bit damaged. In fact, she helped me see that I could be whole again. She helped me realise that in spite of all the darkness that my dog and I had been through, there are still miracles and light in the world.

We'd lost one life, maybe two in Afghanistan. Lance Corporal Ken Rowe and his search dog Sasha were the first dog and handler team the Royal Army Veterinary Corps has lost in action since Northern Ireland operations, over thirty years before. Ranger Justin James Cupples was one of the four-hundred-plus British soldiers lost to the war in Afghanistan – more than the Iraq conflict or even the Falklands war. We will forever remember them.

Their deaths bore upon me heavily, for I felt a strong responsibility for their loss. It was Rachel who gave me the gift of a new life, to help me deal with all of that. She did so when out of the blue she fell pregnant. I'd gone to Afghanistan terrified of losing my dog. I'd come back terrified of what I'd lost out there, and of what I had become. But what Rachel gave me was an impossible hope that Dave Heyhoe was going to bring a life into this world.

I was out driving a few months later, doing a delivery in the truck that I was operating, and I couldn't help myself. I just had to call home.

'Has the baby moved today?' I blurted out, just as soon as Rachel answered.

'Of course she has. She never stops moving!'

I got home and Rachel was fast asleep. I couldn't feel the baby kicking or moving. I went to fetch my stethoscope – the same that I used to listen to Treo's heartbeat when we were out in Afghanistan. I placed it on Rachel's tummy, and I listened for the baby. I heard it kick and turn around . . . and even let out a burp. Luckily, Rachel kept sleeping blissfully.

When we took little Ellie-Ann home from the delivery suite, one of the first things I did was get her out to meet Treo. He's got a big kennel in the garden, and that is the new Kingdom of Treo. I placed her on the grass, and I saw her stretch out her hand to the kennel door.

Treo sniffed it a good few times, then fixed me with a look. *OK, Dad, I can see what you've done here, and I know how proud you are. But hey, I'm still your boy.*

He knew how happy I was, and that made him happy in turn. In time he became very protective of Ellie-Ann. She was the newest and most vulnerable addition to the pack. I'd hold little Ellie-Ann and Treo would come and rest his head in my lap. I had my child and my dog with me, both gazing into my eyes. God, how could life be any better? It just doesn't get any better than that.

For a moment I considered how sad I would be when one day Treo would be gone, and Ellie-Ann would grow up not knowing my wonder dog. And then this thought struck me. Of course she'd know Treo. She'd know my dog because without him, she wouldn't be here. He saved my life so many times out there in the fire and the heat and the dust, and that was what had made another life like hers possible.

One day I was out walking Treo, and a car pulled up, driven by a little old lady. I put Treo in my vehicle, and the old lady paused beside me. She asked me if there were any other dogs around, because last time she was here her little terrier got attacked. I told her no, I hadn't seen any. But I offered to walk with her for a bit if she was afraid.

She asked me what I did for a living. I told her I used to be in the Army, but now I was retired. I told her – a little shyly – that I was a dad now, and I spent a lot of time at home with the baby.

She turned to me: 'You were in the Army, you say? Do you remember that lovely little black dog from Afghanistan, the one who won all the medals? Treo, was it?'

'It was,' I replied. 'And you know, he's not so little.'

I opened the hatchback to my car, and Treo jumped out. I told her it was him. The little old lady couldn't believe it. She was so amazed that she threw her own dog back in her car and bent down to give Treo the biggest ever hug. The funny thing about my dog is that Afghanistan seems to have softened him. It's rare now when he won't let someone – even a complete stranger – cuddle him.

'Thank you,' the little old lady said. 'Thank you.'

She was talking to my dog, not to me.

I drove home, feeling – as I have so many times before – so proud of Treo. As I came through the door I could hear little Ellie-Ann crying. She was teething, Rachel told me, though it didn't mean that much to me. Rachel's been through this twice before – she's got two boys from a former relationship that I now call my own. But all of this baby stuff was totally new and amazing to me.

I was about to rush in and check if Ellie-Ann was OK, but I paused for a moment. I sank into a crouch, until I was eye-to-eye with Treo. Remembering that little old lady's words, I grabbed his front paws and held them in my hands. I gazed into his golden-flecked eyes.

'I asked so much of these pawsies, lad, in Afghanistan. And d'you know what, they never once let me down.'

And, as always with Treo, I meant it from the heart.

INDEX